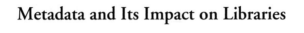

Metadata and Its Impact on Libraries

Recent Titles in the Library and Information Science Text Series

Metadata and Its Impact on Libraries

Sheila S. Intner, Susan S. Lazinger,
and Jean Weihs

Library and Information Science Text Series

LIBRARIES

U N L I M I T E D

A Member of the Greenwood Publishing Group

Westport, Connecticut • London

Library of Congress Cataloging-in-Publication Data

Intner, Sheila S.
  Metadata and its impact on libraries / by Sheila S. Intner, Susan S. Lazinger, and Jean Weihs.
    p. cm. — (Library and information science text series)
  Includes bibliographical references and index.
  ISBN 1-59158-145-1 (alk. paper)
    1. Metadata. 2. Information organization. 3. Cataloging—Standards. 4. Cataloging of electronic information resources. 5. Cataloging of integrating resources. 6. Information storage and retrieval systems. 7. Machine-readable bibliographic data formats. 8. Electronic information resources—Management. 9. Digital preservation. 10. Digital libraries. I. Lazinger, Susan S. (Susan Smernoff) II. Weihs, Jean Riddle. III. Title. IV. Series.
  Z666.7.I58 2006
  025.3—dc22   2005030803

British Library Cataloguing in Publication Data is available.

Library of Congress Catalog Card Number: 2005030803
ISBN: 1-59158-145-1

First published in 2006

Libraries Unlimited, 88 Post Road West, Westport, CT 06881
A Member of the Greenwood Publishing Group, Inc.
www.lu.com

Printed in the United States of America

The paper used in this book complies with the Permanent Paper Standard issued by the National Information Standards Organization (Z39.48-1984).

10   9   8   7   6   5   4   3   2   1

Contents

Part 1

Metadata Concepts and Definitions

Chapter 1

What Is Metadata?

Defining Metadata

Choosing a Definition

Metadata is probably the aspect of electronic data archiving about which there is the greatest number of articles, the most workshops, and the largest community of researchers. It has been defined and redefined, classified, and reclassified by type, put into ever-dynamic categories, expanded and multiplied. This chapter attempts to sort out the confusion of types, categories, association models, and characteristics of metadata. It attempts, in other words, to create a taxonomy that indicates what metadata is and is not, what the relationship among the various aspects of metadata are, and what the primary features of the major metadata models are.

Because the definitions of metadata are so numerous, a sampling of definitions from the literature is probably the best way to start. By far the most widespread definition is the succinct sentence: "Metadata is data about data." This can be found, at least as the opening salvo, in nearly all articles on the subject, although this routine definition by itself doesn't take us very far in understanding what metadata is and why we need it.

Definitions in sources from the United Kingdom and Australia, both countries extremely active in research and projects for digital preservation, remind us that although the term is commonly used to describe information about electronic resources, it can also include library catalog records, including printed ones. Library cataloging records, in fact, are described in many places as metadata, which existed long before the term was coined, a sort of bibliographic version of Moliere's famous sentence in which his bourgeois gentilhomme exclaims rapturously that all these years he didn't know he was talking prose. PADI, an acronym for the National Library of Australia's Web site on Preserving Access to Digital Information, defines metadata as "structured information, perhaps contained in an attached header, that describes other resources. Catalogue records for library materials are a common example of metadata." Michael Day also points out the connection between today's metadata and the traditional library bibliographic record: "When the library and information community discuss metadata, the most common analogy given is the library catalogue record. Priscilla Caplan, for example, has defined metadata as a neutral term for cataloguing without the 'excess baggage' of the *Anglo-American Cataloguing Rules* or the MARC formats" (Day, 1997).

Among metadata experts, a schism has arisen between those who prefer to define metadata broadly, essentially as "data about data," which more or less covers records in all formats, print or electronic, for resources in all formats, print or electronic, and those who prefer to define it narrowly as encoded data about networked electronic resources. In the first category, for example, we find Jane Greenberg and Priscilla Caplan. Greenberg states that distinguishing between cataloging and metadata by maintaining that "*cataloging* is for *physical objects* and *metadata* is exclusively for *electronic resources*.... is not well founded given that it is *common* practice for libraries to catalog computer disks, CD-ROMS, videos, multimedia resources, and other electronic resources, and they have been doing so for nearly three decades" (Greenberg, 2002, p. 246). Caplan acknowledges that "there is inconsistent use of the term 'metadata' even within the library community, some using it to refer to the description of both digital and nondigital resources and others restricting it to electronic resources only" (Caplan, 2003, p. 2). She feels that it is more useful to think of metadata as describing all types of information resources, including print publications, because collections in today's libraries are hybrid collections, made up of both digital and nondigital objects, and in addition, there are publications that appear in both digital and nondigital format. Thus, if we define metadata as describing only electronic resources, we could end up arguing that a cataloging record for an e-journal was metadata whereas a record for the print version of the same publication was not (Caplan, 2003, p. 2).

On the other side of the metadata schism, Hudgins, Agnew, and Brown prefer to narrow it down to the functional definition of metadata. They define metadata by describing its most common function, while at the same time broadening the definition to include some of the new functions data about data acquires in the networked environment: "The term 'metadata' commonly refers to any data that aids in the identification, description and location of networked electronic resources. Another important function provided by metadata is control of the electronic resource, whether through ownership and provenance metadata for validating information and tracking use; rights and permissions metadata for controlling access; or content ratings metadata, a key component of some Web filtering applications (Hudgins, Agnew, and Brown, 1999, p.1).

Like Hudgins, Agnew, and Brown, Dempsey defines metadata functionally, as "data which describes the attributes of a resource. It can therefore be bibliographic data but may also include other description related to content, terms and conditions for use, coverage and technical or access characteristics" (Dempsey, 1998). In an earlier report on the first Metadata Workshop in Luxembourg in December 1997, Dempsey and Makx Dekkers first define metadata with the generic and universal "data about data" phrase, but then narrow it down to its common usage: " In a more narrow sense, however, metadata commonly refers to information available on the Internet. This is also the environment where the necessity of good description mechanisms was becoming the most pressing: on the Internet and most notably the World Wide Web" (Dekkers and Dempsey, 1998).

No one could argue with Caplan that it would be silly to refer to a cataloging record for an e-journal as metadata and a record for the print version of the same journal as something else (traditional cataloging?). Some of the encoding schema or metadata schema described in the following chapters are intended or at least usable to create cataloging records for print resources as well, such as MARC and EAD, which are used to create exclusively electronic *records* but which can describe print *resources or finding aids*). Most, however, will be systems created to produce encoded records for networked resources.

Arlene Taylor, in the recently published second edition of *The Organization of Information* (Taylor, 2004) sums up the reasons for the many varieties of definitions and concepts people include under the umbrella term "metadata":

> People can mean many different things when they refer to "metadata." Discussions of the topic may be about any of the following or any combination of the following conceptual components: the information package and its attributes, content standards (rules for describing the package), metadata schemas, metadata elements, metadata records, and encoding formats…. An example to illustrate this can be found in the MARC format. While many consider MARC to be only an encoding format, others refer to it as a metadata schema. MARC exhibits properties of both, and on close examination it even acts as a content standard by dictating the contents and formats of certain data elements, especially the fixed fields. So it is not surprising that there is some confusion about metadata. (Taylor, 2004, p. 140)

Finally, Greenberg, while advocating an inclusive definition of metadata (information about physical objects as well as electronic resources), acknowledges that there are new circumstances in the world of information organization that "permit, to some degree, a distinction between what has traditionally been labeled as *cataloging* and what is now viewed as *metadata activity* (Greenberg, 2002, p. 247). These "new circumstances" are as follows:

1. the Internet and Web technology have introduced new information formats, new encoding languages (e.g., HTML, XML) and new attribute value schemas (e.g., MIME);

2. the Web has sparked the development of many metadata schemas by different communities outside the library environment; and

3. there is now an unprecedented emphasis on metadata schema standardization and interoperability.

The Chosen Definition

All these new circumstances that distinguish traditional cataloging from metadata activity are the subject of this book. Thus, while granting the validity of the inclusive definition, we concentrate primarily on metadata as it is most commonly thought of both inside and outside of the library community, as "structured information used to find, access, use and manage information resources primarily in a digital environment" (*International Encyclopedia of Information and Library Science*, 2003). Robby Robson gives a similar functional definition of metadata that *includes* cataloging as part of what metadata does but holds that cataloging is only one part of a tripartite function (Robson, n.d.). He says that metadata is "descriptive information associated with digital objects for cataloging, search and discovery," defining *cataloging* as the act of sorting objects for storage and being able to retrieve them later, *search and discovery* as finding objects by matching syntactic or semantic criteria, and *delivery* as causing a copy of an identified object to be available to a user.

We explore the influence on libraries of metadata in the narrower sense—in the sense that it is indeed different from cataloging before the digital revolution and the infiltration of the word "metadata" into the consciousness of all library and information professionals—as anything used to describe and or to organize *electronic, and primarily Web,* resources (born digital and digitized) for management and/or retrieval. At the same time, we relate to metadata as broader than cataloging (at least according to Robson's definition of cataloging) in that it also functions to enable objects to be located by "matching syntactic or semantic criteria" and delivered by "causing a copy of an identified object to be available to a user" (Robson, n.d.). If this sounds like a paradox, it may help to remember that first and most universally accepted definition of metadata as "data about data," which leaves room for virtually every aspect of the content, form, platform, provenance, behavior, and environment of an information object that there is to describe.

Metadata Principles

Having defined the scope and focus of our coverage of metadata, we devote the rest of this chapter to an exploration of the various ways metadata specialists have divided metadata into categories: according to conceptual principles underpinning metadata, by misconceptions about metadata, by metadata creation types, by functional categories of metadata, by metadata association models, and by mixed models that attempt to organize metadata characteristics into comprehensive and comprehensible groups.

Duval et al. (2002) divide metadata into four organizing principles: modularity, extensibility, refinement, and multilingualism.

Modularity, the first principle, allows metadata schema designers to create new metadata applications by combining elements from various previously established metadata schemas. It thus allows them to benefit from the best features of each schema, putting diverse elements together in the most appropriate way for a specific application in a syntactically and semantically interoperable way. Duval et al. use the "Lego metaphor" to explain this concept, comparing the reuse of existing modules of metadata to snapping together individual Lego blocks in order to assemble them into a larger structure. One of the fundamental concepts underlying modularity is the notion of namespaces. This is perhaps a suitable place to clear up some matters of terminology. In the literature about metadata, a number of terms are used to name what is essentially the same concept: a set of encoded fields, each of which is used to contain a different property of an information resource, which are combined to form a record describing that information resource. This set of encoded fields may be called a metadata element set, a metadata scheme, a metadata schema, a metadata system or, finally, a namespace.

Robson defines a metadata schema as "a system used to assign metadata to objects" (Robson, n.d.) and defines the four parts of a schema as *elements* that serve as "labels" with agreed-on interpretations and formats (e.g., a field called "title" with a format of not more than 1,024 characters in length), *taxonomies* that define controlled vocabulary that can be used to populate the elements, *obligations* that require certain elements to be used in any metadata instance, and *extension* rules that say how the schema can legitimately be expanded and altered. Blanchi and Petrone (2001) define what they consider four essential metadata terms—essentially two sets of two terms: *metadata element, metadata element instance, metadata schema, metadata schema instance.* The first term, metadata element, represents an abstract yet specific concept which characterizes data, such as "Creator," whereas the second term, metadata element instance, is a specific example of that concept, such as "Susan Lazinger." The third term, metadata schema, represents a set of unique data elements used to describe information resources, and the fourth term, metadata schema instance, again refers to a specific example of this concept, such as the Dublin Core.

Duval et al. (2002) define a namespace as "a formal collection of terms managed according to a policy or algorithm." An example of a namespace from the library world is *LCSH,* which is a namespace managed by the Library of Congress according to rules *governing* the assignment of subject headings to intellectual artifacts. All metadata element sets are namespaces bounded by the rules determined by the agency which maintains them. Namespace declarations allow the designers of a metadata schema to define the context for a particular term, which ensures that the definition of the term within the bounds of that namespace is unique. At the beginning of an RDF record, for example, is a namespace declaration that gives both the name of the metadata element set or sets used to describe the properties of the information resource and the URL or Internet address at which the official syntax of the metadata element set/schema/system/namespace is set forth. At the beginning of an XML record is a namespace declaration that gives the URL of the site on which the meaning of each field in the particular document type used for the specific XML application of which the record is part is defined. For example, the rules and conventions of the Dublin Core metadata element set —that is, the names of the fields it contains, what each field means, and what rules govern the content of each field—are defined (declared) on the Web site located at the address (URI/URL) of the Dublin Core Metadata Initiative, which is responsible for the development and maintenance of the Dublin Core element set. When various namespaces, that is, metadata element sets or metadata schema, are combined within a single metadata record, the namespace declaration at the beginning of the record enables the elements or fields within the record to be identified as belonging to one or another element set. The concept of namespaces and their role in the syntactic operability of metadata models are discussed in more detail in Chapter 2.

Extensibility, the second metadata principle, refers to the ability of metadata systems to allow for extensions so that the needs of a particular application can be accommodated. There are metadata elements that are likely to be found in any metadata schema such as the concept of the *creator* of an information resource or its *identifier* (URI/URL). On the other hand, there are other terms/fields that will be specific to a specific application for a specific community, such as *degree of cloud cover* in remote sensing data (Duval et al., 2002). For example, there are metadata schemas created and maintained by professional communities that are based on the Dublin Core metadata element set to which domain-specific fields have been added to extend its usefulness to the community's metadata needs. A corollary of the principle of extensibility is that metadata architectures *need* to be constructed so that they easily accommodate the idea of a base schema with additional elements that tailor a specific application to local or domain-specific needs without seriously compromising the interoperability of the base schema. In other words, someone using another application who encounters these extensions should be able to ignore them and still make use of any common elements in the two schemas.

Refinement refers to the ability of a metadata schema to allow its users to choose a level of detail appropriate to a given application. The concept of refinement includes two subconcepts. The first is the addition of qualifiers that make the meaning of an element more specific (i.e., *refine* the meaning). Examples are *Date of creation, Date of modification,* and *Date of acceptance,* all of which refine or make the date attribute narrower and more specific. The second subconcept of refinement is the specification of value sets that define the range of values of a given element. Using the date attribute again, the encoding of dates using a specific encoding standard stating that all dates are input as *yyyy-mm-dd* removes the ambiguity with regard to a string like 06/10/03—which means "June 10, 2003" in North America and "October 6, 2003" in most of the rest of the world—by encoding it as *2003-06-10.* Other elements, such as Subject, can use a traditional library standard such as the controlled vocabulary of *LCSH,* to improve subject access to electronic resources as well. It should be remembered, however, that refinement is a *feature* of metadata, like all the metadata principles discussed in this section, not a *requirement.* That is, metadata schemas such as the Dublin Core may be used without refining the meaning of their fields if the goal of the user is to produce simple records with an absolute minimum of effort or previous expertise. Refinement simply introduces the possibility of producing a much more finely honed description of a resource if the user so desires.

Multilingualism, the last of the four metadata principles, states that it is essential to adopt metadata architectures that "respect linguistic and cultural diversity" (Duval et al., 2002). This last principle presents a paradox. Standards, the concern of the first three principles, foster internationalism and globalization of how we describe our resources. The unspoken subtext below standards utilization is that if we do *not* use tools such as controlled vocabularies and carefully defined namespaces, "the Web will fail to achieve its potential as a global information system" (Duval et al., 2002). At the same time, the need for localization requires adapting these standards to local contexts, a process that can sometimes work at cross purposes with the process of standardization. Although global resource discovery requires international standards, local applications often serve a specific local community better. One of the challenges of metadata development and use is ensuring that the infrastructure can support either strategy or a combination of the two. A starting point for promoting a global metadata architecture is translating metadata standards into a variety of languages. *DDC,* for example, has been translated into a number of languages, promoting the refinement of subject description for global discovery while answering local needs for a controlled vocabulary that can be understood and applied by metadata creators whose native language is not English. Multilingualism, by the way, is one aspect of the broader issue of multiculturalism, which was noted earlier in the way in which dates are represented in different countries. Another multilingual, multicultural issue is the right-left issue, the direction in which text is displayed and read: English and European languages from left to right and Arabic and Hebrew from right to left. Although these issues go beyond the specific context of metadata, they are also part and parcel of the need for metadata to describe the relevant characteristics of resources in ways that take into account and respect linguistic and cultural differences.

Metadata Misconceptions

Although everyone who discusses metadata makes some effort to define what metadata *is*, relatively few make an effort to discuss what metadata *isn't*. Nilsson, Palmer, and Naeve (2002) are an exception, and their architectural guidelines for metadata creation (specifically metadata for e-learning) deserve some attention. The list of misconceptions include the following:

- Metadata is *objective* data about data.

- Metadata for a resource is produced only once.

- Metadata must have a logically defined semantics.

- Metadata can be described by metadata documents.

- Metadata is the digital version of library indexing systems.

- Metadata is machine-readable data about data.

Metadata is objective data about data. Nilsson et al. contend that although all metadata systems contain "indisputable" information such as title, author, identifier (the type of metadata that characterize most of the fields in Dublin Core) when other types of metadata enter the picture—for example, pedagogical purpose, assessments, and learning objectives (concepts in the educational metadata schemas that are the subject of their article)—*interpretative* rather than factual metadata is created. That is, "learning objectives" is not a property that is easily standardized into a controlled vocabulary, and even if it is, different metadata creators may see the learning objectives of a given resource differently. To take their contention a step further, professional catalogers know that even a property as seemingly "indisputable" as title is not really indisputable, because a title can have different parts, different spellings, and different uniform incarnations, as well as different interpretations by different catalogers.

Metadata for a resource is produced only once. Metadata, they stress, needs to be related to as a continuous work in progress. Updating and modifying metadata must be viewed as a natural part of the metadata creation and publishing process, an evolving kind of information that is subject to constant updates and modifications. Competition between descriptions is to be encouraged (a corollary of the first misconception) and combined into single, complex records for the same resource via RDF, the framework that allows the convenient combination of different namespaces into a single record (see Chapter 2). In fact, metadata for a specific resource does not even need to be contained in a single RDF document. For example, translations into different languages might be stored separately, different categories of metadata might be separated, and additional information might be added to an existing record by subsequent metadata creators. The result is what they call a global "meta-data ecosystem," which allows metadata to flourish and cross-fertilize, to evolve and be reused, and to benefit from the participation of everyone who wants to participate. Librarians should probably make the same assumption about ordinary cataloging because of changing subject headings, call numbers, and so on.

Metadata must have a logically defined semantics. There is no language up to the task of capturing all the possible meanings we might want to encode on the Web. Humans prefer to define their semantics whenever they need it. Even RDF, which Nilsson et al. feel is a nice compromise that gives the metadata creator the opportunity to define a vocabulary or reuse vocabulary defined elsewhere, will never be more than a patchwork of many small de facto vocabularies developed in small steps by people who need them for specific tasks. The evolution of these vocabularies approximates the evolution of natural languages, in fact, never arriving at any final form, but instead changing continuously and reflecting the needs of those using it.

Metadata can be described by metadata documents. This misconception has its roots in XML and its popularity as a metadata document format. An XML document is essentially a labeled tree containing text. An XML metadata document cannot be arbitrarily inserted into another XML metadata document, combining metadata element sets in the way that RDF statements do. In Chapter 2, we delve more deeply into the "great RDF-XML debate," but suffice it to say here that in the opinion of Nilsson and his colleagues XML documents, each of which is defined as a document type that cannot be combined modularly with another document type, are not the best way to create metadata. XML documents are more restrictive because each XML schema defines precisely which schema you are allowed to use and each new metadata vocabulary you need to support requires defining a new profile for the new application.

Metadata is the digital version of library indexing systems. Traditional library indexing systems (by which Nilsson et al. seem to mean traditional descriptive and subject cataloging systems) do considerable less than metadata. Metadata, besides carrying out the descriptive and subject defining functions of traditional library systems (e.g., *AACR2, LCSH, DDC*), serves additional functions, such as certifying content, tracking the history of extensions and versions, and monitoring and tracking processes and interactions, to name a few.

Metadata is machine-readable data about data. In the context of this misconception, Nilsson et al. present a long discussion of the Semantic Web that is out of the scope of this book. What is significant for our purposes here is that metadata is not only for machine consumption. Computers are a medium for human-to-human communication, and therefore conceptual metadata that is understandable both to humans and machines (unlike, say, the exclusively machine-readable Leader section of the library community's MARC encoding system described in Chapter 3) can definitely form an important part of that communication. In addition, if machine-readable semantic information is clear and effective for human interpretation, searchers will be less vulnerable to "surfing-sickness" on the Web, which leaves searchers confused about how they got transferred to a new and unfamiliar context from the conceptual context from which they started.

Types of Metadata

Automatically Generated Indexes

The first type of metadata is automatically generated. It includes the indexes used by search engines and other locator services that generate indexes through crawlers and spiders. It does not include indexes such as Yahoo, which use people to classify networked resources into a hierarchical directory.

Automatically generated indexes are what are known as "on-the-fly" records, created electronically for immediate use when a search is implemented on the Web. That is, a user puts in search terms, and a listing of authors, titles, and/or dates, and sometimes the first few lines of the document, are returned. The search may be done on the other type of record—manually created MARC records from a library catalog that has been converted to HTML encoded records to create a Web interface. If the user clicks on a record number in the list, the MARC record is put through the HTML converter that has been written for the catalog so that it can be displayed on the screen (Day, 1997). Although automatically generated indexes cost nothing additional to create, they often contain too little information to be useful.

Manually Created Records

Cataloging records, such as the records libraries worldwide produce in the MARC data format, are examples of manually created metadata, that is, surrogates for the original information resource. Library cataloging records with a Web interface sometimes also contain URLs that link the metadata to the original information source (if it is an online source), just as indexes generated automatically by search engines always do. The Dublin Core, which is discussed in detail in Chapter 2, is an example of a manually created metadata model intended (at least originally) "to mediate these extremes, affording a simple structured record that may be enhanced or mapped to more complex records as called for, either by direct extension or by a link to a more elaborate record" (Weibel, 1995). In the years since Weibel wrote this, other means of enhancing the "simple structured record," *refinements* called "qualifiers" (see Chapter 2) have come into being, providing another means for producing more detailed, elaborate records.

Categories of Metadata

Metadata has usually been divided into three- to five-category taxonomies in the literature. Roy Tennant's 1998 taxonomy divides metadata into three categories:

descriptive metadata, which includes the creator of the resource, its title, subject headings, and other elements that will be used to search for and locate the item;

structural metadata, which describes how an item is structured—for example, if it is an electronic book composed of scanned pages, each of which is a separate computer image file; and

administrative metadata, which includes such things as how the digital file was produced and its ownership (Tennant, 1998, p. 30).

In another early survey of metadata usage and classifications, de Carvalho Moura et al. (1998) suggest a functional classification of metadata based on four metadata component types: metadata for resource discovery, metadata for resource availability, metadata for resource usage, and metadata for resource administration and control. Among the differences, we see that whereas Tennant gives structural metadata an entire category, the de Carvalho classification puts structural metadata into the first category (metadata for resource discovery). The four categories are divided further into the following subcategories:

Metadata for resource discovery

- ◆ Basic bibliographic descriptive metadata (e.g., author, title, series)
- ◆ Metadata for resource unique identification on the Web (e.g., URN, ISBN)
- ◆ Metadata for general content description (e.g., abstract)

- Metadata for subject description (e.g., keywords, subject descriptors)
- Metadata for structure description (e.g., description of images)
- Metadata for relationship description (e.g., elements associating resource to related documents)
- Metadata for describing resource provenance (e.g., data providers)
- Metadata for format and media description (e.g., size, format, compression standards)

Metadata for resource availability

- Metadata for resource distribution (e.g., contact, order process information)
- Terms and conditions for resource access (e.g., access authority permission)
- Terms and conditions for resource use (e.g., copyright notice, restrictions on copying)
- Metadata on resource requirements (e.g., special viewers, hardware or software configurations)
- Metadata for resource location (e.g., URL, access protocol)
- Metadata on resource authenticity (e.g., digital signature)

Metadata for resource usage

- Metadata for resource content classification (e.g., rating labels, security classification control)
- Metadata for describing resource data quality (e.g., degree of reliability, error estimate)
- Metadata for describing resource purpose (e.g., related programs, projects, discussion forums)
- Metadata for resource contextual description (e.g., domain, revision, derivation)

Metadata for resource administration and control

- Metadata for resource modification control (e.g., modification and review dates)
- Metadata for resource administration (e.g., creation date, resource administrators)
- Metadata for resource use history (e.g., copy, edition, removal)
- Metadata for metadata administration (e.g., standard name, standard version)

Anne J. Gilliland-Swetland asserts that metadata in today's information domains needs an even broader scope to provide the data about electronic resources needed by different segments of the academic and business community:

An Internet resource provider might use metadata to refer to information being encoded into HTML metatags for the purposes of making a Web site easier to find. Individuals digitizing images might think of metadata as the information they enter into the header field for the digital file to record information about the image, the imaging process, and image rights. A social science data archivist might use the term to refer to the systems and research documentation necessary to run and interpret a magnetic tape containing raw research data. An electronic records archivist might use the term to refer to all the contextual, processing, and use information needed to identify and document the scope, authenticity, and integrity of a record in an electronic system. (Gilliland-Swetland, 2000a, p. 3)

Metadata, she continues, is needed not only to identify and describe an information object, but also to document how that object behaves, its function and uses, its relationship to other information objects, and how it should be managed. To cover all of these perspectives, she divides metadata into five distinct categories—administrative, descriptive, preservation, use, and technical metadata—according to key aspects of metadata functionality. Her five-category table of metadata types (categories) and functions is shown in Table 1.1.

Table 1.1 Different Types of Metadata and Their Functions

Type	Definition	Examples
Administrative	Metadata used in managing and administering information resources	Acquisition information Rights and reproduction tracking Documentation of legal access requirements Location information Selection criteria for digitization Version control
Descriptive	Metadata used to describe or identify information resources	Cataloging records Finding aids Specialized indexes Hyperlinked relationships between resources Annotations by users
Preservation	Metadata related to the preservation management of information resources	Documentation of physical condition of resources Documentation of actions taken to preserve physical and digital versions of resources, e.g., data refreshing and migration

Type	Definition	Examples
Technical	Metadata related to how a system functions or metadata behaves	Hardware and software documentation Digitization information, e.g., formats, compression ratios, scaling routines Tracking of response times Authentication and security data, e.g., encryption keys, passwords
Use	Metadata related to the level and type of use of information resources	Exhibition records Use and user tracking Content reuse and multi-versioning information

From Gilliland-Swetland, 2000a, p. 3.

Metadata Association Models

Metadata can be created at the time of creation of a digital object, either by or under the auspices of its creator, or added later as part of the traditional cataloging process. Furthermore, there are a number of ways that the created metadata can be stored and managed to facilitate retrieval of the documents.

Storing Metadata in the Items Themselves: Embedded Metadata

Metadata stored as a part of the resource to which it relates can be stored in the HTML Metatag. This implies that the metadata is created at the time that the resource is created, usually by the author. Experts differ concerning whether author-created metadata is preferable to metadata created later by experts or trained practitioners (Duval et al., 2002). In this type of storage metadata about the page is embedded within the page. This embedded metadata is not seen when the page is viewed. The META element is used within the HEAD element of an HTML document to embed document meta-information not defined by other HTML elements. The META element can be used to identify properties of a document (e.g., author, expiration date, a list of key words, etc.) and assign values to those properties.

It is possible to control how your page is indexed by search engines using the META tag to specify additional keywords to index that might reasonably describe your Web site but that you would not necessarily want in the text, as illustrated in the following example (Lazinger, 2001, p. 171):

```
<HTML>
 <HEAD>
 <TITLE>The Web Developer's Virtual Library
 </TITLE>
 <META NAME = "Keywords" CONTENT = "
 HTML, CGI, Java, VRML, browsers, plugins,
 graphics, HTTP servers, JavaScript, Perl,
 ActiveX, Shockwave">
 <META NAME = "Description" CONTENT="
 Locate web authoring & software Internet
 resources at The WDVL, a well-organised
 goldmine with over 500 pages and thousands
 of links about HTML, CGI, Java, VRML,
 browsers, plugins, graphics, HTTP servers,
 JavaScript, Perl, ActiveX, Shockwave,..">
 </HEAD>
```

The problem with the keywords metatag, however, is that in the past it has been used for "spamindexing," (also known as "spamdexing" or "spamming"). That is, the keywords metatag has frequently been misused to repeat keywords over and over or to insert words that really have nothing to do with the Web site but are likely to draw people to the site ("sex" being the example usually used to illustrate this misuse of the keywords metatag; Alimohammadi, 2003). As a result, many of the major search engines began to ignore the entire tag in their indexing, making the usefulness of inserting metadata in the metatag for retrieval purposes uncertain.

The advantages of storing metadata in the HTML Metatag are that it directly associates the metadata with the resource and makes the metadata available to search engines, if they choose to use it. This tight coupling between the metadata and the resource also ensures that "whenever the resource is copied or moved, the metadata goes with it. Whenever the resource is modified, the metadata is right there to be modified as well. When the resource is deleted, the metadata goes away as well" (Architecture for Access …, 1998).

Storing Metadata in Linked Items: Associated Metadata

The alternative to storing the metadata in the resource itself is to store it separately from the resource, which can be done in several ways.

The first method of external metadata storage is in linked items, such as in library catalogs of MARC bibliographic records that link to the item itself. Many library catalogs with Web interfaces have a direct link from the title field of the bibliographic record directly to whatever electronic resource it describes. The disadvantage of storing the metadata and the resources separately, however, particularly if they are on separate servers, is that the automatic linkage is lost. A resource could be copied, moved, deleted, or modified without modifying the associated metadata. The advantage to storing the metadata and the resources separately, on the other hand, is that because the metadata is normally a much smaller file than the resource itself, a single server can store much more metadata, making searching more efficient: fewer servers need to be accessed to search the metadata (Lazinger, 2001, p. 172). Another advantage of associated metadata is the relative ease of managing the metadata without altering the content of the resource itself (Duval et al., 2002).

Storing Metadata in External Catalogs or Finding Aids: Third-party Metadata

Metadata may also be stored in unlinked databases, such as catalogs of bibliographic records without hyperlinks to the resource. Third-party metadata is maintained in a separate repository by an organization that may or may not have any control over or access to the content of the resource (Duval et al., 2002). Furthermore, such metadata may be maintained in a database that is not accessible to harvesters, although the Open Archives Initiative Metadata Harvesting Protocol proposes a system that encourages the disclosure of metadata repositories among federated OAI servers (*The Open Archives Initiative for Metadata Harvesting*, 2001). EAD locator records (see Chapter 3) that point to collections rather than individual records are another example of separately stored, unlinked metadata because obviously a locator record cannot link to a collection, but only to an individual digital resource.

There are several disadvantages to this storage method. First, as mentioned earlier, the metadata may not be directly accessible by public search engines. Second, accessing the metadata may require a published application program interface (API), such as Z39.50 in a records management system, involving an agency-defined database schema and an API that ensures integration with the management of the agency's internal resources. Finally, as with any metadata storage method, linked or unlinked, which maintains the metadata separately from the digital object, the danger of having the resource modified, copied, moved, or deleted while the metadata remains unchanged, and therefore no longer accurate, always exists.

The advantages of metadata storage in unlinked databases are the same as storage in linked databases.

It is worth noting that any information resource may have multiple metadata records reflecting the differing purposes and perspectives of the organizations that create and manage them. For example, a resource may be created with embedded metadata supplied by the author, may also be associated with a separated record created by the issuing organization (such as the publisher) and stored in a separate database, and in addition may have yet another version of metadata created by a third party such as a library, either from scratch or derived from a previous record, and stored in its online catalog (Duval et al., 2002).

Integrating Metadata with the Digital Object in a Repository Structure: Encapsulated Metadata

In addition to the three main methods for storing metadata, it may also be stored in a repository structure that integrates metadata with the digital object, on the same server. Storing all of the metadata with the record content in one encapsulated object ensures that metadata is always stored and transported with the record, simplifies the long-term management, and ensures that the retrieved record is physically self explanatory. Jeff Rothenberg's concept of "encapsulating" data along with all application and system software required to access it, plus a description of the original hardware environment needed to run them—to be used in the future to construct an emulator for the original hardware environment (see Chapter 8)—would require, in addition, the attachment of text only "bootstrap standard" metadata, that is, metadata that would provide contextual information and an explanation of how to decode the record itself.

Although this sort of approach might be useful for preserving, in particular, multimedia publications or complex hypertextual documents with all links maintained, the disadvantage of encapsulation is that much redundant metadata is stored with each record, adding to the cost (Lazinger, 2001, p. 173).

Conclusion: A Summary of Metadata Characteristics

One of the best summaries of all the metadata characteristics described earlier is found in Anne J. Gilliland-Swetland *Introduction to Metadata* (2000b), which divides up the attributes of metadata according to seven characteristics that she calls source, method of creation, nature, status, structure, semantics, and level.

Source

This attribute can be broken down into *internal metadata,* which is generated by the creating agent of an information object at the time when it is first created or digitized, and *external metadata* that is created later, often by somebody other than the original creator (Gilliland-Swetland, 2000a). Gilliland-Swetland gives files names and directory structures as examples of internal metadata and cataloging records and rights information as examples of external metadata. However, internal metadata can also include the kind of metadata found in external cataloging records, such as title and author-created keywords, although this type of metadata, if author created, is often stored as embedded data. External metadata is more commonly stored either as associated or unlinked metadata in separate databases.

Method of Creation

Metadata is either generated automatically by a computer or created manually by humans. Examples of automatic metadata are the keyword indexes generated by search engines and the user transaction logs that serve as the basis for much Internet use and usability research. Examples of manually created metadata are descriptive surrogates for digital objects such as MARC cataloging records and Dublin Core metadata.

Nature

Metadata can be created by persons who are neither specialists in the subject nor information specialists. This type of *lay metadata* is typical of metatags created for personal Web pages and personal filing systems. *Expert metadata,* on the other hand, is created either by subject specialists or information (cataloging) professionals, often not the creator of the information object, as external metadata. Examples of this kind of metadata are *Library of Congress Subject Headings* and other systems of specialized subject headings, MARC finding aids, and archival finding aids, such as EAD records (see Chapter 2).

Status

Metadata can also be categorized by its permanence or status into *static metadata, dynamic metadata,* and *long-term metadata. Static metadata* includes elements that never change once they have been created, such as title, provenance, and creation date of an information object. *Dynamic metadata* may change as the information object is used or manipulated and includes user transaction logs or directory structure. *Long-term metadata* includes those elements that are necessary for ensuring that the information object will remain accessible and usable. Examples of this kind of metadata are rights information, technical format, and preservation management documentation.

Structure

Structured metadata conforms to "a predictable standardized or unstandardized structure" (Gilliland-Swetland, 2000b). Examples of this kind of metadata are all the metadata element sets and encoding systems that are analyzed in detail in Chapters 2 and 3, such as MARC, TEI, and EAD. Examples of the other kind of metadata, *unstructured* metadata that does not conform to a predictable and consistent structure, are certain fields within these element sets or encoding systems, such as unstructured note fields and annotations.

Semantics

Controlled metadata conforms to a standardized vocabulary or authority form. Examples of such standardized systems include Library of Congress Subject Headings (which standardizes metadata vocabulary) and AACR (which standardizes metadata authority forms). *Uncontrolled* metadata does not conform to any standardized vocabulary or authority form and includes such elements as free-text notes and abstracts.

Level

Finally, metadata can be classified according to the level at which it describes an information object. That is, it can be *item metadata,* describing an individual information object, such as a single digitized image on a museum Web site. It can also be *collection metadata,* which relates to collections of information objects, such as the collection to which the single digitized image belongs or an entire collection of letters that form a personal archive.

Blanchi and Petrone (2001) describe metadata as existing in a state of perpetual heterogeneity. On one hand, metadata schema have run into problems of noninteroperability because they describe such a wide range of data genres created in so many diverse environments by such a wide variety of professional communities. This inexorable diversity leads to the constant development of new, data-specific metadata systems, which leads, in turn, to a multiplicity of metadata concepts and namespaces that complicate metadata interoperability. If one recognized metadata standard, such as the Dublin Core, could be adopted as the only metadata system for all the data communities that produce metadata (which has happened to a limited degree), there would be better metadata interoperability, but for practical, technical, and political reasons, this approach is not possible or even desirable. If one metadata system were adopted universally, the resulting metadata records would not be appropriate or adequate for describing all types of data and so would, in the end, not be interoperable anyway. One size simply does not fit all, and such a single universal standard would either provide insufficient information about the described information object or be overwhelmingly complex and difficult to create, resulting also in imprecise descriptions. Multiple metadata schema, therefore, are probably here to stay, and what remains for metadata system creators to do is to simply live with the diversity while channeling the metadata of different communities into frameworks such as RDF or application profiles in XML to achieve varying degrees of syntactic, structural, and semantic interoperability while maintaining the diversity necessary to answer the needs of each metadata community. In Chapters 2 and 3, we describe the different metadata schema of particular communities both within and without the library world, their relationships to each other, and the attempts and systems devised to fit them into interoperable frameworks.

Bibliography

Alimohammadi, Dariush. (2003). "Meta-tag: A Means to Control the Process of Web Indexing." *Online Information Review* 27 (4): 238–42.

Architecture for Access to Government Information. Report of the IMSC—Technical Group. Part B—Main Report [Online]. (1998). Available: http://www.defence. gov.au/imsc/imsctg/imsctg1b.htm

Berners-Lee, Tim. (2000). "Metadata Architecture" [Online]. Available: http://www. w3.org/DesignIssues/Metadata.html

Blanchi, Christophe, and Jason Petrone. (2001). "Distributed Interoperable Metadata Registry." *D-Lib Magazine* 7 (12) [Online]. Available: http://www.dlib.org/ dlib/december01/blanchi/12blanchi.html

Caplan, Priscilla. (2003). *Metadata Fundamentals for All Librarians.* Chicago: American Library Association.

Day, Michael. (1997). "Extending Metadata for Digital Preservation *Ariadne* 9 (May) [Online]. Available: http://www.ariadne.ac.uk/issue9/metadata/

de Carvalho Moura, Ana Maria, Maria Luiza Machado Campos, and Cassia Maria Barreto. (1998). "A Survey on Metadata for Describing and Retrieving Internet Resources." *World Wide Web* 1: 221–40.

Dekkers, Makx, and Lorcan Dempsey. (1998). "Feature: Metadata Workshop in Luxembourg Dec. 1997." *Library Technology* 3 [Online]. Available: http://www. sbu.ac.uk/litc/lt/1998/news634.html

Dempsey, Lorcan. (1998). Metadata: A UK HE Perspective [Online]. Available: http://www.ukoln.ac.uk/services/papers/bl/blri078/content/repor~27.htm

Duval, Eric, Wayne Hodgins, Stuart Sutton, and Stuart L. Weibel. (2002). "Metadata Principles and Practicalities." *D-Lib Magazine* 8 (4) [Online]. Available: http://www.dlib.org/dlib/april02/weibel/04weibel.html

Feather, John, and Paul Sturges, eds. (2003). *International Encyclopedia of Information and Library Science.* London: Routledge.

Gilliland-Swetland, Anne J. (2000a). "Defining Metadata." In *Introduction to Metadata: Pathways to Digital Information.* Edited by Murtha Baca. Los Angeles: Getty Research Institute.

Gilliland Swetland, Anne J. (2000b). "Introduction to Metadata: Setting the Stage" [Online]. Los Angeles, CA: Getty Information Institute. Available: http://www.getty.edu/research/institute/standards/intrometadata/

Greenberg, Jane. (2002). "Metadata and the World Wide Web." *Encyclopedia of Library and Information Science* 72, suppl. 35, 244–61.

Hudgins, Jean, Grace Agnew, and Elizabeth Brown. (1999). *Getting Mileage out of Metadata: Applications for the Library.* Chicago: American Library Association.

Lazinger, Susan S. (2001). *Digital Preservation and Metadata: History, Theory, Practice.* Englewood, CO: Libraries Unlimited.

Nilsson, Mikael, Matthias Palmer, and Ambjorn Naeve. (2002). "Semantic Web Metadata for e-Learning—Some Architectural Guidelines." In *WWW2002. The Eleventh International World Wide Web Conference,* Honolulu, Hawaii, 7–11 May 2002 [Online]. Available: http:// www2002.org/CDROM/alternate/744/

The Open Archives Initiative for Metadata Harvesting, Protocol Version 1.1 of 2001-07-02, Document Version 2001-06-20 [Online]. (2001). Available: http://www.openarchives.org/OAI/openarchivesprotocol.htm

Robson, Robby. (n.d.). "Metadata Matters" [Online]. Available: http://www.library.cornell.edu/dmlib/robson.pdf

Taylor, Arlene G. (2004). *The Organization of Information* (Library and Information Science Texts Series). 2d ed. Westport, CT: Libraries Unlimited.

Tennant, Roy. (1998). "Digital Libraries: 21st-Century Cataloging." *Library Journal* (April 15): 30–31.

Thorneley, Jennie. (1999). "The How of Metadata: Metadata Creation and Standards: Paper Presented at the 13th National Cataloguing Conference, 13-15 October, 1999." *State Library of Queensland Staff Publication* [Online]. Available: http://www.slq.qld.gov.au/pub/staff/catcon99.htm

Weibel, Stuart, Jean Godby, and Eric Miller. (1995). *OCLC/NCSA Metadata Workshop Report* [Online]. Available: http://www.oclc.org:5046/oclc/research/ conferences/metadata/dublin_core_report.html

Chapter 2

Metadata Schemas and Their Relationships to Particular Communities

Metadata Models and Interoperability

Every organization has its own internal language, its own jargon, that has evolved over time so people within it can communicate meaning to each other. Metadata identifies an organization's own "language," and where different terms refer to the same thing, a common term is agreed for all to use. The importance of metadata, then, lies among other things in the fact that "*metadata defines the common language used within an enterprise so that all people, systems and programs can communicate precisely*" (Finkelstein, 2001).

In an irreverent introduction to metadata in 2001, Cory Doctorow debunked the myth of "meta-utopia," an ideal world in which a number of suppliers get together and agree on a metadata standard for a given subject area—say, washing machines—agree to a common vocabulary for describing washing machines (e.g., size, capacity, energy consumption, water consumption, price) and create machine-readable databases of their inventory, so that a consumer can enter the parameters of the washing machine being sought and query multiple sites simultaneously for an exhaustive list of the washing machines that meet the consumer's criteria (Doctorow, 2001). In the real world, Doctorow contends, there are at least seven insurmountable obstacles to this meta-utopia:

1. People lie: Metadata exists in a competitive world ("Suppliers compete to sell their goods, cranks compete to convey their crackpot theories …").

2. People are lazy: Info-civilians are remarkably cavalier about their information ("Your clueless aunt sends you e-mail with no subject line, half the pages on Geocities are called 'Please title this page'…").

3. People are stupid: Even when there's clear benefit in creating good metadata, people steadfastly refuse to be careful and diligent in their metadata creation ("Take eBay: every seller there has a damned good reason for double-checking their listings.... Try searching for a "plam" on eBay. Right now, that turns up *nine* typoed listings for 'Plam Pilots'.").

4. Mission impossible—know thyself: People are lousy observers of their own behavior ("Ask a programmer how long it'll take to write a given module …").

5. Schemas aren't neutral: Any hierarchy of ideas necessarily implies the importance of some elements over others ("The idea that competing interests can come to easy accord on a common vocabulary totally ignores the power of organizing principles in a marketplace").

6. Metrics influence results: Agreeing to a common yardstick for measuring the important stuff in any domain privileges the items that score high on that metric ("Ranking axes are mutually exclusive: software that scores high for security scores low for convenience, desserts that score high for decadence score low for healthiness").

7. There's more than one way to describe something: Reasonable people can disagree forever on how to describe something ("This isn't smut, it's *art*"). (Doctorow, 2001)

Norman Paskin, originator of the Digital Object Identifier (DOI), points out that, in addition to the spectrum of social interoperability considerations, there are at least six types of technical interoperability:

- across media (such as books, serials, audio, audiovisual, software, visual material);
- across functions (such as cataloguing, discovery, workflow, and rights management);
- across levels of metadata (from simple to complex);
- across linguistic and semantic barriers;
- across territorial barriers; and
- across technology platforms. (Paskin, 2002)

The need for interoperability among emerging metadata standards, each of which defines the terminology of a different community or enterprise, has been recognized from the early days of development of metadata element sets and metalanguages by various communities, both within and without the library world.

In a presentation to a European Commission metadata workshop in 1998, Stuart Weibel refers to the need for three kinds of interoperability for electronic data and the standards appropriate for creating each of these three requirements:

A resource community is characterized by common semantic, structural and syntactic conventions for the exchange of resource descriptions. Standards used for semantic interoperability include Dublin Core, *Anglo-American Cataloguing Rules* (AACR2), TEI, and FGDC. Structural interoperability will be based on the Resource Description Framework (RDF). The W3C Extensible Markup Language (XML) will form the basis for syntactic interoperability. (*European Commission DGXIII/E 2nd Metadata Workshop*, 1998)

A year later, in a report on the state of the Dublin Core Metadata Initiative in April 1999, Weibel reiterates the requirements for interchange interoperability, adding the MARC standard to AACR2 for interoperability in library cataloging:

> For two applications to exchange metadata effectively, their metadata must have the same semantics and must share a common structure and syntax. The MARC standard, in conjunction with the second edition of the *Anglo-American Cataloguing Rules* (AACR2) establishes this level of interoperability for library cataloging, and it allows compliant applications to exchange and use metadata which is created according to these standards. (Weibel, 1999)

A few clarifying words are in order here about the meaning of "metadata must have the same semantics and must share a common structure and syntax." As Weibel (1999) states, there are three levels of interoperability required for exchange of metadata: semantic, structural, and syntactic. Semantic interoperability refers to the names of the fields. For example, to be semantically interoperable, the field name *Creator* in *Dublin Core* and *Personal Author* (100) in *MARC* must be understandable to search engines as differently named fields that convey essentially the same information about the resource: who is primarily responsible for it. Structural interoperability means that the fields that compose the schema must be, at least in part, the same fields. For example, many metadata schema used by very different communities (e.g., educational institutions, museums) base their field structure on the Dublin Core, adding additional fields as they see fit in order to describe their specific kinds of resources more precisely. Thus, at least the core fields of the schema are interoperable. Syntactic interoperability refers to the grammar of the metadata—the rules that govern how the information is presented, such as which fields are required and which optional, which fields are repeatable and which are not, what the hierarchical arrangement of the fields should be, what tags are required at the beginning and/or end of nesting subfields, and so on.

At the end of 2000, Weibel stated that the "promise of metadata modularity is only now, after five years of Web metadata development, coming into focus" (Weibel, 2000). Two years later, Weibel and several colleagues formulated the "Lego" approach to metadata modularity:

> In a modular metadata world, data elements from different schemas as well as vocabularies and other building blocks can be combined in a syntactically and semantically interoperable way. Thus, application designers should be able to benefit from significant re-usability as they gather existing modules of metadata and "snap" them together much as individual Lego™ blocks can be assembled into larger structures. (Duval et al., 2002)

In the same year, Ruth Martin remarked that in the past two years the metadata landscape has changed in several ways, with several important efforts at harmonization, combining, mapping, aligning or combining metadata approaches getting underway. These "important activities being discussed in various domains" include the IFLA Functional Requirements for Bibliographic Records (FRBR) model (concentrating on the various forms—conceptual and physical—of content and the relationships between those forms), and the ABC Ontology and model (elaborating a model that looks specifically at interoperability between metadata approaches and concentrates on the activities that are associated with content) (Martin, 2002). Both the IFLA FRBR model and the ABC Ontology and model are discussed more fully in Chapter 3.

In spite of developing approaches featuring reusability, harmonization, and combining metadata schemas, there are still far more metadata applications than anyone can easily follow. Any standardization activity, furthermore, reaches the point where the stable definition of the standard needs to be published, and metadata standards are no different from other standards in this respect. In addition to publication in print form or on a Web site so that a human audience can read and understand them, many metadata standardization activities now see a need for publication of the standard in machine-readable format, that is, as a *schema*. A metadata registry is the mechanism used to publish such schemas, allowing their discovery, interpretation, and reuse (Dekkers, 2001). Another emerging use of registries is for the publication of Application Profiles, which consist of data elements drawn from one or more metadata schemas and combined by implementers to answer the needs of a specific application.

Metadata registries, then, have been established as a way to capture the official definitions of the various defined terms comprising a given metadata standard, to include policies or recommended practice for use of the defined terms and, within the Dublin Core Metadata Initiative (DCMI), to become the definitive repository of DCMI schemas, including formal definitions for defined terms in all of the languages for which there are translations, and to manage changes and additions to the DCMI metadata element set.

The DCMI's Metadata Registry was designed to promote the discovery and reuse of existing metadata definitions. It provides users and applications with an authoritative source of information about the Dublin Core element set and related vocabularies. This simplifies the discovery of terms and related definitions and illustrates the relationship between terms.

The reuse of existing metadata terms is essential to standardization and promotes greater interoperability between metadata element sets. The discovery of existing terms is an essential prerequisite step in this process. It promotes the wider adoption, standardization, and interoperability of metadata by facilitating its discovery and reuse, across diverse disciplines and communities of practice. The application was developed and is distributed as an open-source project, built entirely on open-source/open-standards software (*Dublin Core Metadata Registry*, 2004).

Established in 1999, by the end of 2003 the DCMI Registry Working Group listed its specific goals as follows:

1. Provide a forum for input and discussion of functional requirements.

2. Promote the evolution of the Registry architecture from a centralized to a distributed model.

3. Evaluate, identify, and implement extensions to the registry software that support diverse, heterogeneous communities of practice, and facilitate inter-Registry cooperation.

4. Explore solutions for implementing and distributing authoritative multilingual metadata through a network of distributed registries. (Dublin Core Metadata Initiative, 2004a)

In the following sections of this chapter and in Chapter 3, metadata standards mentioned in the discussion of interoperability are discussed in detail. Here, the history, structure, and current status of some of the more important metadata standards that have been developed and maintained by communities outside the library and archives world are covered, and in Chapter 3, the same is done for those standards that not only influenced libraries and archives but also emerged from within them.

Syntactic Interoperability: Metalanguages

Two important tools for the creation of rich metadata description that have emerged among Web technologies are Standard Generalized Markup Language (SGML) and its subset format, eXtensible Markup Language (XML). Unlike Hypertext Markup Language (HTML), which is a fixed Document Type Definition (DTD) and is therefore discussed in the next section of this chapter, these two document creation languages are *metalanguages,* capable of embedding descriptive elements within the document markup itself. That is, the markup is not set and confined to a specific set of tags, as in HTML, but rather capable of allowing the author to define his own document type both to create and to index Web content.

DTDs are standards developed by various user communities, such as HTML, which is the most widely used markup language on the Web, the Text Encoding Initiative (TEI) developed by the humanities computing domain, or Encoded Archival Description (EAD), an SGML DTD developed by the archives community to digitize collection finding aids. The two metalanguages, SGML and XML, have greatly expanded the potential within the communities, producing and organizing electronic documents because they allow the author to create a DTD that defines the fields to be used and provide rules to govern the application of those fields within the document (Hudgins et. al., 1999, p. 3).

SGML

SGML is a metalanguage because it is a language for describing markup languages, just as metadata is data about data. As mentioned earlier, HTML is an example of a language defined in SGML. SGML is an international standard, ISO 8879, that prescribes a format for embedding descriptive markup within a document and then specifies a method to describe the structure of that document.

The advantage of SGML is that it allows very rich possibilities for document creation and indexing because the markup is not set, as in the simple HTML DTD, to display only text or provide hyperlinks. It not only enables the creation of lists, page breaks, and paragraphs, for example, but also allows different DTDs to provide marking of historical background, ownership, and provenance; controlled vocabulary subject headings within the text; floating tags for information contained within the text (such as author, title, and date); information about the electronic document; and also information about the original—generally print-based—source material. Its three claims to fame are extensibility, structuring capabilities, and validation capabilities. SGML allows one to deal with complex resources in a highly structured fashion and to do it in such a way that allows one to validate the structure as the markup is taking place (Schottlaender, 2003, p. 21).

Because SGML allows parts of the document itself to be labeled or categorized more specifically than HTML, it provides the potential for more precise full-text retrieval. Because it ensures that the indexing is not separated from the text, including indexing both within the text itself and, for descriptive data, within a header, it provides a "reliable method for insuring persistent indexing for electronic texts" (Hudgins et al., 1999, p. 3). This is a critical issue in electronic data archiving in which the digital object and the indexing record must be maintained, updated, and linked over long periods of time and various server architectures.

The major disadvantage of SGML, however, is that despite its feature- richness and flexibility, it is highly complex, and applying it demands a rigor that not everyone is willing to invest. It is SGML's high level of complexity that has inhibited its adoption in a wide variety of environments, including the Web environment. Other disadvantages of SGML include its lack of widely supported style sheets, complex and unstable software because of its broad and powerful options, and obstacles to interchange of SGML data because of varying levels of SGML compliance among SGML software packages.

XML: Namespaces and Application Profiles

XML is a simplified subset of SGML intended for Web applications. It keeps SGML's extensibility, along with SGML's structure and validation capabilities, but it is much simpler to apply. XML was in fact developed "as a means of regaining the power and flexibility of SGML without most of its complexity" (W3C, 1999d). Thus XML preserves most of SGML's power, richness, and commonly used features while making it relatively easy to introduce new elements or additional element attributes. At the same time, it removes many of the more complex features of SGML that make the authoring of suitable software both difficult and expensive (W3C, 1999d).

Defined by the World Wide Web Consortium as a data format for structured document interchange, XML 1.0 was issued in February 1998 by the W3C XML Working Group as a recommended standard (Hudgins et al., 1999, p. 3). XML looks somewhat like HTML, making use of tags (words bracketed by < and >) and attributes of the form name="value", but:

> While HTML specifies what each tag & attribute means (and often how the text between them will look in a browser), XML uses the tags only to delimit pieces of data, and leaves the interpretation of the data completely to the application that reads it. In other words, if you see "<p>" in an XML file, don't assume it is a paragraph. Depending on the context, it may be a price, a parameter, a person, a p…(b.t.w., who says it has to be a word with a "p"?). (W3C, 1999d)

Metadata is published in a DTD file for reference by other systems. A DTD file defines the structure of an XML file or document.

An example of an XML document identifying data retrieved from a PERSON database is illustrated in Figure 2.1. This includes metadata markup tags (surrounded by < … >, such as <person_name>) that provide various details about a person. From this, we can find specific contact information in <contact_details>, such as <email>, <phone>, <fax>, and <mobile> (cell phone) numbers.

Figure 2.1. Example of an XML document identifying data retrieved from a PERSON database.

```
<PERSON person_id="p1100" sex="M">
<person_name>
        <given_name>Clive</given_name>
        <surname>Finkelstein</surname>
        </person_name>
        <company>
            Information Engineering Services Pty Ltd
        </company>
        <country>Australia</country>
        <contact_details>
            <email>cfink@ies.aust.com</email>
            <phone>+61-8-9402-8300</phone>
            <phone>(08) 9309-6163</phone>
            <fax>+61-8-9402-8322</fax>
            <mobile>+61-411-472-375</mobile>
            <mobile>0411-472-375</mobile>
        </contact_details>
        </PERSON>
```

Source: Finkelstein, Clive. (2001). "XML—The Future of Metadata" [Online]. Extract from *Building Corporate Portals with XML.* New York: McGraw-Hill, 1999. Available: http://members.ozemail.com.au/~visible/papers/xml-metadata.htm. Reprinted with permission of McGraw-Hill.

The DTD can also specify that certain tags must exist or are optional, and whether some tags can exist more than once, such as multiple <phone> and <mobile> tags in the example.

Along with XML come namespaces. Simply put, a namespace is "a formal collection of terms managed according to a policy or algorithm" (Duval et al., 2002). Any metadata element set is a namespace bounded by the rules and conventions determined by its maintenance agency. In an XML record, the namespace name in the namespace declaration (e.g., "dc" for Dublin Core) is associated with a URL or URI. The example in Figure 2.2, which shows Dublin Core metadata in an XML document, illustrates the concept of namespaces:

In the example in Figure 2.2, Dublin Core elements are prepended by the namespace name dc: (i.e., it is attached to the beginning of data). The name is associated with the URI http://purl.org/dc/elements/1.1 by the xmlns:dc construct at the beginning of the document. dc:subject is therefore understood to mean "the subject element in the dc namespace as defined at http://purl.org/dc/elements/1.1" (Dornfest and Brickley, 2003).

Figure 2.2. Dublin Core metadata in an XML document.

```
<?xml version="1.0" encoding="iso-8859-1"?>

<rdf:RDF
 xmlns:rdf="http://www.w3.org/1999/02/22-rdf-syntax-ns#"
 xmlns:dc="http://purl.org/dc/elements/1.1/"
 xmlns="http://purl.org/rss/1.0/"
>
 ...
 <item rdf:about="http://www.oreillynet.com/.../metadata.html">
   <title>Distributed Metadata</title>
   <link>http://www.oreillynet.com/.../metadata.html </link>
   <dc:description>This article addresses...</dc:description>
   <dc:subject>metadata, rdf, peer-to-peer </dc:subject>
   <dc:creator>Dan Brickley and Rael Dornfest </dc:creator>
   <dc:publisher>O'Reilly & Associates</dc:publisher>
   <dc:date>2000-10-29T00:34:00+00:00</dc:date>
   <dc:type>article</dc:type>
   <dc:language>en-us</dc:language>
   <dc:format>text/html</dc:format>
   <dc:rights>Copyright 2000, O'Reilly & Associates, Inc.</dc:rights>
   ...
 </item>
```

Source: Dornfest, Rael, and Dan Brickley. (2003). "The Power of Metadata." Openp2p.com [Online]. Available: http://www.openp2p.com/pub/a/p2p/2001/01/18/metadata.html. Reprinted with permission of O'Reilly Media, Inc.

XML is viewed by the digital community as one of the most important developments in Web technology since the creation of HTML, and, in fact, it is expected to replace HTML as the dominant language on the Web within a few years. XML is basically "SGML for the Web" (Hudgins et al., 1999, p. 3), a simplified, browser-enabled version of SGML that retains SGML's richness and is infinitely extensible to allow Web developers and content creators to develop an infinite number of document types. At the same time, as the W3C ecstatically announces in "XML in 10 points," intended for beginners in XML Web development, XML is as easy to use and transmit on the Web as HTML: "The designers of XML simply took the best parts of SGML, guided by the experience with HTML, and produced something that is no less powerful than SGML, but vastly more regular and simpler to use" (W3C, 1999d).

XML Schema Language provides a means for defining the structure, content, and semantics of XML documents. It provides an inventory of XML markup constructs, which can constrain and document the meaning, usage, and relationships of the constituents of a class of XML documents: datatypes, elements and their content, attributes and their values, entities and their contents, and notations. Thus, the XML Schema Language can be used to define, describe, and catalog XML vocabularies for classes of XML documents, such as metadata descriptions of Web resources or digital objects.

XML Schemas have been used to define metadata schemas for a number of specific domains or applications, such as Metadata Encoding and Transmission Standard (METS) (see Chapter 3) and have been combined with XML Namespaces to combine metadata elements from different domains/namespaces into "application profiles" or metadata schemas that have been optimized for a particular application (Hunter, 2003, p. 3). As illustrated earlier, namespace declarations are the XML infrastructure that allows construction of mixed metadata element sets within an application profile. A schema designer can use several namespace declarations to include elements from already-existing schemas that can be combined modularly to form a compound schema. The main goal of application profiles, then, is to increase the "semantic interoperablility" of the resulting metadata instances within a community of practice (Duval et al., 2003).

Semantic Interoperability: Text Markup Languages (XML DTDs)

HTML

HTML, which is, as mentioned earlier, an example of a markup language/DTD defined in SGML, has been given its own separate section because it was the original markup language on which the World Wide Web was constructed, endowing it with enormous historical significance. SGML became ISO Standard 88679 in 1986 and therefore was available for use when the Web began to gain popularity in the early 1990s, but as mentioned earlier, it was too complex to appeal to the heterogeneous group of people who began creating documents for the Web. Schottlaender says that "there is a widespread perception, and frankly it is a misperception, that HTML is 'dumbed down' SGML (Schottlaender, 2003, p. 21). In fact, although HTML is based on SGML, it is not a subset of it. Instead it is meant for marking up hypertext, multimedia, and reasonably small, simple documents. HTML addressed the problem of SGML complexity by specifying a relatively small set of structural and semantic tags suitable for authoring fairly simple documents while adding support for hypertext and later for multimedia. It became wildly popular and before too long outgrew its original purpose as a language for the exchange of scientific and technical documents by non–document specialists. New elements for use within HTML enabling its adaptation by highly specialized markets led to compatibility problems for documents across different platforms and called the suitability of its use across rapidly proliferating software and platforms into doubt. A no less serious failing of HTML for long-term archiving of electronic data is that it is simply too limited in its indexing capacities to allow for the creation of the complex metadata required. XML was conceived basically as "a happy medium, if you will, between HTML and SGML" (Schottlaender, 2003, p. 21).

Selected XML DTDs Created Outside the Library Community

SGML provides the capability for creating thousands of DTDs. HTML was one of the earliest and the one that found the most widespread use to date. Nevertheless, in recent years a number of other markup languages/DTDs have been developed and become popular in specific segments of the digital community. Several of the most successful of these text markup languages are discussed in this section.

Text Encoding Initiative (TEI)

The Text Encoding Initiative Guidelines were first published in 1994 as the result of an international research project that began in 1987. The TEI began as a research effort cooperatively organized by three scholarly societies (the Association for Computers and the Humanities, the Association for Computational Linguistics, and the Association for Literary and Linguisting Computing), funded solely by substantial research grants from the U.S. National Endowment for the Humanities, the European Union, the Canadian Social Science Research Council, the Mellon Foundation, and others.

By 1998, the guidelines consisted of a 1,400-page manual available in print form or as a free electronic document on the Internet (*Electronic Versions of the TEI Guidelines,* 1998). The goal of the TEI project was "to define a set of generic guidelines for the representation of textual materials in electronic form, in such a way as to enable researchers in any discipline to interchange and re-use resources, independently of software, hardware, and application area" (Heery, 1996). *TEI P4* is the current version of the *Guidelines.* The chief objective of this 2002 revision was to implement proper XML support in the *Guidelines* while ensuring that documents produced to earlier TEI specifications remained usable with the new version (Sperberg-McQueen and Burnard, 2002).

The TEI *Guidelines* specify, first of all, that every TEI text must be preceded by a TEI header that describes the text. The header specification was formulated as part of the project by the Committee on Text Documentation, which was composed of librarians and archivists from both Europe and North America, and the overall layout is grounded in cataloging tradition (Heery, 1996). This mandatory TEI Header (TEIH) serves, first of all, as an electronic title page, including metadata such as a description of the encoded text (tagged with file description), the way it was encoded (encoding description), the source (source description), and the revision history (revision history) (Hudgins et al., 1999, p. 8).

The TEI header can be used as a means of bibliographic control in several ways. First, it can be part of the text. The header can be created by the author or publisher as part of the original encoding, or it can be created during the TEI encoding of an existing document when it is used in a research or archival environment. It can be used in a second way by libraries, research sites, and text archives that wish to build up databases of records referring to TEI encoded text held at remote sites. The *Guidelines* lay down a framework for "independent headers," that is, headers that can be stored separately from the text to which they refer. Independent headers are free-standing TEI headers that can be used in catalogs or databases to refer to a remote TEI encoded text (Heery, 1996).

TEI provides an exhaustive tag library in addition to the ability to specify different tag sets: a core set as base, plus additional and auxiliary tag sets. To construct a TEI DTD, the user must always choose one of the six currently defined base tag sets for documents that are predominantly one of the following: prose, verse, drama, transcribed speech, dictionaries, or terminological databases. Another two are provided for use with texts that combine these basic tag sets.

As a well-established DTD, TEI has been used very widely, particularly in academic libraries, for creating digital texts, especially in the humanities, to "insure a standardizing format, with rich markup capabilities for indexing, and to facilitate the sharing of texts in library collections" (Hudgins et al., 1999, p.10).

Computer Interchange of Museum Information

Hudgins, Agnew, and Brown describe several SGML DTDs that they call "off-spring of TEI," DTDs derived from or based on the TEI DTD (Hudgins et al., 1999, p. 10). Probably the most important of the "offspring" DTDs was the Computer Interchange of Museum Information (CIMI), created by a consortium of museums and museum organizations that banded together in 1990 to form the Consortium for the Computer Interchange of Museum Information. As part of its continuing work on standards, the consortium created the CIMI DTD to encode museum-specific information, such as exhibition catalogs, which were the first type of information analyzed as a test case for any text-based museum information resources (*Computer Interchange of Museum Information*, 1999). These standards for interchange of museum information were meant to cover the broad range of information of different types and structures (such as structured texts, full-text documents, and images) offered by the museum communities.

The CIMI Committee was active from 1990 to 1992 and produced *A Standards Framework for the Computer Interchange of Museum Information,* by David Bearman and John Perkins, available as a public domain electronic document (Bearman and Perkins, 1993) and also published as a double issue of the quarterly *Spectra,* (vol. 20, no. 2 and 3), by the Museum Computer Network (MCN). This framework encompassed interchange protocols, interchange formats, and lower-level network and telecommunications building blocks as well as content data standards.

Content data standards included the following:

- ◆ Basic descriptive elements, such as Dates, Object Title Name, Document Title, Editor, and Organization Name;

- ◆ Subject description, such as Classification, Material, Style/Movement, Subject;

- ◆ URIs (not defined);

- ◆ Resource format and technical characteristics (not defined);

- ◆ Host administrative details, such as Organization Name and Place;

- ◆ Administrative metadata, such as Record Type and Document Source;

- ◆ Provenance/source

- ◆ Terms of availability/copyright. (*Computer Interchange of Museum Information*, 1999)

CIMI decided to develop a comprehensive set of museum DTDs, one for each genre of museum information, rather than one overgeneralized DTD for all museum information. It was decided that the DTD should allow for all the significant features of the source document to be marked up (*Computer Interchange of Museum Information*, 1999). CIMI DTD used TEI LITE (a cut-down version of the prose DTD) as a base format, a starting point, and then added additional museum-specific access points, such as materials (e.g., linen, enamel) and process technique. CIMI's Project CHIO (Cultural Heritage Information Online) provides access to databases of museum object records, full texts and library catalog entries, images, and online tools, such as the Art and Architecture Thesaurus (AAT), in an SGML DTD, Z39.50-enabled database. The profile for this type of database was developed for CIMI as a companion profile to the Library of Congress *Z39.50 Profile for Access to Digital Collections*. This profile incorporates extensions for navigation of CHIO resources, such as exhibition catalogs, wall texts, images with text, and object records cataloged in the CIMI format (Hudgins et al., 1999, pp. 10–11).

On December 15, 2003, CIMI ceased operations. On its home page (http://www.cimi.org) the CIMI Executive Committee announced with a mixture of sadness and pride:

> CIMI was very productive for more than a decade and accomplished the original goals established at its founding. We wind up its activities with a bittersweet sense of accomplishment and contribution. We note that the current environment is very different from the one in which CIMI was founded. The fact that much of CIMI's agenda, as well as other important future activities for museums, have been picked up by museum system vendors and taken on by other organizations—such as DIGICULT, IMLS, European Union research consortia, the CCF, and other focus-specific groups—is in some measure due to the influential work done within the CIMI context. (CIMI Consortium, 2003)

Structural Interoperability: Metadata Element Sets

In addition to the text markup languages described earlier, metadata standards include various metadata element sets, both general and discipline-specific, that can be used within a DTD such as HTML to describe electronic resources.

General: Dublin Core Metadata Element Set

The history of the Dublin Core Metadata Element Set began in 1995 with an invitational workshop in Dublin, Ohio, the home of OCLC. This first in the Dublin Core Metadata Workshop Series brought together librarians, digital library researchers, content experts, and text-markup experts to discuss and, ultimately, create an internationally agreed-on set of elements for describing electronic documents that could be "filled in" by the creator of an electronic document (Taylor, 1999, p. 87).

The core list of fifteen metadata elements, with easily understood descriptive names and single-word labels, was agreed on at the OCLC/NCSA Metadata Workshop in March 1995, and the documentation for the Dublin Core element set was published by Stuart Weibel, Jean Miller, and Ron Daniel on the Internet shortly after (see Godby, Miller, Weibel, 1995). A second version, Dublin Core Metadata Element, Version 1.1 (Dublin Core Metadata Initiative, 1999) was published in 1999, superseding the Dublin Core Metadata Element Set, version 1.0 and summarizing updated definitions for the Dublin Core metadata elements as originally defined in RFC2413 (Weibel et al., 1998).

The Dublin Core metadata elements fall into three groups that roughly indicate the type of information stored in them: (1) elements related mainly to the Content of the resource, (2) elements related mainly to the resource as Intellectual Property, and (3) elements related mainly to the Instantiation of the resource (Weibel, Kunze, and Lagoze, 1998):

Content	Intellectual Property	Instantiation
Title	Creator	Date
Subject	Publisher	Format
Description	Contributor	Identifier
Type	Rights	Language
Source		
Relation		
Coverage		

The element descriptions, according to version 1.1, are given in Appendix 2.A at the end of this chapter.

Originally implemented through the use of HTML, widespread implementations of the Dublin Core across the Web inspired other OCLC research projects, such as the Mantis generator project, which used Dublin Core for descriptive metadata, and XML and the RDF metadata framework to ensure interoperability across platforms and search engines. Thus, with the full development of RDF, the Dublin Core can now be encoded with XML, not just HTML, and structured with RDF for transparent metadata exchange.

Another advantage of the Dublin Core, which "might resemble to librarians a somewhat simpler version of MARC tags," is that "Dublin Core elements were designed for flexibility and are mapable to MARC record elements for conversion or for the eventual creation of 'meta'indexing databases that might include both MARC and Dublin Core records" (Hudgins et al., 1999, p. 14). This mapability of the Dublin Core and other metadata element sets to MARC and each other are discussed in more detail in the "Crosswalks" section of this chapter. The original purpose of the Dublin Core, which should not be forgotten in the drive to develop more complex and sophisticated schemes to meet the complex and sophisticated needs of libraries, was to serve as an author-generated description of Web resources that provides consistent indexing but does *not* require cataloging expertise to create, provides semantic interoperability across disciplines and formats, and is available to any publisher or library with electronic resources to describe and index.

The Dublin Core Metadata Initiative (DCMI) continues to lead the international community in the development of structured metadata into the twenty-first century. In a report on DCMI current activities and future directions in the December 2000 issue of *D-Lib,* Stuart Weibel describes what he calls an "active year of progress" that included standardization of the element core foundation and approval of an initial array of Dublin Core Qualifiers (Weibel, 2000). The Dublin Core emerged from the DC-7 workshop in Frankfurt a year earlier with the objective of approving a set of qualifiers intended to "sharpen the semantics" of the original fifteen elements. In determining the makeup of these qualifiers, the subset of the DCMI Advisory Committee charged with managing the approval of changes and additions to the Dublin Core gave preference to vocabularies, notations, and terms already in use by established agencies (Weibel, 2000). Two broad classes of qualifiers were recognized:

- ♦ Element Refinements: qualifiers used to make the meaning of an element narrower or more specific.

♦ Encoding Schemes: qualifiers used to identify schemes that aid in the interpretation of an element value, such as controlled vocabularies. (Weibel, 2000)

Examples of Element Refinement qualifiers, as described in the tabular summary of Dublin Core Qualifiers in Weibel's article, are Table of Contents or Abstract for the *Description* element, or Created, Valid, Available, Issued, or Modified for the *Date* element. Examples of Encoding Scheme qualifiers are *Library of Congress Subject Headings* (LCSH), *Medical Subject Headings* (MeSH), *Dewey Decimal Classification* (DDC), *Library of Congress Classification* (LCC), or *Universal Decimal Classification* (UDC) for the *Subject* element (Weibel, 2000). The addition of qualifiers for each element of the Dublin Core, standardizing the content of each element to increase retrieval interoperability, reflects thinking that brings the Dublin Core closer to MARC.

In subsequent workshops, the DCMI, having more or less completed codifying the structure of Dublin Core and its Qualifiers, has continued to focus on the need to share applications and re-use metadata across communities, as it states on the homepage of DC-2003: "The DC-2003 Conference theme 'Supporting Communities of Discourse and Practice—Metadata Research & Applications' provides an infrastructure for researchers to share inquiries, research methodologies, and results from their latest studies and for system implementers to share application developments, evaluations, and to display their tools through the DC-Lab" (*DC-2003*, 2003). The four basic goals of the Dublin Core—simplicity of metadata creation and maintenance, commonly understood semantics, international scope, and extensibility— continue to hold sway, but the goal of extensibility acknowledges that some projects and domains may find the Core inadequate for their needs. Therefore, while the Dublin Core, more than any other metadata element standard, continues to be a viable standard for resource discovery metadata, as is shown by its very widespread implementation across a large range of communities, its maintainers and developers encourage metadata experts from other domains and communities to extend the Dublin Core with additional elements ("Metadata Debate: Two Perspectives on Dublin Core," 2003).

Selected Specialized Metadata Element Sets/Schemas

Government Information Locator Service (GILS)

GILS is an "information locator" service that was set up by the U.S. Federal Government to provide both the general public and its employees with a means for locating and gaining access to useful information—both digital and nondigital—collected or generated by federal government agencies. A GILS Z39.50 profile was created to enable searching of metadata records mounted on a distributed agency network. The GILS Home Page is available at http://www.gils.net, which provides, among other things, a link to the second (1997) and still current draft of the GILS Application Profile. In addition, a *NonProfit Gateway* providing access to GILS records for federal agencies is available at http://www.nonprofit.gov/links/agencies.html.

A description of the type of resources included makes it clear that it is not the government resources themselves that are available through the GILS records, but rather the *metadata* about the resources, although the word metadata is not used:

> Information providers can describe anything with GILS—not only books and datasets but people, events, meetings, artifacts, rocks.... For networked information, GILS supports "hyperlinks" for network access to the resource described or related resources. (GILS, 199?)

The GILS Core Elements, as defined in Annex E of the *Application Profile for the Government Information Locator Service,* Draft Version 2 (1997), are given at the end of this chapter in Appendix 2.B.

Many of these twenty-eight core elements—nearly double the number of elements in the Dublin Core—have subelements, frequently numerous and extremely detailed, making GILS a much more complex metadata format than the Dublin Core. This is partly because of the breadth of its coverage and partly because its design was heavily influenced by the MARC and Z39.50 communities. Although simple GILS records might be able to be created by untrained staff, the format is detailed enough to permit the creation of very rich and complex records. One of the elements present in GILS and conspicuously absent in Dublin Core is "Date of Last Modification," a piece of information that is of great and growing importance in the dynamic world of the electronic resource if we are to archive these resources with all the relevant data.

In her book on metadata in 1999, Hudgins felt that the potential importance of GILS as a standard for locating electronic government information could hardly be overemphasized. The standardized, efficient access to government information in electronic form that GILS offers, in her opinion, had the potential to help significantly in compensating for the undeniable fact that "in the print world, the sheer enormity of government information has mitigated against efficient and effective access" (Hudgins et al., 1999, p. 18).

Four years later, in her book on metadata, Priscilla Caplan is not so sure. Citing the recommendation from a 1997 evaluation of the first two years of the federal GILS program that the program refocus on identifying and linking to electronically available government information, abandoning the records management function, she concludes that it is unclear what a current evaluation would yield (Caplan, 2003). Although some states have adopted GILS for access to state government information, the GILS core is not universally used for describing government information. Some states have chosen to implement other metadata standards, such as the Dublin Core, as have some non-U.S. governments, such as the Australian Government Locator Service (AGLS), sometimes with a few extensions.

In an e-mail message in April 2004, however, Eliot Christian (1998) of the Geological Survey, a GILS expert, proponent, and documenter, clarified what he felt is a misunderstanding about the significance of GILS. The GILS idea, he explains, is that "the coherence problem should not be dealt with in the creation and maintenance of metadata per se. The coherence problem should be seen as a problem that occurs in the particular context of *searching*. That is we look at the actual case of a searcher trying to deal with diverse metadata and we ask 'What can be done to help this searcher achieve his/her need for coherence without sacrificing the natural diversity of the information space being explored?' " (E. Christian, personal communication, April 18, 2004). GILS, he continues, provides a simple and elegant answer by mapping the metadata from its native format into the concepts that the searcher knows. Sometimes called "semantic mapping," Christian translates the concept into the sentence, "Here's what I want, What do you have that seems to fit with that?" (personal communication, April 18, 2004).

Content Standards for Digital Geospatial Metadata (FGDC)

In June 1992 the Federal Geographic Data Committee (FGDC) began work on a common set of terminology and definitions for documenting geospatial data. Two years later, in June 1994, the standard was approved by the committee as the *Content Standards for Digital Geospatial Metadata* (CSDGM). Since then, it is sometimes referred to as the FGDC standard (*FGDC—Content Standards for Digital Geospatial Metadata*, 1998) and sometimes as CSDGM (Hudgins et al., 1999, p. 19). The second and still-current version was issued in June 1998 and is available online in various formats at http://www.fgdc.gov/metadata/contstan.html. As its name implies—and as is clearly stated on the CSDGM home page—the CSDGM defines strictly metadata content and not the format, delivery, storage, or creation methods for this metadata:

> The standard was developed from the perspective of defining the information required by a prospective user to determine the availability of a set of geospatial data, to determine the fitness of the set of geospatial data for an intended use, to determine the means of accessing the set of geospatial data, and to successfully transfer the set of geospatial data. As such, the standard establishes the names of data elements and compound elements to be used for these purposes, the definitions of these data elements and compound elements, and information about the values that are to be provided for the data elements. The standard does not specify the means by which this information is organized in a computer system or in a data transfer, nor the means by which this information is transmitted, communicated, or presented to the user. (*Content Standard for Digital Geospatial Metadata*, 2003)

The FGDC/CSDGM is a complex metadata standard with more than 300 data elements, arranged hierarchically. Of these, 119 are compound elements or groups of elements describing relationships among other elements. The main categories of metadata are as follows:

- Identification information
- Data quality information
- Spatial data organizational information
- Spatial reference information
- Entity and attribute
- Distribution information
- Metadata reference

Three additional sets of metadata are as follows (Hudgins et al., 1999, p. 19):

- Citation information
- Time period information
- Contact information

All U.S. federal agencies have been required by Executive Order 12906 to document all new geospatial data produced or collected using the CSDGM. Furthermore, the metadata sets created are to be deposited in a Federal Geospatial Data Clearinghouse, which is a distributed network of geospatial data producers, administrators, and users linked electronically. The clearinghouse has, in fact, dealt with a number of issues not covered in the content standard itself.

First, although protocol issues are not addressed (except that Annex D specifies TCP/IP and OSI protocols), the Clearinghouse has implemented variants of the Z39.50 protocol. The draft implementation document (Annex D) proposes the use of Z39.50 compliant software and the GEO profile as a set of FGDC metadata elements. The GEO profile is a "draft specification for Z39.50 programmers that formalizes the data elements within the FGDC Metadata Standard as registered or well-known attributes in a Z39.50 server" (*FGDC Newsletter,* 1996).

Second, the Clearinghouse proposed that the standard use SGML to support loading, exchange, and presentation. As a result, an SGML DTD (FGDC DTD) for parsing FGDC standard metadata against its syntax was developed, as well as SGML software compilers and editors for the CSDGM standard version 2. The Document Type Declaration (DTD) for FGDC-STD-001-1998 (Version 2) is available at http://www.fgdc.gov/metadata/fgdc-std-001-1998.dtd, and the DTD Tagset (alphabetical order) for FGDC-STD-001-1998 is available at http://geology.usgs.gov/tools/metadata/tools/doc/sgmltags.txt, as links from the CDSGM main site.

All federal agencies are mandated by law to document and deposit geospatial data using CSDGM in the Clearinghouse, but the FGDC on the CSDGM home page extends and invitation to other sectors as well to describe their geospatial data with CSDGM: "In addition to use by the Federal Government, the FGDC invites and encourages organizations and persons from State, local, and tribal governments, the private sector, and non-profit organizations to use the standard to document their geospatial data" (*Content Standard for Digital Geospatial Metadata*, 2003).

Educational Metadata Element Sets

GEM

The Gateway to Educational Materials (GEM) (*The Gateway to Educational Materials,* 2003) is a consortium effort, composed of more than 400 organizations and individuals. Its stated goals are to provide educators with quick and easy access to the substantial, but uncataloged, collections of educational materials found on various federal, state, university, nonprofit, and commercial Internet sites. Additional goals delineated on the *Gem Project Site* (2002) are to provide a set of metadata standards and technical mechanisms that provides efficient, simple access to educational materials and, through the Gateway, a searchable, browseable catalog of metadata records for resources from GEM Consortium members Internet sites.

The GEM Project is a project of the U.S. Department of Education, located at the Information Institute of Syracuse at Syracuse University. It is made up of several components. The term *GEM* refers to the project itself, including all of its parts. *The Gateway* is the catalog of educational resources that are the final product of the GEM project. It includes thousands of lesson plans, curriculum units, and other valuable educational materials distributed on Web sites across the Internet, many of which are difficult for most teachers to find efficiently. The goal of the Gateway to Educational Materials (GEM) is to solve this resource discovery problem by providing a "gateway" to quality collections of educational resources. When educators connect to the Gateway, they are able to

- browse through lists organized by subject, keyword, or grade/education level;
- search by subject, keyword, title, or the full-text of the resource's catalog record;
- request retrieval of free resources only; and
- go directly to the resource from the Gateway.

According to information on the Gateway, (www.thegateway.org) GEM included over 40,000 resources by the end of January 2005.

On February 13, 2004, a new interface was introduced that uses an advanced retrieval engine named Seamark, built around a search technique called "faceted searching." Faceted searching combines searching for specific words and phrases with browsing descriptions of resources, based on facets. It enables two ways to find resources. The first, Search & Browse,

1. uses a simple Google-like search using words and phrases *or*
2. browses from a master list of the *facets* in GEM .

The second resource is the Workbench portion of the *Gem Project Site* (http://www.geminfo.org/Workbench/index.html), which concentrates the online documentation for GEM into six resource groups: Cataloging Resources, Creating GEM Metadata for Database Collections, Evaluation Resources for Educational Materials, GEM Element Set and Profile(s), GEM Search Engines, and Technical Implementation Resources. GEM 2.0 (http://www.geminfo.org/Workbench/GEM2_elements.html), the second version of the GEM element set, was previewed at the 2001 GEM Consortium Meeting and was formally adopted by the GEM Governance Board in January 2002. It uses the Dublin Core as the foundation for its metadata set, utilizing the flexibility added to the Dublin Core through the Qualifiers. GEM originally added eight metadata elements to the Dublin Core to tailor the metadata to the information needs of teachers. The elements included description, evaluative elements and a meta-metadata element. The five descriptive elements included information important to educators in finding and evaluating educational resources, but that is not included in the Dublin Core:

- Audience
- Duration
- Essential Resources
- Grade Level
- Pedagogy

While the descriptive elements fill in gaps in the Dublin Core for educational information, the evaluative elements add another dimension. They include:

- Quality Indicators
- Academic Standards

The original eighth GEM element, the Meta-Metadata element, gave an overview of information about the metadata itself, building in accountability and allowing the users to make a decision about whether they consider the metadata to be trustworthy (Lowe, 2000). GEM 2.0 fully integrates the Dublin Core qualifier decisions and recommendations of the Dublin Core Education Working Group. The major changes are as follows:

- GEM.grade is now DC.Audience.level.

- Identifier: GEM is adding "PublicID" as a qualifier (ISSN, ISBN, SICI).

- The Quality element is deprecated in GEM 2.0. The Relation Element is used to link to reviews and other quality assessments.

- Agent fields (cataloging, creator, contributor, publisher, correlator). GEM will no longer capture locational information (e-mail, phone number, etc.) within the metadata for agent elements. (*Gem Project Site. GEM 2.0*, 2002)

ARIADNE/IEEE—LOM

The ARIADNE Project (ARIADNE Project Home Page, 2000) was launched in 1996 as a research and technology development (RTD) project in the "Telematics for Education and Training" sector of the 4th Framework Program for R&D of the European Union. The project's focus was to develop tools for "producing, managing and reusing computer-based pedagogical elements and telematics supported training curricula"(ARIADNE Project Home Page, 2000). The second phase of ARIADNE was completed in June 2000, and in January 2000 ARIADNE released its new Metadata recommendation (ARIADNE version 3 official Metadata) based on the LOM (Learning Objects Metadata) 3.8 specification (*ARIADNE Educational Metadata Recommendation,* 1999). The recommendations stated that its metadata set was meant to be used in the context of *education* (as provided in universities, secondary schools, etc.), but that a very similar scheme could be produced for the purpose of *training* (in the sense of training in skills rather than in knowledge fields) (*ARIADNE Educational Metadata Recommendation,* 1999). ARIADNE grouped its metadata into six categories of metadata descriptors:

1. General information on the resource itself

2. Semantics of the resource

3. Pedagogical attributes

4. Technical characteristics

5. Conditions for use

6. Meta-metadata information

The full metadata set contained thirty-eight required elements (plus an optional category) and was divided among these six categories as shown at the end of this chapter in Appendix 2.C.

The optional category was called Annotations and contained the following descriptors:

1. Annotator name

2. Creation date

3. Content (*ARIADNE Educational Metadata Recommendation,* 1999)

Although the ARIADNE metadata structure included more than twice the number of elements as the Dublin Core, the ARIADNE metadata site (no longer on-line in mid-2004) also included a table mapping its metadata set to the Dublin Core. The set that resulted when it was mapped to the Dublin Core was naturally not nearly as rich as the ARIADNE set (e.g., the only descriptors in Pedagogical attributes that could be mapped to Dublin Core were *3.2. document type* and *3.3. document format,* both of which were mapped to the Type element in the Dublin Core), thereby illustrating the need for specialized metadata element structures for specialized fields.

ARIADNE metadata recommendation ver. 3.1 (May 2001) corresponds to the IEEE LOM WD5.1 Draft 6.1 specification (http://www.tnqit.tafe.net/RLO/metadata/schemas/ieeelommetadata.htm). It is slightly larger than the original element set, with nine categories, forty-four elements, and a number of qualifiers based primarily, but not exclusively, on the Dublin Core Qualifiers. The Categories, however, are quite different from *ARIADNE* 1999. Only two categories, General and Technical, retain the same name, and even they include significantly different elements. ARIADNE metadata recommendation ver 3.1 is given at the end of the chapter in Appendix 2.D.

Art Metadata Element Sets

Murtha Baca, one of the foremost experts on metadata for visual resources, reminds us: "something that people whose task is to build information resources tend to forget or ignore is that there is no 'one-size-fits-all' metadata scheme. There are good reasons why different metadata schemes have been developed over the years" (Baca, 2003). Dublin Core, for example, was not intended to be a metadata scheme for cataloging art objects. Two major schema, each with a different focus, seem to have cornered most of the market for describing art and architecture: the Categories for the Description of Works of Art (CDWA), if the focus is on the art object itself, and the VRA Core categories, if, instead, the focus is on managing and providing access to visual surrogates (e.g., digital images, photographs) or works of art or architecture.

Categories for the Description of Works of Art (CDWA)

"Categories for the Description of Works of Art" is a product of the Art Information Task Force (AITF), formed in the early 1990s to encourage art historians, art information professionals, and information providers to work together to develop guidelines for describing works of art, architecture, groups of objects, and visual and textual surrogates. The work of the AITF was funded by the J. Paul Getty Trust, the National Endowment for the Humanities (NEH), and the College Art Association (CAA).

The Categories describe the content of art databases by articulating a conceptual framework for describing and accessing information about objects and images, identify vocabulary resources and descriptive practices that will make information in diverse systems both more compatible and more accessible, and provide a framework to which existing art information systems can be mapped and on which new systems can be developed.

Which categories are considered core can vary depending on the end users whom the particular art information system are intended to serve, the mission of the specific institution, and other factors. In the current version 2.0 of the Categories, the distinction between information intrinsic to the work (art object, architecture, or group) and information extrinsic to the work has been clarified. It was decided that extrinsic information about persons, places, and concepts related to the work may be important for retrieval, but is more efficiently recorded in separate *authorities* than in records about the work itself, so that this information needs only be recorded once, and it may then be linked to all appropriate work records.

The Categories often deal with differences between information intended for display and information intended for retrieval. Information for display is assumed to be in a format that is easily read and understood by users. In addition, the Categories assume that key elements of information must be formatted to allow for retrieval, often referred to as *indexing* in the CDWA. The CDWA advises that such *indexing* should be performed by catalogers who understand the retrieval implications of their indexing terms and not by an automated method that simply parses every word in a text intended for display into indexes. Furthermore, the Categories advise the use of controlled vocabularies, authorities, and consistent formatting of certain information to ensure efficient end user retrieval (Categories for the Description of Works of Art, 2000).

The Categories are divided into twenty-seven main categories, listed in Appendix 2.E. Each of the main categories is subdivided into anywhere from three to twenty-six appropriate subcategories, some of which are subdivided further. For example, the category RELATED VISUAL DOCUMENTATION subdivides as follows:

```
= RELATED VISUAL DOCUMENTATION
= RELATIONSHIP TYPE
= IMAGE TYPE
= IMAGE MEASUREMENTS
      VALUE
      UNIT
= IMAGE FORMAT
= IMAGE DATE
= IMAGE COLOR
= IMAGE VIEW
      INDEXING TERMS
      VIEW SUBJECT
      VIEW DATE
= IMAGE OWNERSHIP
      OWNER'S NAME
      OWNER'S NUMBERS
= IMAGE SOURCE
      NAME
      NUMBER
= COPYRIGHT/RESTRICTIONS
= REMARKS
= CITATIONS
```

In addition, as mentioned earlier, there is a separate group of AUTHORITIES/CONTROLLED VOCABULARY fields. These fields are divided into five broad categories: *CREATOR IDENTIFICATION*
PLACE/LOCATION IDENTIFICATION
GENERIC CONCEPT IDENTIFICATION
SUBJECT IDENTIFICATION
SUBJECT NAME

Like the categories for information intrinsic to the work, the categories for information extrinsic to the work are subdivided into a varying number of subfields. The *CREATOR IDENTIFICATION* category, for example, has a much richer set of subfields than the *CREATOR* field in the Dublin Core, pointing up how different the needs of a specific community can be from those envisioned by the creators of a standard intended to meet more general needs:

CREATOR IDENTIFICATION
NAME?
VARIANT NAMES
DATES/LOCATIONS?
    BIRTH DATE?
    DEATH DATE?
    EARLIEST ACTIVE DATE
    LATEST ACTIVE DATE
    PLACE OF BIRTH
    PLACE OF DEATH
    PLACES OF ACTIVITY
NATIONALITY/CULTURE/RACE ?
    NATIONALITY/CITIZENSHIP
    CULTURE
    RACE/ETHNICITY
GENDER
LIFE ROLES?
RELATED PEOPLE
    RELATIONSHIP TYPE
    NAME
REMARKS
CITATIONS ("Categories for the Descriptions of Works of Art," 2000)

VRA Core Categories

The *VRA Core Categories, Version 3.0* consist of a single element set that can be applied as many times as necessary to create records to describe *works* of visual culture as well as the *images* that document them. The Data Standards Committee followed the "1:1 principle," developed by the Dublin Core community, that is, only one object or resource may be described within a single metadata set. How the element sets are linked to form a single record is a local implementation issue. The order of the categories in the *VRA Core 3.0* is arbitrary, with local implementations encouraged to decide on the field sequence that most appropriate for their data.

The *VRA Core 3.0*, unlike the CDWA, is intended to be a point of departure—not a completed application. The elements that comprise the Core are designed to facilitate the sharing of information among visual resources collections about *works* and *images*. The Visual Resources Association acknowledges that these elements may not be sufficient to describe fully a local collection and that additional fields can and may need to be added for that purpose. They also recommend the use of qualifiers with certain elements in the *VRA Core 3.0* so that the data values contained in the element may be more precisely identified. In addition, every element may be repeated as many times as necessary within a given set to describe the *work* or *image*.

By *work*, the *VRA Core 3.0* refers to a physical entity "that exists, has existed at some time in the past, or that could exist in the future," an artistic creation such as a painting; a performance, composition or literary work; a building; or an object of material culture. A work may be a single item, or it may be composed of many parts. An *image* is a visual representation of a work in photomechanical, photographic, or digital format, typically a reproduction of a *work* that is owned by the cataloging institution. The same visual resources collection may include several *images* of a single *work*. Relationships between two works may be either *essential* or *informative,* the first type existing when the described work includes the reference work, and the second type existing when the described and referenced works could each stand alone and the relationship is informative but not essential either physically or logically. Only those elements that are relevant for a specific record should contain data, and all categories and qualifiers are repeatable (Visual Resources Association Data Standards Committee, 2002).

The seventeen elements of the *VRA Core 3.0* are as follows:

Record Type	ID Number
Type	Style/Period
Title	Format
Material	Culture
Technique	Subject
Creator	Relation
Date	Description
Geographic	Source
Rights	

The definitions on the VRA Web site for each basic category include mapping to the much more complex CDWA and to Dublin Core, but according to site information, the *VRA Core 3.0* is a work in progress, and both mapping to other metadata standards, such as MARC, and further guidance on recommendations for the use of controlled vocabularies are planned (Visual Resources Association Data Standards Committee, 2002).

Rights Metadata

Digital Object Identifier (DOI)

In 1999, Hudgins et al. wrote that rights metadata, which was then still in the developmental stage, is intended to ensure that clicking on a hyperlink would retrieve a rights page describing authorized access, display and use permissions for the object and a way to require the agreement of the user to the access, and display and use limitations before the object could be displayed (Hudgins et al., p. 19). Although electronic rights metadata could be used to charge a fee for access, this was not to be a requirement; the basic goals would be to provide access to the most complete copyright and use for a digital object and to provide an easy way to seek and obtain permission to use it by imposing rights metadata between discovery of a digital object and display of that object. The Dublin Core has a Rights Management element.

Rights management metadata is meant to interoperate with a Digital Object Identifier (DOI), "a unique and extensible identification scheme which can apply to entire books, to a book chapter or even to a photograph within a chapter of a book. The DOI is a simple identifier, relevant only to associated rights and permissions metadata or service" (Hudgins et al., p. 23).

In the same year Norman Paskin, director of the International DOI Foundation (IDF), defined the DOI as "a unique identifier of a piece of content" ("Executive Briefing: The Digital Object Identifier," 1999). He offered four reasons to add DOI metadata:

- ◆ To enable reverse look-up
- ◆ To enable development of DOI services
- ◆ For cost effectiveness
- ◆ For quality control

Launched at the Frankfurt Book Fair in October 1997 and called the Digital Object Identifier System, the DOI was meant only to link users of the material named by those identifiers with rights holders. International publishers had begun to realize that as a new environment for commerce of information, the Internet required new enabling technologies to provide services and to protect customers, publishers, and rights owners and that systems needed to be developed to identify, authenticate, and protect intellectual property (About the DOI, 2000).

In an article from the May 1999 *D-lib*, the entire issue of which was devoted to the current status and outlook of the DOI, Paskin described the origin of the DOI as a persistent identifier for managing copyrighted materials and its development under the nonprofit International DOI Foundation into a system providing identifiers of intellectual property. An outgrowth of a program of the Association of American Publishers to develop tools to enable management of copyrightable materials in an electronic environment, the DOI was to be a specifier for routing to an occurrence of a piece of material on a publisher's Web site, because "to protect something, it is first necessary to uniquely and unambiguously designate what that entity is" (Paskin, 1999). Paskin went on to explain the concept of the DOI as a "persistent" identifier, not subject to change, as URLs are: the DOI provides a persistent identifier ("name") for a resource or entity, which allows the designation of the entity directly, in contrast to a URL, which designates a location at which an instance is held. Thus, DOIs allow an infrastructure for managing digital objects independent of locations (Paskin, 1999).

The need for persistent names has long been recognized in the development of the Internet, and requirements for Uniform Resource Names (URN) have been specified. These requirements provide a set of principles, which the DOI takes as a fundamental starting point:

- Global scope: A name has a global scope, which does not imply a location. It has the same meaning everywhere.

- Uniqueness: The same URN will never be assigned to two resources.

- Persistence: It is intended that the lifetime of a URN be permanent. That is, the URN will be globally unique forever and may well be used as a reference to a resource well beyond the lifetime of the resource it identifies or of any naming authority involved in the assignment of its name.

- Scalability: URNs can be assigned to any resource that might conceivably be available on the network.

- Legacy support: The scheme must allow support of existing legacy naming systems, if these satisfy the other requirements described here.

- Extensibility: Any scheme for URNs must permit future extensions to the scheme.

- Independence: It is solely the responsibility of a name issuing authority to determine the conditions under which it will issue a name. (Paskin, 1999)

Nearly a decade after its rather modest beginnings as a tool for maintaining a persistent URN and linking a rights page to a digital object, the DOI has developed into a far more versatile system. It has turned into an entire system for providing a framework for managing intellectual content, for linking customers with content suppliers, for facilitating electronic commerce, and for enabling automated copyright management for all types of media (International DOI Foundation, 2004).

The DOI has two components, the prefix and the suffix, which together form the DOI and may be assigned to any item of intellectual property and which must be precisely defined by means of structured metadata. The DOI itself remains persistent and unaltered once assigned. A prefix is assigned to an organization that wishes to register DOIs. Following the prefix (separated by a forward slash) is a suffix (unique to a given prefix) to identify the entity. The combination of a prefix for the Registrant and unique suffix provided by the Registrant avoids any necessity for the centralized allocation of DOI numbers.

The value of the DOI system lies in its combination of Resolution, Metadata, and Policy. The DOI system uses a Resolution System that ensures persistence by resolving the DOI to a current associated value such as a URL; users of DOIs need not be aware of changes to URLs to use the system. The Resolution System is the Handle System, an open standard scalable architecture. Resolution may be to multiple pieces of data. The DOI system uses a Metadata system based on the <in*d*ecs> (interoperability of data in ecommerce systems) activity (see next section). The DOI metadata enables mappings between application areas to be made consistently.

Added value services that may be built using DOI features include the use of multiple resolution (associating DOIs with several items of data); associating related pieces of intellectual property (versions, derivations, etc.); use with other tools (e.g., OpenURL for contextual local use). By integrating an identifier into a DOI, the identifier becomes actionable as a standard hyperlink (but unlike URL, persistent) and can function in DOI applications across a variety of platforms. DOIs may be used to identify related entities or linked material in any form. Using one system enables one set of tools to be applicable across many platforms, media, standard identification schemes, and so on and promotes interoperable transactions of intellectual property (International DOI Foundation, 2003).

For libraries and other institutions that have traditionally administered copyright protection for the materials in their collections, the DOI and its role in rights metadata is critical to the continuing implementation of this responsibility in the electronic environment. For businesses, the content management capabilities—as illustrated on the *DOI Demonstrations* page of the DOI Web site (International DOI Foundation, 2004b) and shown in Figure 2.3—that enable a publisher's potential customers, for example, to link from a single title to a whole range of related titles on the subject may be even more useful.

Figure 2.3. DOI content management capabilities.

Source: International DOI Foundation, *doi: The Digital Object Identifier System. DOI Demonstrations* [Online]. Available: http://www.doi.org/demos.html (retrieved April 12, 2004). Reprinted by permission of the International DOI Foundation.

<in*d*ecs>

<in*d*ecs> (Interoperability of Data for Electronic Commerce Systems) was a project backed by the European Commission that brought together a global group of organizations with an interest in managing content in the digital environment. The <in*d*ecs> Project was created to address the need to put different identifiers and their supporting metadata into a framework where they could operate side by side in the digital environment. It especially aimed to support the management of intellectual property rights. A timed project, which finished its work in 2000, <in*d*ecs> produced

outputs that are highly regarded and have been adopted in a number of implementations, most important of which is the DOI.

The <indecs> model underlies all DOI metadata. The fundamental requirements defined within the indecs project and used within DOI are as follows:

- Unique identification: every entity needs to be uniquely identified within and identified namespace.

- Functional granularity: it should be possible to identify an entity when there is a reason to distinguish it.

- Designed authority: the author of metadata must be securely identified.

- Appropriate access: everyone requires access to the metadata on which they depend and privacy and confidentiality for their own metadata from those who are not dependent on it. (Paskin, 2002)

The <indecs> data model was created to cover the same field of endeavor as the DOI, that is, all types of intellectually property, or "creations" in <indecs> terminology. The project focused on the practical interoperability of digital content identification systems and related rights metadata within multimedia e-commerce. It was an international project aimed at generating a formal structure for describing and uniquely identifying intellectual property, the people and the businesses trading intellectual property on the Internet, and the agreements made about those online sales. The project intended to create a structure that would provide the foundation for online commercial transactions for copyrighted works in all media: text, audiovisual, music, and multimedia works. It was directed toward ensuring filmmakers, musicians, visual artists and writers, producers and publishers that they would receive fair payment for work traded in the digital world ("<indecs>: Putting Metadata to Rights …," 2000).

<indecs> is an open model, designed to be extensible to fit the needs of specific communities of interest and to be readily extensible into the field of rights management metadata essential for managing all e-commerce and intellectual property. A core concept of both <indecs> and DOI is that there is no logical separation of rights metadata from other metadata.

The adoption of the <indecs> metadata model gave DOI metadata a basis in an intellectual analysis of the requirements for metadata in a network environment that has been tested in real applications. The <indecs> model is alone in having demonstrated its extensibility to real-world transactions, through rights management. DOI uses the indecs dictionary, creating a mechanism to provide a description of what is identified in a structured way and allowing services about digital content object to be built for any desired purpose (Paskin, 2002).

Preservation Metadata: OAIS

Most digital preservation strategies depend on capturing, creating, and maintaining metadata. Preservation metadata is all of the various kinds of data that will allow the recreation and interpretation of the structure and content of digital data over time. So far, preservation metadata initiatives have tended to originate in one of three contexts: national and research libraries, archives and records management domains, and digitization projects (Day, 2003).

In the first group, the initiatives have tended to be either pragmatic responses to management needs, such as the element set developed by the National Library of Australia (NLA), or metadata frameworks based on the *Reference Model for an Open Archival Information System (OAIS)*, such as the specifications developed by CEDARS (CURL Exemplars in Digital Archives) or the NEDLIB (Networked European Deposit Library) project.

The National Library of Australia's preservation metadata for digital collections (National Library of Australia, 1999) was influenced by many models, as they state on their metadata Web site:

> Some are of broad relevance, (eg the Reference Model for an Open Archival Information System [OAIS] Draft Recommendation for Space Data System Standards ...), while some came to us as results of data modelling exercises for particular projects (the NEDLIB project ... and the NLA's own PANDORA project ...). Some were more refined metadata specifications developed for particular programs or projects (the Library of Congress-CNRI Experiment Project ...; The Making of America II Project ...; the CEDARS project ...; the National Archives of Australia's Recordkeeping Metadata Standard ...). One particular starting point for our exercise was the metadata set proposed by the Research Libraries Group (RLG) PRESERV Working Group on Preservation Uses of Metadata ... which mainly addressed digitisation projects. RLG invited us to adapt this set to describe a wider range of materials. (National Library of Australia, 1999)

The NLA Preservation Metadata Set differs from all the other sets described earlier in that it is meant to be a data output model, not a data input model. It indicates the information that the NLA wants out of a metadata system, and not necessarily what data should be entered, how it should be entered, or how the metadata should be associated with what it is describing. Therefore, this model was, from the outset, intended to be applicable to many implementations that record this information in a variety of ways. This model simply says, "however you do it, this is what you have to deliver so we can manage preservation" (National Library of Australia, 1999). It focuses solely on preservation requirements and is a very different set from both the Dublin Core and the specialized metadata element sets of the various special groups. Recommended elements include the following (National Library of Australia, 1999):

Persistent Identifier—type and identifier

Date of Creation

Structural Type

Technical Infrastructure of Complex Object

File Description (including a number of subelements)

Known System Requirements

Installation Requirements

Storage Information

Access Inhibitors

Finding and Searching Aids, and Access Facilitators

Preservation Action Permission

Validation

Relationships

Quirks

Archiving Decision (work)

Decision Reason (work)

Institution Responsible for Archiving Decision (work)

Archiving Decision (manifestation)

Decision Reason (manifestation)

Institution Responsible for Archiving Decision (manifestation)

Intention Type

Institution with preservation responsibility

Process (including a number of subelements)

Record Creator

Other

The OAIS model provides terms of reference, conceptual data models, and functional models for interoperable open archives and defines the nature of "information packages" in terms of both the content and what is necessary to understand, access, and manage the content. Two projects— the NEDLIB project in the Netherlands and the CEDARS project in the United Kingdom—are full implementations of this model. NEDLIB adopted the OAIS model as a framework on which to build its archiving model for deposit libraries and added a Preservation Module that included provision for both emulation approaches and digital migrations resulting from changed content, and CEDARS implemented the OAIS model for a distributed digital archive of library resources.

The concept of emulation, using physical or logical structures called "containers" or "wrappers" to provide a relationship between all information components such as the digital object and its metadata and software specifications, underlies the OAIS Reference Model, which utilizes the concepts of "information packages" (IPs) composed of "content information" and "preservation description information" contained by "packaging information." The content information includes the digital object itself and the representation information needed to interpret it. The preservation description information includes information about provenance and context, reference information such as unique identifiers, and a wrapper that protects the digital object against undocumented alteration.

The basic idea of the NEDLIB project was to test whether emulating obsolete computer hardware on future computer hardware can be used to confer longevity on digital publications by enabling their obsolete software to be run on future platforms. The results indicated that even using off-the-shelf emulation that was not specifically designed to be used for preservation, the experimental outcome was impressive (Lazinger, 2001, p. 102).

As part of the UK Electronic Libraries Programme (eLib), the CEDARS project was funded to explore issues and practical examples for the long-term preservation of digital materials. The Consortium of University Research Libraries (CURL) represents the major national, academic and research libraries in the UK, and CEDARS stands for "CURL Exemplars in Digital Archives." Funded for three years, from 1999 to 2002, and led by the universities of Oxford, Cambridge, and Leeds, in partnership with the UK Office of Library Networking, the particular focus of CEDARS was on metadata issues for long-term preservation. Its distributed archive architecture is based on an implementation of the OAIS Reference Model, using a framework that facilitates three "information packages," each based on specific functions within the archive itself. Each information package contains two elements:

- ◆ The primary data, including the digital object being preserved and metadata that specifies systems and software needed to render this data in a meaningful way

- ◆ Other metadata that describes the digital object in relation to its preservation

The first type of information package, known as an Archival Information Package (AIP), encapsulates preserved digital objects and is physically stored in the archive. Pointers to metadata that allows its rendering and describes its preservation process is stored separately from the digital object itself so that the archive can update the representation network without having to go through every AIP and incorporate the change. The second type of information package, the Submission Information Packages (SIP) includes information transmitted at the time of submission of the digital object to an archive that is sufficient to enhance the understanding of the digital object, a particularly useful approach, for example, for complex, multilayered objects.

The third information package type is called a Dissemination Information Package (DIP) and includes an access component that relies on a system of metadata that are relevant to retrieving and rendering the digital object on the requested platform (Lazinger, 2001, p. 103).

Preservation metadata initiatives emanating from the archives and record management communities are discussed in Chapter 3, but the third type of preservation metadata initiative contexts, independent digital initiatives include, for example, the IEEE-LOM initiative, discussed earlier, and the Open Archives Initiative Protocol for Metadata Harvesting (OAI-PMH), which is discussed later in this chapter. Both of these standards contain terms that have relevance to digital preservation, although they are intended for use in specific domains.

Crosswalks between Metadata Element Sets

By mapping one metadata standard to another, Margaret St. Pierre explained in 1998, crosswalks provide the ability to make the contents of elements defined in one metadata standard available to communities using related metadata standards (St. Pierre, 1998). Arlene Taylor describes crosswalks as visual instruments for showing which value in one metadata standard corresponds to a particular value in another standard (Taylor, 1999, p. 95). Five years later, she narrows the definition down to "tools used to achieve interoperability, specifically semantic interoperability." Lacking the "golden, one-size-fits-all schema," she continues, crosswalks help users and creators equivalence relationships among metadata elements in different schemas. For example, a crosswalk shows that the 700 field in a MARC record is approximately equivalent to the Contributor element in a Dublin Core record (Taylor, 2004, p. 154).

As the number, size, and complexity of content metadata standards grows, supplying the metadata for each standard becomes more and more repetitious and time-consuming. To minimize the amount of time needed to create and maintain the metadata and to maximize its usefulness to the broadest user community, metadata created and maintained in one standard needs to be accessible through crosswalks of related content metadata standards. A fully specified crosswalk "provides the ability to create and maintain one set of metadata, and to map that metadata to any number of related content metadata standards. In the future, fully automated crosswalks will enable search engines to function with any given family of content metadata standards" (St. Pierre, 1998).

Like so many of the most promising technologies associated with digital preservation, the specification of a crosswalk is a difficult and expensive task. It requires in-depth knowledge and specialized expertise in the associated metadata standards, expertise that is particularly problematic to obtain because the metadata standards themselves are often developed independently, and specified differently using specialized terminology, methods, and processes. In addition, maintaining the crosswalk as the metadata standards change becomes even more problematic because of the need to sustain both a historical perspective and ongoing expertise in the associated standards (St. Pierre, 1998).

Despite these difficulties, a surprising number of crosswalks are publicly available online. An extensive list of crosswalks is referenced at the metadata web pages of the UK Office for Library Networkings (UKOLN) at http://www.ukoln.ac.uk/metadata/interoperability/ (Day, 2002). It includes LC's Dublin Core/MARC/GILS Crosswalk; the Monticello Electronic Library's Dublin Core to EAD/GILS/USMARC crosswalk; the TEI header to USMARC/Dublin Core crosswalk by Richard Giordano (University of Manchester, Department of Computer Science); the FGDC to USMARC crosswalk by Elizabeth Mangan (Geography and Map Division, Library of Congress); and several crosswalks to national MARC standards, such as FINMARC, among others. The Getty Research Institute has developed a *Crosswalk of Metadata Element Sets for Art, Architecture, and Cultural Heritage Information and Online Resources* that maps among several metadata standards, showing commonalities and differences. Standards mapped by the Getty include Categories for the Description of Works of Art (CDWA), VRA Core Categories, Dublin Core, and CIMI access, as well as several library and archival standards (Crosswalk of Metadata Element Sets for Art, Architecture, and Cultural Heritage Information and Online Resources, 2003).

Beyond Crosswalks: The Resource Description Framework (RDF)

The Resource Description Framework (RDF), produced under the auspices of the World Wide Web Consortium, is an XML application that allows different metadata models to be expressed within a single well-defined model and syntax. RDF is intended for situations in which the information provided by these metadata models needs to be processed by applications, rather than being displayed only to people. RDF provides a common framework for expressing this information so it can be exchanged between applications without loss of meaning (*RDF Primer,* 2004).

RDF Schemas express these models (e.g., Dublin Core) within an XML structure that provides a machine-readable system for defining these individual vocabularies. Each metadata model has its own semantics, or meaning, as well as its own syntax, or systematic arrangement of its data elements. Structure, the third element that is needed, in addition to semantics and syntax, for the effective use of metadata among applications, "can be thought of as a formal constraint on the syntax for the consistent representation of semantics" (Miller, 1998).

By wrapping such element sets as Dublin Core within the syntax of RDF, it becomes easier to move between Dublin Core metadata and other metadata types. RDF provides a common structure for integrating data records of different kinds, "just as MARC21 enables library systems to integrate data bibliographic, authority, and community information records in a single system" (Hearn, 1999).

RDF creates a structure that allows the properties of one resource to be described by reference to other resources. The infrastructure it provides enables the encoding, exchange, and reuse of structured metadata. It promotes metadata interoperability by "helping to bridge semantic conventions and syntactic encodings with well defined structural conventions" (Bearman, 1999). It does not stipulate semantics, but instead provides the ability for each resource description community to define its own semantic structure and its own metadata element set and then utilizes XML as a common syntax for the exchange and processing of the metadata. By exploiting XML features, RDF imposes a structure that permits the unambiguous expression of semantics and, in so doing, enables the consistent encoding, exchange, and machine-processing of standardized metadata. RDF can probably best be thought of as a framing system that provides transparent support for the metadata schemas defined and utilized within its wrapper (Hudgins et al., 1999, p. 35).

RDF, then, is a general-purpose language for representing information in the Web, which specifies no particular vocabulary, instead letting communities of users define their own vocabularies. RDF properties may be thought of as attributes of resources and in this sense correspond to traditional attribute-value pairs. RDF properties also represent relationships between resources. RDF however, provides no mechanisms for describing these properties, nor does it provide any mechanisms for describing the relationships between these properties and other resources. That is the role of the RDF vocabulary description language, RDF Schema. RDF Schema defines classes and properties that may be used to describe classes, properties, and other resources. All things described by RDF are called *resources* and are instances of the class rdfs:Resource.

All other classes are subclasses of this class. rdfs:Resource is an instance of rdfs:Class (*RDF Vocabulary Description Language 1.0: RDF Schema.* 2004).

RDF vocabularies can describe relationships between vocabulary items from multiple independently developed vocabularies. The example in Figure 2.4, for instance, represents the simple description of a set of resources in RDF using the Dublin Core vocabulary.

Figure 2.4. A Web page described using Dublin Core properties.

```
rdf:RDF
  xmlns:rdf="http://www.w3.org/1999/02/22-rdf-syntax-ns#"
  xmlns:dc="http://purl.org/dc/elements/1.1/">
  <rdf:Description rdf:about="http://www.dlib.org">
  <dc:title>D-Lib Program - Research in Digital Libraries</dc:title>
  <dc:description>The D-Lib program supports the community of people
      with research interests in digital libraries and electronic
      publishing.</dc:description>
  <dc:publisher>Corporation For National Research Initiatives
</dc:publisher>
      <dc:date>1995-01-07</dc:date>
      <dc:subject>
        <rdf:Bag>
          <rdf:li>Research; statistical methods</rdf:li>
          <rdf:li>Education, research, related topics</rdf:li>
          <rdf:li>Library use Studies</rdf:li>
        </rdf:Bag>
      </dc:subject>
      <dc:type>World Wide Web Home Page</dc:type>
      <dc:format>text/html</dc:format>
      <dc:language>en</dc:language>
    </rdf:Description>
  </rdf:RDF>
```

Source: RDF Primer. W3C Recommendation 10 February 2004 [Online]. (2004). Available: http://www. w3.org/TR/rdf-primer/ (retrieved May 24, 2004). Reprinted by permission of the W3C.

Note that both RDF and the Dublin Core define an (XML) element called "Description" (although the Dublin Core element name is written in lowercase).

An RDF description identifies each property type with a prefix (such as "dc" in the example in Figure 2.4), which is in turn mapped to a specific URI of a specific metadata set using the XML namespaces mechanism (Luh, 1998). A given set of metadata elements can be registered as an RDF schema on the Web, thereby specifying the semantics and the structure of the metadata set. By providing the encoding syntax and the XML-namespace facility, RDF makes it straightforward to mix element sets in a given metadata description without the danger of element names colliding. Once an element is established as a component of one namespace, such as the Dublin Core, it is in no danger of being confused with an element of the same name from another namespace. The ability to specify metadata schemas in RDF makes it possible for applications to access a particular schema from a publicly accessible registry on the Web and retrieve the semantics of the element set (Weibel, 1999).

Finally, as a metadata framework rather than a semantic metadata standard, RDF is intended to be highly extensible. It should be able to encompass semantic description standards for large numbers of metadata element sets created by large number of user communities and to allow those standards to interoperate. RDF is meant to be transparent with regard to application domain, user/subject domain, and semantic metadata model employed. It should prove of tremendous benefit in describing, indexing, and retrieving digital objects over the long term because it provides a consistent framework for metadata creation that is extensible to multiple semantic standards, including both those that currently exist and are in use, such as Dublin Core, and those that have yet to be developed, while providing a transparent framework for the global interoperability of these metadata models (Hudgins et al., 1999, p. 36).

Conclusion: Interoperability, the OAI, and Its Problems

In April 2001, an editorial was published in *D-Lib Magazine* in which Associate Editor Peter Hirtle noted that an experience with a publisher who confused OAI with OAIS "made it clear that even in our narrow community interested in digital libraries and electronic publishing, our wealth of acronyms can lead to confusion," ("OAS and OAIS: What's in a Name?" 2001). The OAIS, he goes on to clarify, is the draft ISO reference Model for an Open Archival Information System (described earlier), developed by the Consultative Committee for Space Data Systems. It is an archive, consisting of an organization of people and systems, that has accepted responsibility for preserving information and making it available for a Designated Community by providing a framework needed for long-term digital preservation and access. OAI, on the other hand, stands for the Open Archives Initiative and seeks to develop and promote interoperability standards that facilitate the efficient dissemination of content. Whereas the OAIS initiative arose from a desire to ensure that scientific data would remain accessible into the future, OAI arose from a desire to enhance access to e-print archives today, in order to enhance the availability of scholarly communication. It began as an initiative in scholarly self-publishing and interoperable dissemination and ended up with the term *archives* in its name because in the e-prints community where it originated, the term archive is generally accepted as a synonym for any repository of scholarly papers.

The beginnings of the OAI can be traced back to the early 1990s, when the Los Alamos Preprint Archive was created by Paul Ginsparg. "Preprint," one of the key concepts handed on from the Los Alamos experience, means in the Los Alamos sense, a non-peer-reviewed paper in electronic format, made available before formal peer-reviewed publication. Since the creation of the Los Alamos Archive in 1991, however, the definition of what might be archived has changed, and the OAI now talks about "e-prints," a significantly different concept. The categories of what might be archived has expanded to include "post-prints"—documents for which harvestable metadata is available after the peer-review process—as well, and collectively, they are all "e-prints."

An important convention held in Santa Fe in 1999, initiated by Paul Ginsparg, Rick Luce, and Herbert Vand de Soempel, established the OAI. Its two main points of focus were to be the speeding up of scholarly communication and a general opening up of access to communities interested in these scholarly resources. The convention established organizational principles and technical specifications for facilitating a minimal but highly functional level of interoperability among scholarly e-print archives.

The OAI, then, laid down a minimal set of requirements for interoperability through a protocol that is principally about the exchange of metadata. The OAI protocol is not about the specification of particular metadata formats, although it expects as a minimum something like Dublin Core metadata. It specifies the following (Hunter and Guy, 2004, p. 169):

- a protocol for the exchange of metadata;
- that XML should be the syntax for representing and transporting the metadata;

- that metadata should be exposed to end-user services; and

- that metadata should be harvested to facilitate the discovery of content stored in distributed e-print archives.

"Exposing" metadata means simply making your metadata available to third parties. In this case, it means specifically placing your metadata, wrapped in the appropriate XML, in a place that can be accessed by third parties, in other words, being a data provider. This can mean maintaining an e-prints archive, but it can also mean only supplying metadata for resources available somewhere else, in a full-text archive, the location of which can be indicated in the metadata records. To conform to the OAI definition of a data provider you have to register with a third party that can harvest your exposed metadata and provide user services, so that the service providers know you are exposing metadata for them to harvest.

One other set of terms that need clarifying within the OAI context are the terms *repository* and *archives*. Originally, an archive meant an e-prints archive of full-print texts, and a repository held the metadata for this archive. Since mid-2002, it has become clear that the use of the term archives within the OAI is no longer restricted to document objects but can also refer to collections of metadata.

Another recent change, this one in practice rather than terminology, is that whereas most of the early adopters of OAI belonged to the e-prints or e-theses communities, its application by now is not limited to the disclosure of metadata about e-prints. It is being adopted by a wide range of communities, including commercial communities, as an extensible and interoperable metadata exchange protocol. Libraries are finding that the OAI protocol, supported and encouraged by OCLC, makes it easy to send a query to a database over the Web and receive the results in XML. The protocol thus makes it possible to perform searches of multiple databases simultaneously without the need for proprietary hooks into local databases (Banerjee, 2002).

Despite the promise OAI has shown, there are still many challenges that need to be met with regard to collaborating for metadata harvesting. The first problem, as Martin Halbert put it, writing about the OAI-based MetaScholar Initiative, is that "collaboration among many institutions is exceedingly difficult" (Halbert, 2003). The academic libraries and archives that are candidates for collaborating in the project are chronically underfunded and understaffed; local digital library metadata systems are in transition; metadata quality is sometimes an issue despite the fact that the partner institutions involved in Halbert's project are all research libraries that presumably, produce high- quality metadata.

In addition to specific library problems, there is still a widespread lack of understanding about what the Open Archive Initiative Protocol for Metadata Harvesting (OAI-PMH) is intended to do. One unanticipated problem that has arisen in applications is what is termed "conceptual collisions of metadata formats" (Halbert, 2003). The OAI-PMH allows OAI provider systems to serve up any metadata schema that can be validated against an available XML Schema Definition, although the minimum standard is at least unqualified Dublin Core. In practice, project staff are faced with many practical decisions about mapping metadata from one representation into unqualified Dublin Core, and it has quickly become obvious that some metadata formats map (or "crosswalk") into one another better than others. This problem is so troubling because when formats don't map well—for example, because one format is hierarchical and the other is not or because one is simple and the other very complex—the result is degradation of the metadata. Another problem is that authority control, the pillar of the library cataloging world, is "virtually impossible in the rough-and-ready OAI world of heterogeneous metadata streams, where the only common ground is the loose standard of unqualified Dublin Core metadata elements" (Halbert, 2003). Another problem is duplication of records, which may be likely if a metadata provider is harvesting from databases with records for the same items. Legacy print data, that is, metadata for a collection (particularly an archival collection) in the form of printed catalogs, has also been a surprise, unpleasant experience. Project staff call this "the 'stone table' syndrome; an archive might have God's own scrapbook, but if it is carved on stone tablets, you are looking at recon work" (Halbert, 2003).

Interoperability among all the rich and varied metadata formats created and used by all the rich and varied communities to describe and access their digital objects still has a long way to go. Like the widespread use of the term metadata itself, widespread efforts to foster metadata interoperability are little more than a decade old. Although there has been progress toward a default global metadata standard—unqualified Dublin Core—as well as toward a global metalanguage in which to describe the digital objects of various communities—XML—and a metadata framework in which to wrap the multiplicity of metadata schema these communities have created to describe these objects—RDF—implementing the OAI has shown, among other things, that the problem of interoperability still requires a variety of assessment activities to guide plans for the long-term sustainability of the services established.

Bibliography

About the DOI [Online]. (2000). Available: http://www.doi.org/about_the_ doi.html

Agnew, Grace. (2003). "Developing a Metadata Strategy." *Cataloging & Classification Quarterly* 36 (3/4): 31–46.

Application Profile for the Government Information Locator Service, Version 2 [Online]. (1997). Available: http://www.gils.net/prof_v2.html

ARIADNE Educational Metadata Recommendation [Online]. (1999). Version 3.0. Available: http://ariadne.unil.ch/Metadata/ariadne_metadata_v3final1.htm [no longer available online]

ARIADNE Project Home Page [Online]. (2000). Available: http://ariadne. unil.ch/main.content.html [no longer available online]

Aschenbrenner, Andreas. (2004). "The Bits and Bites of Data Formats—Stainless Design for Digital Endurance." *RLG DigiNews* [Online] 8 (1). Available: http://www.rlg.org/preserv/diginews8-1.html

Baca, Murtha. (2003). "Practical Issues in Applying Metadata Schemas and Controlled Vocabularies to Cultural Heritage Information." *Cataloging & Classification Quarterly* 36 (3/4): 47–55.

Banerjee, Kyle. (2002). "How Does XML Help Libraries?" *Computers in Libraries* [Online] 22 (8). Available: www.infotoday.com/cilmag/sep02/Banerjee.htm

Bearman, David. (1999). "A Common Model to Support Interoperable Metadata: Progress Report on Reconciling Metadata Requirements from the Dublin Core and INDECS/DOI Communities." *D-Lib Magazine* [Online] (January). Available: http://www.dlib.org/dlib/january99/ bearman/01bearman.html

Bearman, David, and John Perkins. (1993). "A Standards Framework for the Computer Interchange of Museum Information" [Online]. Available: http://www. cni.org/pub/CIMI/framework.html

Caplan, Priscilla. (2003). *Metadata Fundamentals for All Librarians.* Chicago: American Library Association.

"Categories for the Description of Works of Art" [Online]. (2000). Edited by Murtha Baca and Patricia Harpring. Available: http://www.getty.edu/research/ conducting_research/standards/cdwa/m.html

Christian, E. (1998). *Experiences with Information Locator Services.* Available: http://www.w3.org/TandS/QL/QL98/pp/experiences.html

CIMI Consortium. (2003). *Publications* [Online]. Available: http://www.cimi. org/CIMI_operations_announcement.html

Computer Interchange of Museum Information (CIMI) [Online]. (1999). Available: http://www.ukoln.ac.uk/metadata/desire/overview/rev_04.htm

Content Standard for Digital Geospatial Metadata (CSDGM) [Online]. (2003). Available: http://www.fgdc.gov/metadata/contstan.html

Crosswalk of Metadata Element Sets for Art, Architecture, and Cultural Heritage Information and Online Resources [Online]. (2003). Compiled by Murtha Baca, Anne Gilliland-Swetland, Patricia Harpring, and Mary Woodley. Available: http://www.getty.edu/research/conducting_research/standards/intrometadata/3_crosswalks/index.html

Day, Michael. (2002). "Metadata: Mapping Between Metadata Formats" [Online]. Available: http://www.ukoln.ac.uk/metadata/interoperability/

Day, Michael. (2003). "Integrating Metadata Schema Registries with Digital Preservation Systems to Support Interoperability: A Proposal" [Online]. Available: http://www.siderean.com/dc2003/101_paper38.pdf

DC-2003. 28 September–2 October 2003. Seattle, Washington, USA [Online]. (2003). Available: http://dc2003.ischool.washington.edu/

de Carvalho Moura, Ana Maria, Maria Luiza Machado Campos, and Cassia Maria Barreto. (1998). "A Survey on Metadata for Describing and Retrieving Internet Resources." *World Wide Web* 1: 221–40.

Dekkers, Max. (2001). *Metadata Watch Report #7* [Online] (SCHEMAS-PWC-WP2-D28-Final-20011217). Available: http://www.schemas-forum.org/ metadata-watch/d28/mwr7.pdf

Doctorow, Cory. (2001, August). "Metacrap: Putting the Torch to Seven Straw-Men of the Meta-utopia" [Online]. Version 1.3. Available: http://www.well. com/~doctorow/metacrap.htm

Dornfest, Rael, and Dan Brickley. (2003). "The Power of Metadata." *Openp2p.com* [Online]. Available: http://www.openp2p.com/pub/a/p2p/2001/01/18/metadata.html

Dublin Core Metadata Initiative. (1999). *Dublin Core Metadata Element Set, Version 1.1: Reference Description* [Online]. Available: http://dublincore.org/documents/1999/07/02/dces/#rfc2413

Dublin Core Metadata Initiative. (2004a). *Dublin Core Metadata Element Set, Version 1.1: Reference Description* [Online]. Available: http://dublincore.org/documents/dces/

Dublin Core Metadata Initiative [Online]. (2004b). *DCMI Registry Working Group.* Available: http://dublincore.org/groups/registry/

Dublin Core Metadata Registry [Online]. (2004). Available: http://dublincore.org/dcregistry/

Duval, Eric, Wayne Hodgins, Stuart Sutton, and Stuart L. Weibel. (2002). "Metadata Principles and Practicalities." *D-Lib Magazine* 8 (4) [Online]. Available: http://www.dlib.org/dlib/april02/weibel/04weibel.html

Electronic Versions of the TEI Guidelines [Online]. (1998). Available: http://www-tei.uic.edu/orgs/tei/p3/elect.html [no longer available]

The EOR Toolkit [Online]. (2001). Available: http://eor.dublincore.org

European Commission DGXIII/E 2nd Metadata Workshop, Luxembourg, 26 June 1998 [Online]. (1998). Available: http://www2.echo.lu/oii/en/meta-lib.html

Erpanet. (2003). *ERPANET OAIS Training Seminar Report* [Online]. Available: http://www.erpanet.org/www/content/documentation.html

"Executive Briefing: The Digital Object Identifier." (1999). *Information Services & Use* 19: 179.

FGDC—Content Standards for Digital Geospatial Metadata [Online]. (1998). Available: www.ukoln.ac.uk/metadata/desire/overview/rev_09.htm

FGDC Newsletter [Online] (1996, March). (March). Available: http://www.fgdc.gov/publications/documents/geninfo/fgdcnl0396.html

Finkelstein, Clive (2001). "XML—The Future of Metadata [Online]." Extract from *Building Corporate Portals with XML.* McGraw-Hill (1999, September). Available: http://members.ozemail.com.au/~visible/papers/ xml-metadata.htm

The Gateway to Educational Materials [Online]. (2003). Available: http://www.thegateway.org

Gem Project Site [Online]. (2002). Available: http://www.geminfo.org

Gem Project Site. GEM 2.0 [Online]. (2002). Available: http://www.geminfo.org/Workbench/gem2.html

GILS. (n.d.). *FAQ (Frequently Asked Questions)* [Online]. Available: http://www.gils.net/faq.html#q_1_1

Guidelines for Using XML for Electronic Data Interchange. Version 0.0.5 [Online]. (1998). Available: http://www.geocities.com/WallStreet/Floor/5815/guide.htm

Halbert, Martin. (2003). "The Metascholar Initiative: AmericanSouth.Org and MetaArchive.Org." *Library Hi Tech* 21 (2): 182–98.

Hearn, Stephen S. (1999). "Metadata Structures and Authority Control." *Technicalities* 19 (6): 7–9.

Heery, Rachel. (1996). *Review of Metadata Formats* [Online]. Available: http://www. ukoln.ac.uk/metadata/review.html

Hudgins, Jean, Grace Agnew, and Elizabeth Brown. (1999). *Getting Mileage out of Metadata: Applications for the Library.* LITA Guides #5. Chicago: American Library Association.

Hunter, Jane. (2003). "A Survey of Metadata Research for Organizing the Web." *Library Trends* 52 (2): 318–44.

Hunter, Philip, and Marieke Guy. (2004). "Metadata for Harvesting: the Open Archives Initiative, and How to Find Things on the Web." *The Electronic Library* 22 (2): 168–74.

"<indecs>: Putting Metadata to Rights. Summary Final Report" [Online]. (2000). Available: http://www.indecs.org/project.htm

International DOI Foundation. (2003). *doi: The Digital Object Identifier System. Introductory Overview* {Online]. Available: http://www.doi.org/overview/sys_overview_021601.html

International DOI Foundation. (2004a). *doi: The Digital Object Identifier System* [Online]. Available: http://www.doi.org/

International DOI Foundation. (2004b). *doi: The Digital Object Identifier System. DOI Demonstrations* [Online]. Available: http://www.doi.org/demos.html

Lazinger, Susan S. (2001). *Digital Preservation and Metadata: History, Theory, Practice.* Englewood, CO: Libraries Unlimited.

Lowe, Carrie. (2000). "GEM: Design and Implementation of a Metadata Project for Education." In *Metadata and Organizing Educational Resources on the Internet.* Edited by Jane Greenberg. New York: Haworth Information Press, 109–26.

Luh, James C. (1998). "Tech ABS: The Resource Description Framework." *Internet World* [Online],(August 10). Available: http://www.internetworld.com/print/1998/08/10/webdev/19980810-techabc.html

Martin, Ruth. (2002). *Metadata Watch Report #8* [Online] (SCHEMAS-PWC/WP2/WP3-D29/D35-Final-20020131). Available: http://www.schemas-forum.org/metadata-watch/d29/d29.pdf

"Metadata Debate: Two Perspectives on Dublin Core." (2003). *Digicult.Info* 6 [Online]. Available: http://www.digicult.info/downloads/dc_info_issue6_december_20031.pdf

Miller, Eric. (1998, May). "An Introduction to the Resource Description Framework." *D-Lib Magazine* [Online]. Available: http://www.dlib.org/dlib/may98/miller/05miller.html

National Library of Australia. (1999). "Preservation Metadata for Digital Collections. Exposure Draft" [Online]. Available: http://www.nla.gov.au/preserve/pmeta.html

"OAS and OAIS: What's in a Name?" (2001, April). *D-Lib Magazine* [Online]. Available: http://www.dlib.org/dlib/april01/04editorial.html

Paskin, Norman. (1999). "DOI: Current Status and Outlook." *D-Lib Magazine* [Online] 5 (5). Available: http://webdoc.sub.gwdg.de/edoc/aw/d-lib/dlib/may99/05paskin.html.

Paskin, Norman. (2002). "Digital Object Identifiers." *Information Services & Use* 22 (2/3): 97–112.

RDF Primer. W3C Recommendation 10 February 2004 [Online]. (2004). Available: http://www.w3.org/TR/rdf-primer/

RDF Vocabulary Description Language 1.0: RDF Schema. W3C Recommendation 10 February 2004 [Online]. (2004). Available: http://www.w3.org/TR/rdf-schema/

Schottlaender, Brian E. C. (2003). "Why Metadata? Why Me? Why Now?" *Cataloging & Classification Quarterly* 36 (3/4): 19–29.

Sperberg-McQueen, C. M., and Burnard, L., eds. (2002). *TEI P4: Guidelines for Electronic Text Encoding and Interchange* [Online]. Text Encoding Initiative Consortium. XML-compatible edition: Oxford, Providence, Charlottesville, Bergen. Available: http://www.tei-c.org/P4X/

St. Pierre, Margaret. (1998). "Issues in Crosswalking Content Metadata Standards" [Online]. Available: http://www.niso.org/crsswalk.html

Taylor, Arlene G. (1999). *The Organization of Information.* Englewood, CO: Libraries Unlimited.

Taylor, Arlene G. (2004). *The Organization of Information.* 2d ed. Library and Information Science Text series. Westport, CT: Libraries Unlimited.

Visual Resources Association Data Standards Committee. (2002). "VRA Core Categories, Version 3.0" [Online]. Available: http://www.vraweb.org/vracore3.htm

W3C. (1999d). "XML in 10 Points" [Online]. Available: http://www3.org/XML/1999/XML-in-10-points

W3C. (2004). *Extensible Markup Language (XML) 1.0.* 3rd ed. W3C Recommendation 04 February 2004. [Online]. Available: http://www.w3.org/TR/REC-xml

Weibel, Stuart. (1999, April). "The State of the Dublin Core Metadata Initiative April 1999." *D-Lib Magazine* [Online]. (April). Available: http://www.dlib.org/dlib/april99/04weibel.html

Weibel, Stuart. (2000, December). "The Dublin Core Metadata Initiative: Mission, Current Activities, and Future Directions." *D-Lib Magazine* [Online]. Available: http://www.dlib.org/dlib/december00/weibel/12weibel.html

Weibel, Stuart, Jean Godby, and Eric Miller. (1995). *OCLC/NCSA Metadata Workshop Report* [Online]. Available: http://www.oclc.org:5046/oclc/ research/ conferences/metadata/dublin_core_report.html

Weibel, S.[tuart], J. Kunze, and C. Lagoze. (1998). "Dublin Core Metadata for Resource Discovery" [Online]. (Network Working Group Request for Comments: 2413). Available: http://www.ietf.org/rfc/rfc2413.txt

APPENDIX 2.A: Dublin Core Metadata Elements, Version 1.1

Element: Title

Name:	Title
Identifier:	Title
Definition:	A name given to the resource.
Comment:	Typically, a Title will be a name by which the resource is formally known.

Element: Creator

Name:	Creator
Identifier:	Creator
Definition:	An entity primarily responsible for making the content of the resource.
Comment:	Examples of a Creator include a person, an organization, or a service.
	Typically, the name of a Creator should be used to indicate the entity.

Element: Subject

Name:	Subject and Keywords
Identifier:	Subject
Definition:	The topic of the content of the resource.
Comment:	Typically, a Subject will be expressed as keywords, key phrases, or classification codes that describe a topic of the resource.
	Recommended best practice is to select a value from a controlled vocabulary or formal classification scheme.

Element: Description

Name:	Description
Identifier:	Description
Definition:	An account of the content of the resource.
Comment:	Description may include but is not limited to an abstract, table of contents, reference to a graphical representation of content, or a free-text account of the content.

Element: *Publisher*

Name:	Publisher
Identifier:	Publisher
Definition:	An entity responsible for making the resource available
Comment:	Examples of a Publisher include a person, an organization, or a service. Typically, the name of a Publisher should be used to indicate the entity.

Element: *Contributor*

Name:	Contributor
Identifier:	Contributor
Definition:	An entity responsible for making contributions to the content of the resource.
Comment:	Examples of a Contributor include a person, an organization, or a service. Typically, the name of a Contributor should be used to indicate the entity.

Element: *Date*

Name:	Date
Identifier:	Date
Definition:	A date associated with an event in the life cycle of the resource.
Comment:	Typically, Date will be associated with the creation or availability of the resource. Recommended best practice for encoding the date value is defined in a profile of ISO 8601 [W3CDTF] and follows the YYYY-MM-DD format.

Element: *Type*

Name:	Resource Type
Identifier:	Type
Definition:	The nature or genre of the content of the resource.
Comment:	Type includes terms describing general categories, functions, genres, or aggregation levels for content. Recommended best practice is to select a value from a controlled vocabulary (for example, the working draft list of Dublin Core Types [DCT1]). To describe the physical or digital manifestation of the resource, use the FORMAT element.

Element: Format

Name: Format
Identifier: Format
Definition: The physical or digital manifestation of the resource.
Comment: Typically, Format may include the media type or dimensions of
                 the resource. Format may be used to determine the software,
                 hardware, or other equipment needed to display or operate the
                 resource. Examples of dimensions include size and duration.
                 Recommended best practice is to select a value from a con-
                 trolled vocabulary (for example, the list of Internet Media
                 Types [MIME] defining computer media formats).

Element: Identifier

Name: Resource Identifier
Identifier: Identifier
Definition: An unambiguous reference to the resource within a given context.
Comment: Recommended best practice is to identify the resource by means
                 of a string or number conforming to a formal identification
                 system. Example formal identification systems include the
                 Uniform Resource Identifier (URI) (including the Uniform Re-
                 source Locator (URL)), the Digital Object Identifier (DOI),
                 and the International Standard Book Number (ISBN).

Element: Source

Name: Source
Identifier: Source
Definition: A Reference to a resource from which the present resource is derived.
Comment: The present resource may be derived from the Source resource in
                 whole or in part. Recommended best practice is to reference
                 the resource by means of a string or number conforming to a
                 formal identification system.

Element: Language

Name: Language
Identifier: Language
Definition: A language of the intellectual content of the resource.
Comment: Recommended best practice for the values of the Language element is
                 defined by RFC 1766 [RFC1766] which includes a two-letter Lan-
                 guage Code (taken from the ISO 639 standard [ISO639]), followed
                 optionally, by a two-letter Country Code (taken from the ISO 3166
                 standard [ISO3166]). For example, "en" for English, "fr" for
                 French, or "en-uk" for English used in the United Kingdom.

Element: Relation

Name:	Relation
Identifier:	Relation
Definition:	A reference to a related resource.
Comment:	Recommended best practice is to reference the resource by means of a string or number conforming to a formal identification system.

Element: Coverage

Name:	Coverage
Identifier:	Coverage
Definition:	The extent or scope of the content of the resource.
Comment:	Coverage will typically include spatial location (a place name or geographic coordinates), temporal period (a period label, date, or date range) or jurisdiction (such as a named administrative entity). Recommended best practice is to select a value from a controlled vocabulary (for example, the Thesaurus of Geographic Names [TGN]) and that, where appropriate, named places or time periods be used in preference to numeric identifiers such as sets of coordinates or date ranges.

Element: Rights

Name:	Rights Management
Identifier:	Rights
Definition:	Information about rights held in and over the resource.
Comment:	Typically, a Rights element will contain a rights management statement for the resource, or reference a service providing such information. Rights information often encompasses Intellectual Property Rights (IPR), Copyright, and various Property Rights. If the Rights element is absent, no assumptions can be made about the status of these and other rights with respect to the resource.

Note: From the Dublin Core Metadata Initiative (1998). Each element is optional and repeatable, and the elements may appear in any order.

APPENDIX 2.B: GILS Core Elements

- **Title** (Not Repeatable): This element conveys the most significant aspects of the referenced resource and is intended for initial presentation to users independently of other elements.

- **Originator** (Repeatable): This element identifies the information resource originator.

- **Contributor** (Repeatable): This element is used if there are names associated with the resource in addition to the Originator, such as personal author, corporate author, coauthor, or a conference or meeting name.

- **Date of Publication** (Not Repeatable): The discrete creation date in which the described resource was published or updated, although not for use on resources that are published continuously, such as dynamic databases.

- **Place of Publication** (Not Repeatable): The city or town where the described resource was published. May also include country if location of city is not well known.

- **Language of Resource** (Repeatable): This element indicates the language(s) of the described resource as represented by the MARC three-character alpha code. If a resource is multilingual, repeat this element for each applicable language.

- **Abstract** (Not Repeatable): This element presents a narrative description of the information resource.

- **Controlled Subject Index** (Repeatable): This element is a grouping of subelements that together provide any controlled vocabulary used to describe the resource and the source of that controlled vocabulary:

- **Subject Terms Uncontrolled** (Not Repeatable): This element is a grouping of descriptive terms to aid users in locating resources of potential interest, but the terms are not drawn from a formally registered controlled vocabulary source.

- **Spatial Domain** (Not Repeatable): This element is a grouping of subelements that together provide the geographic a real domain of the data set or information resource.

- **Time Period** (Repeatable): This element provides time frames associated with the information resource.

- **Availability** (Repeatable): This element is a grouping of subelements that together describe how the information resource is made available.

- **Sources of Data** (Not Repeatable): This element identifies the primary sources or providers of data to the system, whether within or outside the agency.

- **Methodology** (Not Repeatable): This element identifies any specialized tools, techniques, or methodology used to produce this information resource. The validity, degree of reliability, and any known possibility of errors should also be described.

- **Access Constraints** (Not Repeatable): This element is a grouping of subelements that together describe any constraints or legal prerequisites for accessing the information resource or its component products or services.

- **Use Constraints** (Not Repeatable): This element describes any constraints or legal prerequisites for using the information resource or its component products or services.

- **Point of Contact** (Not Repeatable): This element identifies an organization, and a person where appropriate, serving as the point of contact plus methods that may be used to make contact.

- **Supplemental Information** (Not Repeatable): Through this element, the record source may associate other descriptive information with the GILS Core locator record.

- **Purpose** (Not Repeatable): This element describes why the information resource is offered and identifies other programs, projects, and legislative actions wholly or partially responsible for the establishment or continued delivery of this information resource.

- **Agency Program** (Not Repeatable): This element identifies the major agency program or mission supported by the system and should include a citation for any specific legislative authorities associated with this information resource.

- **Cross Reference** (Repeatable): This element is a grouping of subelements that together identify another locator record or related information resources likely to be of interest.

- **Schedule Number** (Not Repeatable): This element is used to record the identifier associated with the information resource for records management purposes.

- **Control Identifier** (Not Repeatable): This element is defined by the information provider and is used to distinguish this locator record from all other GILS Core locator records.

- **Original Control Identifier** (Not Repeatable): This element is used by the record source to refer to another GILS locator record from which this locator record was derived.

- **Record Source** (Not Repeatable): This element identifies the organization that created or last modified this locator record.

- **Language of Record** (Not Repeatable): This element indicates the language of the locator record as represented by the MARC three-character alpha code.

- **Date of Last Modification** (Not Repeatable): This element identifies the latest date on which this locator record was created or modified.

- **Record Review Date** (Not Repeatable): This element identifies a date assigned by the Record Source for review of this GILS Record.

Note: From *Application Profile for the Government Information Locator Service, Version 2* (1997).

APPENDIX 2.C: ARIADNE Version 3 Official Metadata (Categories and Subcategories)

1. General information on the resource itself

   1.0 identifier

   1.1 title

   1.2 authors

   1.3 date

   1.4 language

   1.5 publisher

   1.6 sources

2. Semantics of the resource

   2.1 discipline

   2.2 subdiscipline

   2.3 main concept

   2.4 main concept synonyms

   2.5 other concepts

3. Pedagogical attributes

   3.1 end-user type

   3.2 document type

   3.3 document format

   3.4 usage remarks

   3.5 didactical context

   3.6 course level

   3.7 difficulty level

   3.8 interactivity level

   3.9 semantic density

   3.10 pedagogical duration

4. Technical characteristics

   4.1 document handle

   4.2 file media types

   4.3 package size

   4.4 operating system type

   4.5 OS version

        4.6   other platform requirements

        4.7   installation remarks

5.   **Conditions for use**

        5.1   cost

        5.2   copyright and other restrictions

        5.3   usage remarks

6.   **Meta-metadata information**

        6.1   author name

        6.2   creator name

        6.3   last modified date

        6.4   language

        6.5   validator name

        6.6   validation date

APPENDIX 2.D: ARIADNE Metadata Recommendation ver. 3.1

1. General

    1.1.   Identifier

    1.2.   Title

    1.3.   Catalog Entry

    1.4.   Language

    1.5.   Description

    1.6.   Keywords

    1.7.   Coverage

    1.8.   Structure

    1.9.   Aggregation level

2. Life Cycle

    2.1.   Version

    2.2.   Status

    2.3.   Contribute

3. Meta-metadata

    3.1.   Identifier

    3.2.   Catalog

    3.3.   Contribute

    3.4.   Metadata Scheme

    3.5.   Language

4. Technical

    4.1.   Format

    4.2.   Size

    4.3.   Location

    4.4.   Requirements

    4.5.   Installation remarks

    4.6.   Other platform requirements

    4.7.   Duration

5. Educational

    5.1.   Interactivity type

    5.2.   Learning resource type

APPENDIX 2.E: Categories for the Description of Works of Art

OBJECT, ARCHITECTURE, OR GROUP

OBJECT/WORK

CLASSIFICATION

ORIENTATION/ARRANGEMENT

TITLES OR NAMES

STATE

EDITION

MEASUREMENTS

MATERIALS AND TECHNIQUES

FACTURE

PHYSICAL DESCRIPTION

INSCRIPTIONS/MARKS

CONDITION/EXAMINATION HISTORY

CONSERVATION/TREATMENT HISTORY

CREATION

OWNERSHIP/COLLECTING HISTORY

COPYRIGHT/RESTRICTIONS

STYLES/PERIODS/GROUPS/MOVEMENTS

SUBJECT MATTER

CONTEXT

EXHIBITION/LOAN HISTORY

RELATED WORKS

RELATED VISUAL DOCUMENTATION

RELATED TEXTUAL REFERENCES

CRITICAL RESPONSES

CATALOGING HISTORY

CURRENT LOCATION

DESCRIPTIVE NOTE

Chapter 3

Library and Information-Related Metadata Schemas

The Content Standards

Content standards are the guidelines that prescribe the kind of information recorded in the description of an information object, printed or digital. The term *description* in our definition is used in the broadest sense, including both the data elements of descriptive cataloging (author, title, date, publisher, etc.) and of subject cataloging (classification number, subject headings, etc.) of a resource. Most metadata schemes, including those described in the previous chapter, concentrate on syntax rather than semantics, that is, on the *grammar* of the schema, for example, what fields are repeatable and what tags must be used at the beginning and end of a data element in an XML scheme. Content standards, in contrast, are concerned with the semantics of the bibliographic record, for example, how the date in a field giving the date of publication should be formatted, or whether a subject term should be expressed in its natural order or with the noun and adjective reversed in order to put the most important word first. Whatever the decisions, content standards all have the same ultimate goal: to standardize the data in records describing information objects to facilitate interoperability that will maximize retrieval.

Collocation—bringing together like objects (or in our case, records) by unifying descriptive formats or subject terms describing the objects—has been used to optimize retrieval since cataloging was invented. The introduction of digital objects to the information scene has not changed this need for collocation, and content standards are as useful today for achieving it as they were a hundred years ago. One of the most eloquent examples of the ongoing need for collocation, which sometimes conflicts with the need for simplicity, is the gradual increase in the use of content standards such as controlled vocabularies, within the Dublin Core. The Dublin Core began as a thirteen-field metadata element set meant to be simple enough for nonlibrarian digital object creators to use. Only the structure and syntax were prescribed, with the semantics of what went into the uniformly structured fields left to

73

the creator's choice. In the relatively few years since Dublin Core became an international standard, content standards have been introduced more and more into Dublin Core applications, because without them only the syntax is interoperable, while the content of the fields is a wild and colorful jungle of forms. Creative, perhaps, but not very useful for retrieval.

In practice, content standards have long been produced almost exclusively by the library and archives communities. When we discuss "traditional cataloging standards," we refer to the tools that have been developed for cataloging purposes. Some of the most widely used library-based content standards—AACR2, Dewey Decimal Classification (DDC), and Library of Congress Subject Headings (LCSH)—are examined in the first section of this chapter. They are discussed in light of the changes that the need to describe digital information objects has brought about, and continues to inspire, in them. In the next section, the encoding standards that the library community devised to express the traditional content standards in machine-readable form—MARC, in its current and planned implementations, and EAD, the archival community's encoding scheme—is discussed. Finally, in the third section, efforts at harmonization, the "process of ensuring consistency in the specification of related content metadata standards" (St. Pierre and LaPlant, 2004), are examined through the prism of the leading ontologies and models developed with this aim in mind.

Michael Gorman, in a seminal article on cataloging electronic resources, refers to "the impossible thing that librarians have been doing for a long time … classification—the reduction of the almost infinite dimensions of knowledge to a straight line from 000-999 or A to Z" (Gorman, 2003, p. 6). The new impossible thing librarians need to do today—bring order to a vast sea of electronic documents and make them "part of an arranged and harmonious world—in short, to apply some kind of bibliographic control to the disorder of the Internet and the Web" (Gorman, 2003, p. 6), is the purpose of the content standards and the subject of this section.

DESCRIPTIVE CONTENT: AACR2

AACR2 is an internationally recognized standard for descriptive cataloging that contains rules for describing all types of library materials. It includes rules to describe and provide access to books, serials, electronic resources, maps, films, sound recordings, and so on through library catalog records. It is also a standard for providing headings and references for linking bibliographic items with similar characteristics. AACR2 was completely different from its predecessor *Anglo-American Cataloging Rules* (1968) in that it was published as a single text (unlike its predecessors, which came in separate American and British versions) and "quickly transcended even the historic achievement of being a unitary English-language cataloguing code to become the nearest approach to a world code we have" (Gorman, 2003, pp. 9–10). It worked out the principles of author/title cataloguing set forth in the Paris principles, which were based on the pioneering work of Seymour Lubetsky (*The Future of Cataloging*, 2000), and in the nearly thirty years since its publication it has been revised and updated several times. It is this constant updating in response to changes in the realities of the cataloging world that have kept AACR2 a relevant standard for so many years:

AACR2 may serve as an example of a cataloging standard that was developed for traditional cataloging, but was sufficiently flexible to adapt to new formats. AACR2 was developed and expanded to accommodate new formats. When microforms became the accepted format for preserving paper formats, AACR2 developed a chapter on cataloging of these materials. With the appearance of Internet resources, AACR2 added a chapter on handling this format. (El-Sherbini and Klim, 2004, p. 244)

The revisions to the rules in AACR2 for cataloging electronic resources are probably the changes that have proven most significant in keeping it "a metadata standard that remains as viable today as any of the other metadata standards being used to organize electronic information" (Huthwaite, 2003, p. 88).

Radical changes in the cataloging environment led up to the 2002 revisions. First, the rise of the Internet redefined what we mean by the term *information.* A proliferation of the variety of information media gave rise of formats that were no longer clearly defined and recognizable. If the "electronic resource" was not in direct-access form (for example, on a CD-ROM), but rather accessible only remotely, it was not only intangible, requiring cataloging without any physical item-in-hand, it was often unstable, moving across boundaries that sometimes seemed to defy description. Nonetheless, if electronic resources were to be retrievable, they had to be described, and so the 2002 revisions focusing mainly on electronic resources, continuing serial resources, and integrating resources were issued.

AACR2 2002 Revisions

In 2002, a number of changes were made that affect all resources. Because the focus of this book is electronic resources, we concentrate only on the changes that specifically influence the cataloging of these electronic resources.

Electronic Resources (Chapter 9)

The scope of this chapter was narrowed to exclude continuing resources such as Web sites, and the chief source of information for an electronic resource was changed to the resource itself (not just the title screen).

Continuing Resources (Chapter 12)

The title of Chapter 12 was changed from "Serials" to "Continuing Resources." The scope of the chapter was expanded beyond serials to encompass all continuing resources. Continuing resources were defined as "bibliographic entities which are issued over time, either in a succession of discrete parts (serials) or by means of additions or changes that are integrated into the document itself (integrating resources)" (*Notice of AACR2 Revisions*, 2002). Obvious typographical errors in the title proper (which seem to occur more frequently on Web sites than in print materials) were now permitted to be corrected by the cataloger, and if an initialism and a full-name form appeared on the chief source of information, preference was to be given to the full form.

Serials

Significant changes were made to distinguish between major and minor title changes to reduce the number of cases in which new records need to be created.

Description is to be based on the first or earliest available issue. More flexibility in the numbering area is allowed, enabling the cataloger to alter punctuation, supply chronological designation for first issues, and supply wording for new sequences of numbering (*Notice of AACR2 Revisions*, 2002).

Integrating Resources

An integrating resource was defined as "a bibliographic resource that is added to or changed by means of updates that do not remain discrete and are integrated into the whole" (*Notice of AACR2 Revisions*, 2002). These include updating loose-leaf publications, databases, and Web sites. To accommodate this new characterization of documents, a new Bibliographic Level (BibLvL) was added to MARC 21 and implemented by OCLC after July 2003. Description is based on the latest iteration of the integrating resource and changed in the bibliographic record whenever the resource changed. The chief source of information for an electronic resource is the resource itself, including title screens, metadata, HTML headers, and splash screens (screens that you have to click through to get to a site). Preference is given to the most complete presentation of the title. The date on which the electronic resource is viewed is always to be recorded in a note.

One might ask what the advantages are of continuing to use AACR2 given that the metadata content standard to describe resources that are constantly changing, being updated, integrating new portions into the old versions in a chaotic and unpredictable manner? First, it is an international standard, used by an increasing community of catalogers globally. It is used in virtually all English-speaking countries and has been translated into other languages. AACR2 has made widespread sharing of cataloging records possible worldwide. Second, it provides rules for describing information resources in all formats, so it can be used in a print, Internet, or hybrid environment. Third, it is more precise than many other metadata standards, such as Dublin Core, which, if used without modification, produces records with content that can be accessed by keywords but not by the precisely formulated content description in all fields which AACR2 cataloging creates. Additionally, AACR2 provides for authority control of names and places, a factor that has a critical impact on the relevance of items retrieved in catalog searches. Finally, AACR2 allows what Huthwaite calls "a principled approach for resource discovery" (Huthwaite, 2003, p. 91). It gives the user searching a catalog the assurance that the catalog is organized by a set of operating principles, for example, the principle of authorship, so the user can be confident that the "author" of a work has a particular, known type of relationship with the work.

The revision process for serials in AACR2 had three basic goals: creation of descriptive cataloging rules for new kinds of resources; integration of the rules for seriality throughout the cataloging code, and harmonization of serial cataloging practices internationally (Hirons, 2003). In a report on the impact of the 2002 AACR2 Amendments on SabiCatweb at the end of 2002, Ina van der Merwe of the Joint Steering Committee for Revision of AACR remarks that "the burning question at the time was whether to proceed with another revision of AACR2 or to proceed with a bibliographic neutron bomb—an AACR3" (van der Merwe, 2002). Despite the success of the 2002 revisions in dealing with the new kinds of rules needed to catalog the new kinds of resources, the answer to that question ultimately was affirmative with regard to the perceived need to publish a whole new edition of the code,

AACR3. Three more sets of revisions lay between the very significant 2002 changes and the "bibliographic neutron bomb" scheduled, at this writing, to be released in 2008—the 2003 Revisions, 2004 Revisions, and the 2005 update to AACR2.

AACR2 2003 Revisions

The 2003 revisions were not nearly as extensive as those issued in 2002, but need to be mentioned. They included the following changes:

- Binding information can now been added when there is only one ISBN (1.8E1).

- The term *earth* will now be capitalized whenever it refers to the planet (1.10C2b; 3.0A1; A.27A).

- Two examples of "summary" notes for integrating resources were added (12.7B18).

- Minor changes to a title proper now includes rearrangement of existing words in the title (21.2A2i).

- A title added entry is now made for all items entered under a name heading or entered under a uniform title heading (21.30J1; 25.2E1; 26.4B1, footnote 2).

- Headings for heads of governments and heads of international intergovernmental organizations can now contain the name of an incumbent and the incumbent's dates, bringing these headings into accord with headings for heads of state and heads of religious organizations (24.20C1; 24.20C2; 24.20C3).

- The abbreviation for "Newfoundland and Labrador" has been changed to "N.L."; (b) "Newfoundland" and its abbreviation "Nfld." have been added (Appendix B.14A) (Cataloging Policy and Support Office, 2003).

AACR2 2004 revisions

Some of the 2004 revisions were corrections to previous changes, such as the rule for the physical description of sound recordings (MARC field 300), rule 6.5B1, which now included an option to use "a term in common usage to record the specific format of the physical carrier" instead of one of the specific material designations prescribed in the rule. The revisions noted that the Library of Congress, however, had issued an LCRI that instructs its staff not to apply this option and that other libraries following LC practice will also follow the LCRI (Gonzalez, 2004). In addition to this and other corrections, there are changes to Chapter 9, for electronic resources. Area 3 is eliminated (the general statement of the type of electronic resource in MARC field 256) and moved to an optional note (9.7B8). Rule 9.5 provides an option to record a physical description of a remotely available electronic resource, using a term either from an appropriate subrule or from common usage (for example, Web site). This rule also allows for other physical details, including file type to be given. Other changes directly affecting the cataloging of electronic resources include the rule addressing sources of information (1.0A). This rule has been lengthened to include a new subrule (1.0A3), which explains more fully the concept of "chief source of information." There is also a discussion of the basis of the description for continuing resources (both serials and integrating resources).

AACR2 2005 Update

The Library of Congress implemented the 2005 Update to the 2002 AACR2 on August 1, 2005. The major amendments included in this, AACR2's final update, were as follows:

- Rules A.2A, A.4A, and A.30 have been revised to cover capitalization of single letters used to represent words, and multiple-letter prefixes in compound terms, in headings for corporate bodies and in titles, for example, "eBay" and "drkoop.com, Inc."

- Rule A.40 on German capitalization has been revised in line with changes to German orthography.

- The definition of "coloured illustration" in the Glossary has been revised.

- The Turkish word "bir" has been removed from Appendix E, Initial Articles.

- Minor changes arising from the preparation of the new edition of *Cartographic Materials: A Manual of Interpretation for AACR2* have been made. (Joint Steering Committee, 2005a)

It is worth noting that with the publication of AACR3, the name "AACR" may disappear from the professional lingo. In April 2005, the Joint Steering Committee announced that it has decided to take a different approach to the new edition, and therefore a decision was made to use a new working title: *RDA: Resource Description and Access* (Joint Steering Committee, 2005b).

The Next Big Thing: AACR3 (or *RDA: Resource Description and Access*)

On May 17, 2004, the Joint Steering Committee for Revision of AACR (JSC) issued its "Strategic Plan for AACR" (Beacom, 2004), stating seven goals for AACR3:

1. The rules will continue to be based on principles and include attributes for all types of materials.

2. They will be used worldwide, but will be derived from English language conventions and customs.

3. They will be easy to use and interpret.

4. They will be applicable to, and operate in, an online, Web-based environment.

5. They will provide effective bibliographic control of all types of media (analogue and digital).

6. They will be compatible with other standards for resource description and retrieval.

7. They will be used beyond the library community.

Three targets for the accomplishment of these goals were outlined, along with the specific tasks for achieving each target:

Target 1, the principal target, declares that a new edition of AACR is intended for publication in 2008, with the rules designed for use in a Web-based environment. The tasks for accomplishing this are as follows:

1. A new introduction will be completed, including a statement of the principles of AACR, a description of the functions of the catalogue, and conceptual information to assist cataloguers in understanding the methods of the procedure.

2. New introductions to part I (description) and part II (access) will also be completed.

3. The concept of authority control will be incorporated in the rules.

4. Concepts and terminology from *Functional Requirements for Bibliographic Records (FRBR)* will be incorporated in the rules.

5. Ambiguous and inconsistent terminology in the rules will be revised, for example, "main entry," "added entry," and "entry."

6. Terminology will be revised to extend consistency within the chapters of part I, and redundancy will be eliminated.

7. Problems associated with the class of materials concept and the related issue of GMDs (general material designators) will be resolved.

8. Residual problems associated with cataloguing resources that change over time, including multipart items, will be resolved.

9. Chapter 21 will be revised to address issues associated with the concept of "authorship" as it is currently reflected in the rules, and restrictions imposed by the "rule of three."

10. Chapter 25 (Uniform Titles) will be revised to incorporate the concept of expression-level citations.

11. The examples throughout the rules will be reviewed and updated where necessary. (Oliver, 2004)

Target 2 states that there will be outreach to other resource description communities to achieve closer alignment with other standards. Target 3 is that a Web-based version of the new edition of the rules, to complement the loose-leaf product, will be produced.

In notes accompanying a 2004 presentation on AACR3, LC's Barbara Tillett discusses why it is necessary to have a new set of rules. The intention is not to cause changes like those experienced when AACR2 was published, but to change the approach to cataloging and go back to principle-based rules that build cataloger's judgment, are simple to use, and provide more consistency across various types of content and media. The cataloging rules need to remain independent of communication formats and provide a content standard for elements of bibliographic description that can be used by any of the emerging metadata standards, like Dublin Core. Metadata standards, she says, "give us the categories of data elements to include in the record, but usually do not tell us how to structure the content of those elements or what we should use as the source for finding the content of those elements—they just give us labels to use—like saying 'title' or 'date' " (Tillett, 2004). It is to supply content structure and sources so that AACR3, like its predecessors, will continue to be essential for organizing resources both digital and analog for the foreseeable future.

Subject Content: LCSH, LCC, DCC

Subject cataloging consists of either assigning a number from a classification system or assigning a heading from a controlled vocabulary, or both, to a resource. There are a large number of controlled vocabularies and classification systems in existence, both general and specific to individual knowledge domains. Nonetheless, a few dominate globally. *Library of Congress Subject Headings* (LCSH) is the most widely used controlled vocabulary in the world, and *Library of Congress Classification* (LCC) and *Dewey Decimal Classification* (DCC) are the two most widely used general classification systems. Therefore, it is on these three global subject content standards that we concentrate.

LCSH

Within the library community, there is widespread use and acceptance of LCSH worldwide (Subject Access to Digital Collections, 2004). Nevertheless, the introduction and increasing popularity of free-text or natural language searching over the past few decades has brought with it a key question: Is there still a need for controlled vocabulary? To information professionals, there was never a question but that the answer is "yes." Outside the profession the need for controlled vocabulary sometimes became clear only when searching started bogging down because of the sheer size of retrieved results. Controlled vocabulary provides consistency, accuracy, and control and improves retrieval results by alleviating the burden of synonym and homograph control placed on the user (Chan, 2000). Despite these benefits, Chan notes, questions arise about the efficacy of traditional tools for providing subject access to Internet resources: "How well can existing subject access tools fulfill the requirements of networked resources? More specifically, how adequate are traditional tools, such as LCSH, LCC and DDC in meeting the challenges of effective and efficient subject retrieval in the networked environment?" (Chan, 2000).

Vizine-Goetz, for example, carried out a number of practical, statistical research projects testing the use of classification schemes for internet resources (see the later section on DDC and LCC). Research on the usefulness of LCSH for networked resources tends to be more theoretical. Chan reports that when the Association for Library Collections & Technical Services (ALCTS) Subcommittee on Metadata and Subject Analysis deliberated whether a new controlled vocabulary more suited to the requirements of electronic resources should be constructed, they eventually came to the conclusion that LCSH, with or without modification, was most suitable for the following reasons: (1) LCSH is a rich vocabulary covering all subject areas, easily the largest general indexing vocabulary in the English language; (2) there is synonym and homograph control; (3) it contains rich links (cross-references indicating relationships) among terms; (4) it is a precoordinate system that ensures precision in retrieval; (5) it facilitates browsing of multiple-concept or multifaceted subjects; and (6) having been translated or adapted as a model for developing subject headings systems by many countries around the world, LCSH is a de facto universal controlled vocabulary (Chan, 2000).

Despite the potential contribution of LCSH vocabulary, or semantics, to the subject control of networked resources, Chan believes that the way it is currently applied has serious limitations: (1) because of its complex syntax and application rules, assigning LC subject headings according to current Library of Congress policies requires trained personnel; (2) subject heading strings in bibliographic or metadata records are costly to maintain; (3) LCSH, in its present form and application, is not compatible in syntax with most other controlled vocabularies; and (4) it is not amenable to search engines outside of the OPAC environment, particularly current Web search engines (Chan, 2000). Her suggested solution to these problems is to rework LCSH into a faceted system—that is, primarily post-coordinated (made up of single terms combined at the time of use), not pre-coordinated (made up of predetermined long strings of main subject headings and subdivisions). If LCSH evolves into a more faceted system, with each term standing alone rather than in combination with other concepts, it will be more flexible with regard to the addition of new terms and new relationship, because changes can usually be made in a facet more easily without disturbing the rest of the thesaurus. A faceted LCSH will be easier to maintain and could also be used as the basis for generating subject- or discipline-specific controlled vocabularies, or special-purpose thesauri (Chan, 2000).

DCC and LCC

According to a 1997 report on the role of classification schemes in Internet resource description, "DDC is used by more libraries than any other classification scheme" (*The Role of Classification Schemes in Internet Resource Description and Discovery: The Dewey Decimal System (DDC)* (1997). Three years later, Lois Chan attributed DDC's continuing ascendancy in adapting to the networked environment and becoming a useful tool for organizing electronic resources to the early development of WebDewey. This product contained, in addition to the DDC/LCSH mapping feature OCLC first developed for their Dewey for Windows product, an automated classification tool that generated likely DDC numbers while creating metadata records (Chan, 2000). LCC, in contrast, had just converted its voluminous schedules to MARC format and lagged behind OCLC in the market.

DDC, first produced by Melvil Dewey in 1876, was bought by OCLC in 1988, and is currently in its 22nd edition. Because it consists solely of digits and decimal points, it is not tied to one language. DDC has been translated into more than 30 languages other than English and serves library users in 135 countries. Translations that have been completed or are in progress are Arabic, Chinese, French, German, Greek, Hebrew, Icelandic, Italian, Korean, Norwegian, Russian, and Spanish (*Dewey Services,* 2004). DDC numbers are linked to LCSH headings by most major bibliographic services. OCLC also selects LC subject headings from recent Weekly Lists accompanied by candidate numbers from the current DDC editions and maps them to new numbers on its Web site, "to provide classifier assistance for topics of recent interest not mentioned explicitly in Edition 22" (*Dewey Services,* 2004).

Wikepedia, the free online encyclopedia, accurately notes, "DDC's cleverness is choosing decimals for its categories: this allows it to be both purely numerical and infinitely hierarchical. It is also a faceted classification, combining elements from different parts of the structure to construct a number representing the subject content (often combining two subject elements with linking numbers and geographical and temporal elements) and form of an item rather than drawing upon a list containing each class and its meaning" (*Dewey Decimal Classification,* 2004).

The system is made up of ten main categories:

- ◆ 000 Generalities
- ◆ 100 Philosophy and Psychology
- ◆ 200 Religion
- ◆ 300 Social Science
- ◆ 400 Language
- ◆ 500 Natural Science and Mathematics
- ◆ 600 Technology (Applied Sciences)
- ◆ 700 Arts
- ◆ 800 Literature
- ◆ 900 Geography and History

OCLC states that DDC "was conceived to accommodate the expansion and evolution of the body of human knowledge. That's why 22 unabridged print editions and 14 abridged editions over nearly 139 years, as well as about 10 Web editions since 2000 have been published" (*Dewey Services,* 2004). Funded by OCLC, Diane Vizine-Goetz conducted a large study in 1999 and a follow-up in 2002 to determine the efficacy of using library classification schemes (primarily DDC) for Internet resources (Vizine-Goetz, 1999, 2002). Comparing DDC's category structure and Internet subject trees in both studies, she found "both Internet subject trees and the DDC provide hierarchical and alphabetical access to collections. Both have category structures that can be applied in a multilingual environment. The DDC would seem to have an advantage here since it has been translated into 30 languages.... Overall, the findings suggest that the prospects are very good for developing DDC-based browsing structures to large collections" (Vizine Goetz, 2002).

In the United States, LCC is used in most research and university libraries, although most public libraries continue to use DDC. Originally developed for use by the Library of Congress in the late nineteenth century, LCC has been criticized as lacking a sound theoretical basis. Classification decisions were driven mainly by the specific needs of LC, rather than considerations having wider applicability. It divides subjects into broad categories from A to Z and is essentially enumerative in nature, unlike DDC, which emphasizes hierarchy and number building.

The letters and titles of the main classes of LCC are as follows:

- ◆ A—General Works
- ◆ B—Psychology, Psychology, Religion
- ◆ C—Auxiliary Sciences of History
- ◆ D—History (General) and History of Europe
- ◆ E—History: America
- ◆ F—History: America
- ◆ G—Geography, Anthropology, Recreation

- ✦ H—Social Sciences
- ✦ J—Political Science
- ✦ K—Law
- ✦ L—Education
- ✦ M—Music and Books on Music
- ✦ N—Fine Arts
- ✦ P—Language and Literature
- ✦ Q—Science Student
- ✦ R—Medicine
- ✦ S—Agriculture
- ✦ T—Technology
- ✦ U—Military Science
- ✦ V—Naval Science
- ✦ Z—Bibliography, Library Science, Information Resources (General)

Letter classes I, O, W, X, and Y are not used, except in a few libraries such as the U.S. National Library of Medicine, which uses Ws and selected Qs. Online access to the LCC outline, including all subclasses, is available online free of charge at http://www.loc.gov/catdir/cpso/lcco/lcco.html.

In 2001, the Library of Congress made LCSH and LCC Web accessible via the *Classification Web* software, a subscription product with the goal of allowing full-text display of all Library of Congress classification schedules and correlations between LC classification numbers and LC subject headings. In addition, users of *Classification Web*, through a cooperative agreement with OCLC also have access to the following correlations with Dewey classification numbers in Classification Web:

LC Subject Headings—Dewey Classification Numbers

LC Classification—Dewey Classification Numbers

With this feature, users can enter a Dewey classification number and display a list of matches to LC subject headings or LC classification numbers as they appear in LC bibliographic records (Cataloging Distribution Service, 2004). In other words, catalogers may now enjoy a complete online mapping among the world's three main subject content standards. As to their long-term usefulness, Lois Chan suggests that not only are they viable content standards for general metadata schemes, but also, and perhaps even more significantly, they deserve a place in domain-specific metadata schemes as well if we are to work toward achieving true global interoperability in our cataloging of online resources. She states:

> For domain- and subject-specific organizing schemes I suggest a modular approach. In building special-purpose thesauri mentioned earlier, LCSH could serve as the source vocabulary, and DDC or LCC could be used to facilitate the identification and extraction of terms related to specific subjects or domains and could provide the underlying hierarchical structure. Where more details are needed in a particular scheme, terms can be added to the basic structure as needed, thus making the specialized scheme an extension of the main structure

and vocabulary. Developing these modules with a view of fitting them as nodes, even on a very broad level, into the overall classification structures of meta-schemes such as DDC and LCC can go a long way to ensure their future interoperability. (Chan, 2000)

Encoding Standards for the Content Standards

MARC21

The relationship between the Dublin Core and MARC (MAchine Readable Cataloging) has been widely discussed in the literature. The level of bibliographic control of the Dublin Core is usually considered to be midway between the detailed approaches of MARC and the automatic indexing of commercial search engines. The options and problems in mapping Dublin Core to USMARC are also well known. Because unqualified Dublin Core elements are less specific than MARC, some fields cannot be sufficiently identified to tag them correctly. For example, the author field in MARC is identified as being a personal or corporate name, but Dublin Core does not make this difference.

MARC format originated in the 1960s. It answered the need for a standard format libraries could use to exchange newly automated cataloging records. MARC was created by LC's Network Development and MARC Standards Office, which is still responsible for the maintenance and development of all the formats (for example, Bibliographic, Authority, MARC LITE, etc.). It defines them as "standards for the representation and communication of bibliographic and related information in machine-readable form" (Network Development and MARC Standards Office, 2004b). The use of MARC spread rapidly, and outside users adapted it to their needs. Outside the United States, national libraries developed automation systems using MARC variants suitable for their national, language, or cultural requirements.

Unlike Dublin Core, which was originally created for use by nonexperts such as electronic document creators and publishers, MARC was never intended to be used by nonlibrarians. The creation of high-quality MARC records requires training and expertise in the use of cataloging rules if the record creator is to format information correctly into the MARC record. Like the Dublin Core, however, the MARC standard only governs record structure or encoding; it does not prescribe the content of the record within that structure. MARC records consist of a record label called the leader, a directory, variable length fields with content designators consisting of three-digit tags, data field separators, and record separators. Fields containing data with similar function are organized into groups identified by the first number in the tag:

- 0XX control numbers, provenance
- 1XX main entry
- 2XX titles and related information
- 3XX physical description
- 4XX series statements
- 5XX notes
- 6XX subject access

- 7XX added entries; linking fields
- 8XX series added entries
- 9XX reserved for local fields

The last two digits in the tags indicate further subdivision of content, and parallel content designation is preserved across the groups, for example:

- X00 personal author
- X10 corporate name
- X11 meeting name
- X30 uniform title

Within this pattern, the digit 9 is used to indicate a local implementation.

The fields are further subdivided into subfields, and many fields also have indicators of two characters following the tag. Indicators generate displays and indicate types of content. The content of the fields, as mentioned, is formulated according to the *Anglo-American Cataloguing Rules* and International Standard Bibliographic Description (ISBD), not by the MARC format. Within this general structure, different national implementations of the standard have used different numbered tags and different subfield codes to identify the same type of bibliographic data (Lazinger, 2001, pp. 157–8).

Because MARC is a very complex and detailed metadata system, it is not suitable for untrained electronic document creators or publishers to create descriptive metadata. They would have to formulate the metadata according to AACR2 and ISBD and then encode it using the proper MARC fields, subfields, and indicators. Nonetheless, MARC has an important relationship to other metadata standards. For example, The *GILS Core Element Set* documentation contains corresponding MARC fields, and EAD, an archival encoding standard discussed later in this chapter, includes the ability to code MARC fields, making it possible to generate MARC records from EAD-encoded finding aids automatically.

Significant changes and developments in the MARC fields have occurred to deal with remote-access electronic resources. First, the 856 field was added to allow the coding of URLs for hyperlink displays in systems with Web interfaces. Later, other data elements designed specifically for use in describing electronic resources were added, such as the following:

Type of resource: 256$a	Computer file characteristics
Frequency of update: 310$a	Current publication frequency
Access restriction notes: 506$a	Restrictions on access note
Mode of connection and resource address: 538$a	Systems details note
Host administrative details contact: 856$m	Contact for access assistance

William Moen and Penelope Benardino analyzed 400,000 MARC 21 records from OCLC's WorldCat database and reported in their preliminary findings that less than 4 percent of available MARC 21 content designation accounts for 80 percent of all occurrences of the content designation (Moen and Bernardino, 2002). In other words, 96 percent of MARC 21's fields account for only 20 percent of MARC field use. Of the nearly 2,000 discrete structures for content designation, less than 50 percent actually occurred in the large dataset of records they analyzed. This study calls into question the necessity for such a rich encoding structure, although "one might suggest that the rich encoding structure provides a capability in case we need it" (Moen and Bernardino, 2002, p. 7). Noting that as metadata schemes such as Dublin Core or Metadata Object Description Schema (MODS) develop and evolve, there will always be calls to extend the capability of the metadata scheme to accommodate new requirements of communities and users, they suggest lessons from the evolution of MARC point to a need for policies to identify "thresholds of needs" (Moen and Benardino, 2002, p. 8).

Traditionalists, who consider MARC the only plausible encoding standard for bibliographic description because of its richness and ubiquity, tend to minimize the fact that "MARC is costly, labor-intensive, and requires special technical knowledge about AACR2 rules and MARC encoding" (Chandler and Westbrook, 2002, p. 208). Nonetheless, in addition to the undeniable fact of its richness, MARC'S "ubiquity" may in itself be a reason inhibiting its abandonment for a simpler, less labor-intensive metadata standard: "XML-only proponents overlook the enormous costs of switching from the standard for sharing bibliographic resources from MARC to XML ... 'Switching costs' are the cost of changing from one technology standard to another. When switching costs are very high, the user(s) of the standard may be said to be 'locked-in' " (Chandler and Westbrook, 2002, p. 208).

MARCXML

Switching costs notwithstanding, MARC 21 is built on the well-established worldwide standard, IS0 2709. Despite the wide use of this format structure for many years and in many MARC and MARC-type formats, many new protocols are more "comfortable" with an XML-based structure for bibliographic records. In response to that need, new and alternative structures for the MARC 21 data elements have been developed over recent years. MARCXML, one of the most important, provides a pathway from MARC 21 to MARC in XML, and then back again, as needed. The MARCXML version of MARC 21 is a good vehicle for moving data among other XML formats, such as MODS (discussed later) and Dublin Core (McCallum, 2004).

Even though sharing data between library catalogs is easy because of the widespread use of the MARC format, being able to express MARC data in XML is useful for libraries trying to develop tools that combine MARC data, such as the online catalog, with non-MARC resources, such as a nonlibrary database. In addition, the development of MARCXML has opened up the enormous stores of MARC 21 data to easier exchange with XML protocols, for example, the harvesting protocol of the OAI and the Metadata Encoding and Retrieval Standard (METS), which is also discussed later in the chapter.

Metadata Object Description Schema (MODS)

According to LC's Sally McCallum, the Metadata Object Description Standard developed from the need for an XML format for electronic resources that staff could use to expedite records for those resources (McCallum, 2004). To this end, it was created with language-based tags rather than numeric tags, special characteristics for e-resources, and compatibility with MARC 21. It can be used for an alternative view of MARC data for digital conversion of items that have already been cataloged using MARC 21 for the library's catalog, when a subset of that metadata is needed for a repository that archives and disseminates the e-resource version of the item. It is also a relatively simple format for original cataloging of "born-digital" items and high-volume resources such as Web sites. MODS has an important related item capability that enables inclusion of hierarchically related information on the electronic resource, and a capability for indicating the language, script, and transliteration for each data element.

As a subset of MARC elements, and with its language-based tags replacing the harder-to-understand numerical ones, MODS is a simpler MARC, particularly appropriate to digital library objects that require rich descriptions compatible with the ones already existing in library catalogs, but not as complex as full MARC 21 or MARCXML formats, and therefore easier and quicker to create. It is intended to complement other metadata formats and provide an alternative between a very simple metadata format with a minimum of fields and little or no substructure, such as Dublin Core, and a very detailed format with many data elements and numerous structural complexities, such as MARC 21 (Guenther, 2003).

Most elements defined in MODS have equivalents in the MARC 21 format. In the MODS XML schema, the documentation sections specify where the semantics for the element can be found in MARC 21, and, in addition, LC has made available mappings between MARC and MODS and vice versa. All elements and attributes are optional. Attributes are not in a mandated sequence and not repeatable (per XML rules). "Ordered" below means the subelements must occur in the order given. All elements and subelements are repeatable.

"Authority" attributes are either followed by codes for authority lists (e.g., iso639-2b) or "see" references that link to documents that contain codes for identifying authority lists.

There are nineteen Top Level Elements in MODS Version 3.0, each of which also has a list of subelements and attributes (Metadata Object Description Schema Official Web Site, 2003d):

- titleInfo
- name
- typeOfResource
- genre
- originInfo
- language
- physicalDescription
- abstract
- tableofContents
- targetAudience
- note
- subject
- classification
- relatedItem
- identifier
- location
- accessCondition
- extension
- recordInfo

Because MODS is a subset of MARC, decisions were made regarding which elements should be included, which elements could be combined with other elements to form a single element, and which could be dropped altogether. For example, numerous types of relationships expressed in the MARC 76X-78X linking entry fields are expressed in MODS under relatedItem, with a type attribute to express the type of relationship. Some elements having multiple values in MARC did not keep all their values, especially when they expressed very fine distinctions. On the other hand, a comparison between the Dublin Core metadata element set and MODS differs depending on whether one is comparing it to unqualified or qualified Dublin Core. Simple Dublin Core has fifteen main elements and Qualified Dublin Core now has sixteen main elements (including the new element "audience," added in October 2001), whereas MODS has nineteen top level elements. Dublin Core has twenty-eight additional subelements that refine its elements, and MODS has forty-seven subelements, not counting those used under more than one top level element. MODS also has substructure that Dublin Core lacks, which provides further richness. For example, the Dublin Core Publisher element has no further substructure or qualifiers defined for it and cannot be associated with the place or date of publication, so that if there are several publishers and issuing dates, these cannot be associated with one another. The publicationInfo element in MODS, in contrast, has subelements for place, publishers and various forms of dates (Guenther, 2003).

All in all, while Dublin Core, particularly simple Dublin Core, remains the easiest to use of all the widely utilized metadata schemes today, MODS provides an alternate encoding standard that, although considerably simpler than full MARC 21, is much richer and more compatible with the great sea of MARC records already existing in library catalogs worldwide. However, MODS "does not target round-tripability with MARC 21" (Metadata Object Description Schema Official Web Site, 2003c), despite the mapping between the standards that LC provides on the MODS Web site. In other words, the original MARC 21 record converted to MODS may not convert back to MARC21 without some loss of specificity in tagging or loss of other data, because the reconverted record may not have the data placed in exactly the same field that it started or because the MARC 21 element may not have an equivalent in MODS, in which case the data will be lost, not just misplaced.

Metadata Encoding and Transmission Standard (METS)

The Metadata Encoding and Transmission Standard can be called "a technique for recording, in a highly flexible manner, metadata about all aspects of a digital object. This includes the descriptive metadata that we use MARC and MODS to encode and also technical, preservation, administrative, structural, etc." (McCallum, 2004). METS e-resource packages can include or point to this metadata and specify the format of the metadata. Thus, the METS schema is a standard for encoding descriptive, administrative, and structural metadata for objects within a digital library, expressed using the XML schema language of the World Wide Web Consortium. This standard, like MARC and MODS, is maintained by the Network Development and MARC Standards of the Library of Congress and is being developed as an initiative of the Digital Library Federation (Metadata Encoding & Transmission Standard Official Web Site, 2003).

METS provides an XML document format for encoding metadata necessary for both management of digital library objects within a repository and exchange of such objects between repositories (or between repositories and their users). Depending on its use, a METS document could be used in the role of Submission Information Package (SIP), Archival Information Package (AIP), or Dissemination Information Package (DIP) within the OAIS Reference Model.

A METS document consists of seven major sections:

1. **METS Header.** The METS Header contains metadata describing the METS document itself, including such information as creator, editor, and so on.

2. **Descriptive Metadata.** The descriptive metadata section may point to descriptive metadata external to the METS document (for example, a MARC record in an OPAC or an EAD finding aid maintained on a Web server), contain internally embedded descriptive metadata, or both. Multiple instances of both external and internal descriptive metadata may be included in the descriptive metadata section.

3. **Administrative Metadata.** The administrative metadata section provides information regarding how the files were created and stored, intellectual property rights, metadata regarding the original source object from which the digital library object derives, and information regarding the provenance of the files comprising the digital library object (i.e., master/ derivative file relationships and migration/transformation information). As with descriptive metadata, administrative metadata may be either external to the METS document or encoded internally.

4. **File Section.** The file section lists all files containing content that comprise the electronic versions of the digital object. <file> elements may be grouped within <fileGrp> elements to provide for subdividing the files by object version.

5. **Structural Map.** The structural map is the heart of a METS document. It outlines a hierarchical structure for the digital library object and links the elements of that structure to content files and metadata pertaining to each element.

6. **Structural Links.** The Structural Links section of METS allows METS creators to record the existence of hyperlinks between nodes in the hierarchy outlined in the Structural Map. This is of particular value in using METS to archive Web sites.

7. **Behavior.** A behavior section can be used to associate executable behaviors with content in the METS object. Each behavior within a behavior section has an interface definition element that represents an abstract definition of the set of behaviors represented by a particular behavior section. Each behavior also has a mechanism element which identifies a module of executable code that implements and runs the behaviors defined abstractly by the interface definition. (Metadata Encoding & Transmission Standard Official Web Site, 2003)

By using XML to provide a vocabulary and syntax to identify the "digital pieces" that together comprise a digital entity, specify the location of these pieces, and express the relationships between these digital pieces (Calanag, Tabata, and Sugimoto, 2004), the METS schema can provide a useful standard for exchanging digital library objects between repositories and provide the ability to associate a digital object with behaviors or services.

Encoded Archival Description (EAD)

A great divide between library cataloging and archival cataloging has long existed because, among other things, the former concentrates on individual manifestations of works and the latter concentrates for the most part on creating finding aids for collections of documents (Gorman, 2003, p. 12). Library catalog records have traditionally made poor substitutes for the rich descriptive documents that archivists have created to represent their collections, and the limitations of MARC, with its lack of hierarchical structure, "mask the true intellectual work of arrangement and description done by archivists. MARC was created to make representations of items, while repositories wanted to describe collections of items" (Wisser and Roper, 2003, p. 72).

The EAD Document Type Definition (DTD) is a standard, first published in 1998, for encoding archival finding aids using the Standard Generalized Markup Language (SGML). In 1995, three years earlier, seeds for EAD first took root with an online finding aid project at Berkeley. At this point, "the creation of a metadata mark-up language became a marriage between archival theory and information technology" (Wisser and Roper, 2003, p. 72), with EAD intended to supplement, not replace, existing structures. Today it is maintained in the Network Development and MARC Standards Office of the Library of Congress (LC) in partnership with the Society of American Archivists and can be retrieved through the Library of Congress Web site at http://lcweb.loc.gov/ead. The current site includes the EAD Version 2002 Tag Library in both the printed edition and the Web (HTML) edition, application guidelines in both the printed edition and the Web (HTML) edition, and EAD tools and helper files (*Encoded Archival Description*, 2004).

The development of EAD was motivated by a desire to provide an enduring standard for machine representation of archival description and facilitate uniform network access to archive and manuscript library collections. Furthermore, as mentioned, it was designed to be complementary to traditional MARC cataloging records, which were to provide summary description and access, whereas EAD was to provide detailed description and access. That is, MARC records provide summary representation of collections in bibliographic databases that lead to the detailed EAD-based finding aids, such as detailed catalogs. EAD is intended primarily to accommodate registers and inventories describing the full range of archival holdings in various media.

In addition to providing for both collection-level, hierarchically structured finding aids and MARC-like individual cataloging records, EAD, like other SGML/XML DTDs, allows simple or complex markup for varying degrees of sophistication in indexing and retrieval, allowing libraries to decide which tags to use and what degree of detail to include. Tags for personal, corporate, family, and geographic names may be combined with controlled vocabulary thesauri and authority files, such as *Library of Congress Name Authority File* (LCNAF), *Library of Congress Subject Headings* (LCSH), *Thesaurus for Graphic Materials* (TGM2), or *Art & Architecture Thesaurus* (AAT).

At the most basic level, then, encoded archival finding aids consist of two segments: (1) a segment that provides information about the finding aid itself (its title, compiler, compilation date, etc.) and (2) a segment that provides information about a body of archival materials (a collection, a record group, or a series). The EAD DTD splits the first segment into two high-level elements known as EAD Header <eadheader> and Front Matter <frontmatter>. The second segment, consisting of information about the archival materials, is contained within the third high-level element named Archival Description <archdesc>. All three of these high-level elements are contained within the outermost element named Encoded Archival Description <ead>, which wraps around the entire document (Lazinger, 2001, pp. 148–9).

With the arrival of the new millennium, the need to reconsider some existing SGML/XML elements and to examine certain design aspects of the EAD DTD had grown to the point where formal suggestions were solicited from users of the DTD. A series of sixty-seven suggestions for changes and additions were received from users via a Web-based suggestions form made public on the EAD Web site. The suggestions were consolidated into a list that was circulated internally and discussed during a special meeting of the EAD Working Group including representatives from Australia, Canada, France, the United Kingdom, and the United States, held in Washington, D.C., April 27–29, 2001.

The discussions resulted in the deprecation of only eight EAD elements that had been part of the Version 1.0 (1998) EAD DTD. A few new elements were also added to the EAD DTD. The revision introduced some structural changes that unbundled certain pieces of information in a finding aid, thus facilitating a more logical arrangement of information, and opened up certain existing elements for use inside elements where they had not been allowed earlier (*Encoded Archival Description,* 2004). The EAD Elements section presents information for each element as shown in Figure 3.1.

Availability of the 2002 version of the EAD DTD came at a time when more and more users were moving from SGML to XML markup. The entire suite of DTD and entity reference files was reengineered to meet the needs of XML and related technologies.

EAD finding aids "have the major potential in a networked environment to revolutionize the archival researcher's world" (Hudgins, Agnew, and Brown, 1999, p. 7) by allowing researchers from remote locations to query collection-level finding aids with links to individual item-level records. These, in turn, provide links to the digital object itself. As the official EAD Web site states in its discussion of changes in the 2002 version of EAD, "it is hoped that the new 2002 version of the EAD DTD is even more stable and useful than the popular 1998 version 1.0. As with related standards, the EAD DTD will certainly continue to evolve to meet the needs of a growing user base" (*Encoded Archival Description,* 2004).

Figure 3.1. EAD elements section.

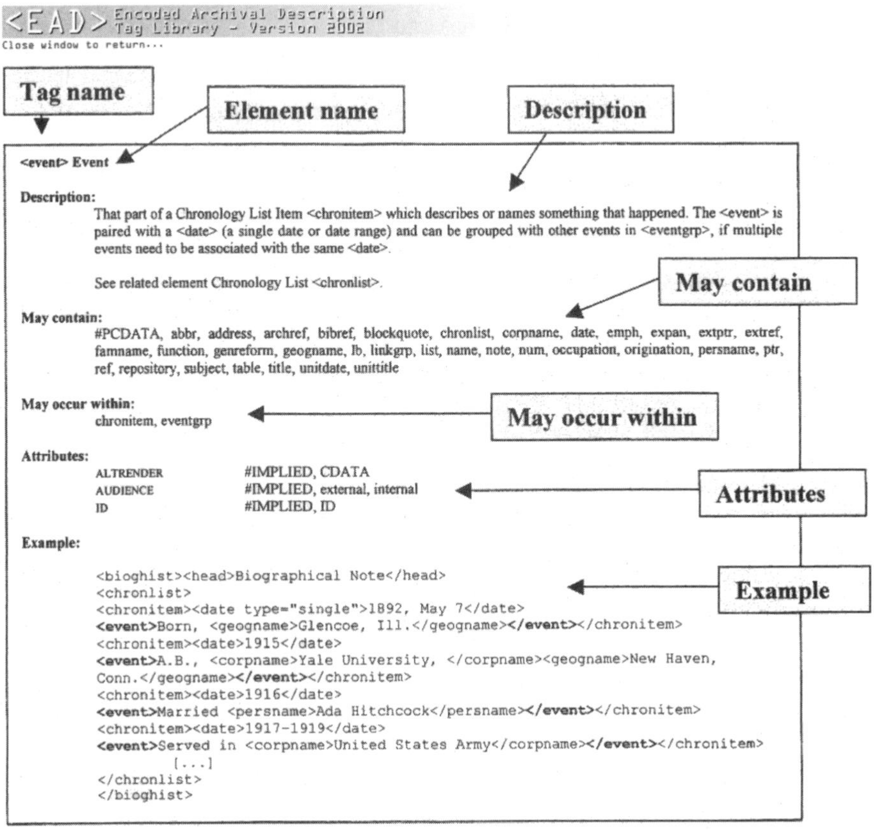

Source: *Encoded Archival Description (EAD): Official EAD Version 2002 Web Site. Tag Library Conventions* [Online]. (2004). Available: http://www.loc.gov/ead/tglib/tlc.html (retrieved 22 November, 2004). Reprinted by permission of Society of American Archivists.

Library Metadata Standards-Settings Groups: Efforts at Harmonization

Harmonization

Harmonization is "the process of enabling consistency across metadata standards" (St. Pierre and LaPlant, 2004). This is accomplished in a number of ways, some of which have already been discussed, such as creating pathways or crosswalks between metadata standards to map the elements of one standard to those of another. By extracting the common terminology, properties, organization, and processes which many metadata standards have in common, metadata researchers have been able to move toward creating a generic framework within which to develop new standards or revise existing ones. Some of the shared properties of metadata standards are the following:

- a unique identifier (e.g., tag, label, field name) for each element;

- a semantic definition for each element;

- rules determining whether a metadata element is optional or mandatory;

- rules determining whether a metadata element is repeatable;

- rules determining hierarchical parent-child relationships of metadata elements;

- constraints on the value of an element (for example, free text, numeric range, date, controlled vocabulary); and

- whether there is support for locally defined metadata elements. (St. Pierre and La Plant, 2004)

Another type of harmonization has become the focus of international groups in recent years. In collaboration with permanent international standards-setting organizations such as IFLA, working groups have been set up to develop and maintain conceptual models aimed at helping solve the problem of semantic interoperability between the documentation structures used for library and museum information. The most important goals of these international efforts at harmonization have been the following:

- to enable all equivalent information to be retrievable under the same notions;

- to enable all directly and indirectly related information to be retrievable regardless of its distribution over individual data sources; and

- to ensure that knowledge encoded for a specific application can be reused.

Toward these ends, three projects in particular have been devoted and have met with varying degrees of success: Functional Requirements for Bibliographic Records (FRBR), the CIDOC Conceptual Reference Model (CRM), and the Harmony Project and the ABC Harmony Data Model Version 2 (2001).

Functional Requirements for Bibliographic Records (FRBR)

In August 2003, a new alliance between the International Association of Library Associations and Organizations (IFLA) and various national libraries was established to continue and to expand the coordination work formerly done by the IFLA Universal Bibliographic Control and International MARC (UBCIM) and Universal Dataflow and Telecommunications (UDT) Core Programme Offices. Designed to work in close collaboration with the Conference of Directors of National Libraries (CDNL), the new alliance was dubbed the "IFLA-CDNL Alliance for Bibliographic Standards (ICABS)" (IFLA Core Activity, 2004). Its purpose is to offer a practical way to improve international coordination and steer developments in these key areas, as well "to maintain, promote, and harmonize existing standards and concepts related to bibliographic and resource control, to develop strategies for bibliographic and resource control, and to advance understanding of issues related to long-term archiving of electronic resources" (IFLA Core Activity, 2004). An important action of this group was supporting the work of IFLA's Cataloguing Section FRBR Review group in developing and maintaining the conceptual model and related guidelines for the Functional Requirements for Bibliographic Records (FRBR) and promoting use of this model. The British Library was the responsible entity.

As Gunilla Jonsson, the current head of IFLA's Cataloguing Section, noted in a 2003 article on the FRBR, "a common structure doesn't achieve anything if we do not agree on the contents of the structure" (Jonsson, 2003). In recent years, the proliferation of electronic resources and growing use of electronic networks for disseminating the resources have led to a reexaminination of the content of the catalog record. In line with this rethinking, the IFLA Working Group on Functional Requirements for Bibliographic Records (FRBR) completed a study in 1997 in which it defined user tasks in relation to four primary entities: the **work**—a distinct intellectual or artistic creation—for example, Shakespeare's *Hamlet;* the **expression**—the intellectual or artistic realization of a work—for example, a Norwegian translation of the work *Hamlet;* the **manifestation**—the physical embodiment of an expression—for example, a book of that translation; and the **item**—a specific exemplar of a manifestation—for example, the copy of the book of the translation held in a particular library collection. The graphic model of the relationships among the four primary entities appears in Figure 3.2.

Figure 3.2. Relationships among the four primary entities.

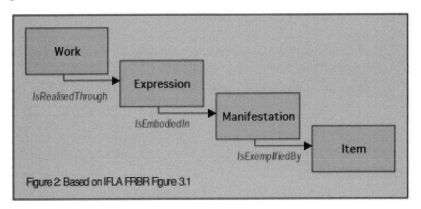

Source: David Bearman, et al. (1999). "A Common Model to Support Interoperable Metadata: Progress Report on Reconciling Metadata Requirements from the Dublin Core and INDECS/DOI Communities," *D-Lib Magazine* 5(1) [Online]. Available: http://www.dlib.org/dlib/january99/bearman/01bearman.html. Reprinted with permission of the Corporation for National Research Initiatives (CNRI).

The study also defined four generic user tasks and mapped each task to the specific attributes and relationships of the primary entities defined in the model. These user tasks are the things brought into play in the resource discovery process, things a user wants to do relative to the bibliographic universe: **find, identify, select,** and **obtain** the resource. To **find** an entity is to locate materials that correspond to the user's stated search criteria. To **identify** an entity is to confirm that the information object described in a record corresponds to the object sought by the user. To **select** an entity is to choose an object appropriate to the user's needs (for example, in a language the user understands). To **obtain** the entity means to acquire it by submitting a request for a loan, for example, or accessing online an electronic document stored on a remote computer.

On a more detailed level, for example, the first task—to find entities that correspond to the user's stated search criteria—involves locating either a single entity or a set of entities in a database as the result of a search using an attribute or relationship of the entity. To **find** a particular *work*, the user will typically search using the name of the person or group responsible for creating the work (*Hamlet*). To find a particular *expression* of the work, the user will typically search using the name of the person responsible for that realization of the work (the translator of the Norwegian version of *Hamlet*). To find a particular *manifestation,* the user may search using the title as it appears on the on the title page or container, or possibly by a numeric identifier such as an ISBD number or publisher number. Finally, to find a specific *item* (i.e., a specific copy), the user would search using an item identifier, such a call number for the copy in the library's collection.

In a 2003 interview, Barbara Tillett (2003b), a member of IFLA's Study Group on the Functional Requirements of the Bibliographic Record (FRBR) from its inception, discusses both the uses of the FRBR model and its acceptance so far within the library community. She maintains it should help provide a theoretical framework for understanding cataloging, would ensure navigation among related works and bring together multiple manifestations of the same works, and would give system designers the conceptual structure to build systems that enable more automated authority work and more direct linking of related works and linking of various manifestations to their related expressions and works. As for the reaction of the library community, she notes that the National Library of Australia embraced it and used it for development of its AustLit project (http://www.austlit.edu.au/); the Library and Archives Canada (formerly National Library of Canada) used a similar model in developing its integrated library system; several places in Europe have applied it; but the United States has been "rather late to catch on, which is why I've been doing a lot of speaking over the past couple of years to raise awareness" (Tillett, 2003).

CIDOC Conceptual Reference Model (CRM)

FRBR is a reference model. It is a framework for commonly shared understanding that allows us to compare data that may not be structured the same way. FRBR does not strive to account for temporal aspects explicitly, such as changes over time. The CIDOC Conceptual Reference Model (CRM), in contrast, models *events* that occur over the lifetime of a document, while the ABC model also discussed in this chapter, models *states* that exist between these changes (Le Boeuf, 2004).

The "CIDOC object-oriented Conceptual Reference Model" (CRM) originates from earlier standards proposals produced by The International Committee for Documentation of the International Council of Museums (ICOM-CIDOC). Since September 2000, the CRM has been progressing as an ISO standard (ISO/A WI 21227). It represents an ontology for cultural heritage information, that is, it describes, in a formal language, "the explicit and implicit concepts and relations underlying documentation structures used for cultural heritage" (Doerr, Hunter, and Lagoze, 2002). The main role of the CRM model is to serve as the semantic "glue" needed to transform disparate, localized information sources into a coherent global resource. Like FRBR, it is a conceptual model that can be used to facilitate wide area information exchange and integration of heterogeneous sources. The term *cultural heritage collections* covers all types of material collected and displayed by museums and related institutions and includes collections relating to natural history, ethnography, archaeology, historic monuments, as well as collections of fine and applied arts. The CRM's intended scope includes the exchange of relevant information with libraries and archives and the harmonization of the CRM with their models (Doerr, Hunter, and Lagoze, 2002).

Like all the harmonization models described in this section, CIDOC/CRM defines and is restricted to the *underlying semantics* of metadata schema and document structures. It does not define any of the terminology itself but rather foresees the characteristic relationships for its use. Its goal does not aim at proposing what cultural institutions should document but at explaining the logic of what they actually do document and, in this way, enabling semantic interoperability. In other words, "it intends to provide an optimal analysis of the intellectual structure of cultural documentation in logical terms" (ICOM /CIDOC CRM Special Interest Group, 2003). CIDOC/CRM is extensible, and users are encouraged to create extensions for communities whose needs are more specialized.

Key terminology in the model includes **classes** with **properties, instances** (items belonging to a class), and **subclasses.** In addition, there are **superclasses,** that is, generalizations of one or more other classes (and subclasses), **extensions** that are the set of all real-life instances belonging to the class, and **scope notes** to describe textually the **intension** (intended meaning) of a property or class (ICOM/CIDOC CRM Special Interest Group, 2003). Thus, the CIDOC/CRM uses attributes (properties) on attributes to denote a dynamic subtyping of roles and to enable the integration of data structures based on concepts at different levels of abstraction, such as Dublin Core and the Categories for the Description of Works of Art (CDWA).

The following naming conventions apply throughout the CRM:

- Classes are identified by numbers preceded by the letter "E" (historically classes were sometimes referred to as "Entities") and are named using noun phrases (nominal groups) using title case (initial capitals). For example, E63 Beginning of Existence.

- Properties are identified by numbers preceded by the letter "P" and are named in both directions using verbal phrases in lower case. Properties with the character of states are named in the present tense, such as "has type," whereas properties related to events are named in past tense, such as "carried out." For example, *P126 employed (was employed by) (Definition of the CIDOC Conceptual Reference Model. Version 4.0,* 2004).

The CIDOC/CRM class hierarchy is structured as follows:

E1 CRM Entity

E2 -Temporal Entity

E3 —Condition State

E4 —Period

E5 —-Event

E7 ——Activity

E8 ——-Acquisition Event

E9 ——Move

E10 ——Transfer of Custody

E11 ——Modification Event

E12 ———Production Event

E79 ———Part Addition

E80 ———Part Removal

E13 ——Attribute Assignment

E14 ———Condition Assessment

E15 ———Identifier Assignment

E16 ———Measurement Event

E17 ———Type Assignment

E65 ——Creation Event

E83 ———Type Creation

E66 ——Formation Event

E63 ——Beginning of Existence

E67 ——Birth

E81 ——Transformation

E12 ——Production Event

E65 ——Creation Event

E83 ———Type Creation

E66 ——Formation Event

E64 ——End of Existence

E6 ——Destruction

E68 ——Dissolution

E69 ——Death

E81 ——Transformation

E77 -Persistent Item

E70 —Stuff

E72 —-Legal Object

E18 ——Physical Stuff

E19 ——Physical Object

E20 ———Biological Object

E21 ———-Person

E22 ———Man-Made Object

E84 ———-Information Carrier

E24 ———-Physical Man-Made Stuff

E22 ———Man-Made Object (ICOM /CIDOC CRM Special Interest Group, 2003).

A graphic representation of the CIDOC/CRM class hierarchy is shown in Figure 3.3.

Figure 3.3. CIDOC/CRM class hierarchy.

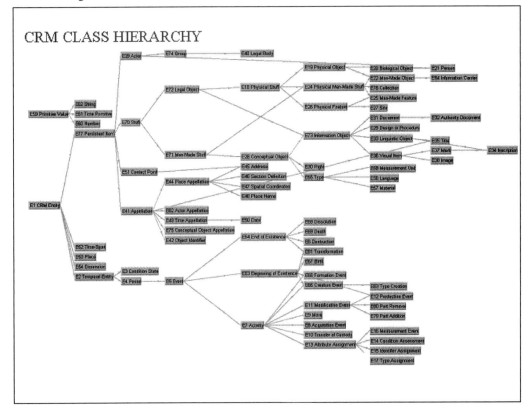

Source: *The CIDOC Conceptual Reference Model: CRM Class Hierarchy* [Online]. (2003). Available: http://cidoc.ics.forth.gr/cidoc_graphical_representation/crm_class_hierarchy.htm. Reprinted by permission of the International Committee for Documentation of the International Council of Museums.

CIDOC/CRM is "event aware." The definition of event is "something which happens." Events are in causal interrelationships. Time is connected to temporal phenomena. Location (Place), people (Actors), material, and immaterial items (Stuff) are connected primarily to temporal entities. For example, that a thing resides at a place is seen as a result of a temporal entity, such as the building of a house (Doerr, Hunter, and Lagoze, 2002). The time-span relationships between the classes (which begin with letter "E") and the properties (which begin with the letter "P") is graphically depicted in Figure 3.4.

Figure 3.4. Time-span relationships between the classes ("E") and properties ("P").

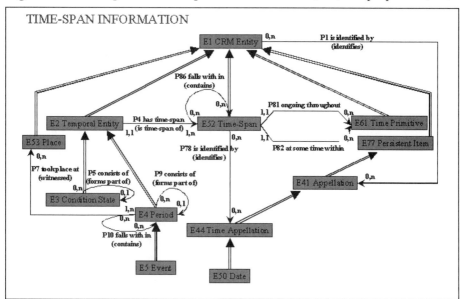

Source: *The CIDOC Conceptual Reference Model: Time-Span Information* [Online], (2003). Available: http://cidoc.ics.forth.gr/cidoc_graphical_representation/time_span_information1.htm. Reprinted by permission of the International Committee for Documentation of the International Council of Museums.

The current official version of the CIDOC CRM as of this writing, Version 4.0, was published in April 2004.

The Harmony Project and the ABC Harmony Data Model Version 2

Version 2

Both the CIDOC/CRM and ABC ontologies reflect a commitment to the expression of the common concepts underlying the data structures used by their communities. Both ontologies are models of reality that overlap but simultaneously reflect specific perspectives and scope in certain ways. Perhaps the most striking of these ways is seen in the difference in the temporal aspects of both models. Although both models attempt to model change over time, the nature of that *change* is quite different. The CIDOC/CRM model, motivated by the requirements of cultural artifacts and museums, focuses more on changes in context than on object transformation itself. A typical example of this is the movement of an object between museums. The ABC model, driven by digital library requirements, was originally motivated by the need to describe how objects change over time. Examples of this type of change are the versioning of digital objects or the production of derivative works (Doerr, Hunter, and Lagoze, 2002). This difference in perspective derives directly from the fact that the Harmony model covers more digital objects and CIDOC/CRM covers more physical objects.

The CRM influenced the ABC Harmony Data Model Version 2, which was published in 2001. Furthermore, in a meeting between representatives of Harmony and the CRM in September 2000 in Lisbon, it was noted that despite the differences in perspective and scope of the two models, the CRM and the Harmony Model "exhibit deep similarity in the sense, that they [both] … regard an event-centric analysis as the key to the semantics of the metadata under consideration." In light of this similarity, it was decided that the CRM and the Harmony Model should not develop independently (*DELOS Workshop on Ontology Harmonization co-sponsored by the Harmony Project, 2001*).

A summary of the draft of the first version of the ABC model in 1999 stated the following principles:

- ABC is built on a number of fundamental concepts and assumptions including universally identified resources, properties (as a special type of resource), and classes that create sets of resources (and properties).

- ABC defines a set of fundamental classes (sets of resources) including creations, events, agents, and relationships. These fundamental classes provide the building blocks for expression (through subclassing) of application-specific or domain-specific metadata vocabularies.

- ABC provides an event-centric view for modeling the relationship between the various manifestations of a creation. This event-centric view provides semantically clear attachment points for the association of properties among the various manifestations and contributors (agents) to the manifestations.

The ABC vocabulary defines and declares a core set of resource categories that are common across metadata communities—these are represented by ABC's *abstract base classes*. These base classes are intended to provide the proper attachment points (i.e., entities) for different properties (or metadata) that are associated with information content and its lifecycle, and are defined as follows:

- *Creation*, with properties such as Title, Subject, Description, and Language.

- *Events* are enacted on resources and produce other resources. Properties of events include the agent(s) associated with the event and the time and place at which the event was enacted. One important side effect of an event is the transformation of properties associated with a creation. For example, an event that is the translation of a resource may output a new resource with a different Language property.

- *Agents*, with properties such as name, affiliation, contact information, and so on.

- *Contributions* made by these agents in the context of some particular event. One important item of information associated with a contribution is the *role* played by that agent. Additional information items associated with a *contribution* might include details of financial transactions, specific timing information, and so on.

- *Other relationships* between resources. These are relationships that, unlike events, do not occur at a specific time or place but that establish a time-independent fact. Examples of these relationships include structural and containment relationships and references or citations. (*ABC: A Logical Model for Metadata Interoperability—Harmony discussion note 19991019-abc-draft*, 1999)

Graphically, the hierarchical relationship among the ABC classes and their properties can be seen in Figure 3.5.

Figure 3.5. Hierarchal relationship among the ABC classes and their properties.

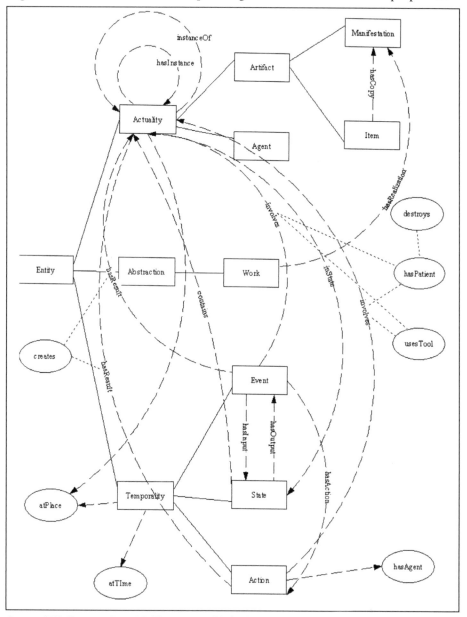

Source: ABC Harmony Data Model Version 2 [Online]. (2001). Available: http://metadata.net/harmony/ABCV2.htm. Reprinted by permission of the Harmony Project.

In 2002, the IFLA Cataloging Section formed a Working Group on FRBR to provide a focal point within the organization for the ongoing support and development of the conceptual model and to encourage the implementation of FRBR as a data model and a reference model for the bibliographic universe. Patrick Le Boeuf, who was chair of this working group, observed with regard to this ABC class structure that "it seems that the FRBR distinction between Work and Expression was deemed too subtle—perhaps too unhelpful?—to be kept in ABC: Work and Expression are mashed into a single Work class, which in turn is subsumed in the Abstraction class, along with Concepts" (Le Boeuf, 2004).

In conclusion, all of these efforts at harmonization indicate a fundamental change in the metadata landscape in the past few years. First, they reflect a growing realization that it is important to avoid or reduce duplication of effort. Second, in several domains, the relationship between domain-specific standards and the Dublin Core have been under investigation, with a view toward wider, cross-domain interoperability. Third, a shifting emphasis from schema design to more fundamental modeling approaches has been occurring in the metadata community. All the harmonization models grew out of a common, cross-domain attempt to solve the mapping/common understanding problem by identifying commonalities in different metadata formats. This identification of commonalities has allowed for building of an additional semantic layer on top of metadata descriptions, which, in turn, may help to foster consistent metadata modeling throughout the world's online catalogs of print and, in particular, digital resources.

Bibliography

All URLs checked October 24, 2004, unless otherwise noted.

ABC: A Logical Model for Metadata Interoperability—Harmony discussion note 19991019-abc-draft [Online]. (1999). Available: http://www.ilrt.bris.ac.uk/discovery/harmony/docs/abc/abc_draft.html#Vocabulary%20Overview

ABC: A Logical Model for Metadata Interoperability—Workshop Notes [Online]. (2000). Available: http://archive.dstc.edu.au/RDU/staff/jane-hunter/harmony/workshop_notes.html

ABC Harmony Data Model Version 2 [Online]. (2001). Available: http://metadata.net/harmony/ABCV2.htm

About Harmony [Online]. (2000?). Available: http://metadata.net/harmony/

Anglo-American Cataloging Rules. (1968). North American Text. Chicago: American Library Association.

Arms, Caroline R. (2003). "Available and Useful: OAI at the Library of Congress." *Library Hi Tech* 21 (2): 129–39.

Banerjee, Kyle. (2003). "How Does XML Help Libraries?" *Computers in Libraries* [Online] 22 (8). Available: http://www.infotoday.com/cilmag/sep02/Banerjee.htm

Beacom, Matthew. (2004*). Strategic Plan for AACR* [Online]. Available: www. collectionscanada.ca/jsc/docs/chair79rev3.pdf

Bearman, David, et al. (1999). "A Common Model to Support Interoperable Metadata: Progress Report on Reconciling Metadata Requirements from the Dublin Core and INDECS/DOI Communities." *D-Lib Magazine* 5(1) [Online]. Available: http://www.dlib.org/dlib/january99/bearman/01bearman.html

Brickley, Dan. (1999). *ABC: A Logical Model for Metadata Interoperability* [Online]. Available: http://www.ilrt.bris.ac.uk/discovery/harmony/docs/abc/abc_draft.html

Bowen, Jennifer. (2004). "FRBR and AACR: Expressions in Our Catalogs?" *American Association of Law Libraries. 97th Annual Meeting and Conference,* July 10–14, 2004, Boston, Massachusetts [Online]. Available: http://aall.omnibooksonline. com/2004/papers%5C35_F-5%20-%20Bowen%201.pdf

Calanag, Maria Luisa, Koichi Tabata, and Shigeo Sugimoto. (2004). "Linking Preservation Metadata and Collection Management Policies." *Collection Building* 23 (2): 56–63.

Cataloging Distribution Service. (2004). *Classification Web: Web Access to LC Classification and LC Subject Headings* [Online]. Available: http://www.loc.gov/ cds/classweb/

Cataloging Policy and Support Office. (2002). *Library of Congress Implementation of the 2002 Edition of AACR2—Significant Changes* [Online]. Available: http:// www.loc.gov/catdir/cpso/aacr2002.html

Cataloging Policy and Support Office. (2003). *Library of Congress Implementation of the 2003 Update to the 2002 AACR2* [Online]. Available: http://www. lcweb.loc.gov/catdir/cpso/2003upd.html

Chan, Lois Mai. (2000). *Exploiting LCSH, LCC, and DDC to Retrieve Networked Resources: Issues and Challenges* [Online]. Available: http://www.loc.gov/catdir/ bibcontrol/chan_paper.html

Chandler, Adam, and Elaine L. Westbrooks. (2002). "Distributing non-MARC Metadata: The CUGIR Metadata Sharing Project." *Library Collections, Acquisitions, and Technical Services* 26 (3): 207–17.

The CIDOC Conceptual Reference Model: CRM Class Hierarchy [Online]. (2003). Available: http://cidoc.ics.forth.gr/cidoc_graphical_representation/crm_class_ hierarchy.htm

The CIDOC Conceptual Reference Model: Results [Online]. (2001). Available: http://cidoc.ics.forth.gr/testproject_results.html

The CIDOC Conceptual Reference Model: Scope Definition of the CIDOC Conceptual Reference Model [Online]. (2003). Available: http://cidoc.ics.forth.gr/ scope.html

The CIDOC Conceptual Reference Model: Time-Span Information [Online]. (2003). Available: http://cidoc.ics.forth.gr/cidoc_graphical_representation/time_span_ information1.htm

The CIDOC Conceptual Reference Model: Who We Are [Online]. (2003). Available: http://cidoc.ics.forth.gr/scope.html

Committee on Cataloging: Description and Access. (2005). *Minutes of the meeting held at the 2004 Annual Conference in Orlando, FL June 26 and 28, 2004* [Online]. Available: http://www.libraries.psu.edu/tas/jca/ccda/min0406.html

Definition of the CIDOC Conceptual Reference Model. Version 4.0 [Online]. (2004). Available: http://cidoc.ics.forth.gr/official_release_cidoc.html

DELOS Workshop on Ontology Harmonization co-sponsored by the Harmony Project. [Online]. (2000). Available: http://metadata.net/harmony/Darmstadt_Rep.doc

DELOS Workshop on Ontology Harmonization co-sponsored by the Harmony Project. Full Report from the First Meeting at CNR in Rome [Online]. (2001). Editor [sic]: Martin Doerr, Jane Hunter. Available: http://cidoc.ics.forth.gr/docs/rome_full_rep_v2.pdf

DELOS Workshop on Ontology Harmonization co-sponsored by the Harmony Project. Managerial Report from the Second Meeting at TU Darmstadt [Online]. (2001). Available: http://metadata.net/harmony/Darmstadt_Rep.doc

Delsey, Tom. (2003). "Functional Requirements for Bibliographic Records. User Tasks and Cataloguing Data: Part I." *Catalogue & Index* 150 (Winter): 1–3.

Dewey Decimal Classification [Online]. (2004). Available: http://en.wikipedia.org/wiki/Dewey_Decimal_Classification

Dewey Services [Online]. (2004). Available: http://www.oclc.org/dewey

Doerr, Martin, Jane Hunter, and Carl Lagoze. (2002). *Towards a Core Ontology for Information Integration Darmstadt* [Online]. (2002). Available: http://www.cs.cornell.edu/lagoze/papers/core_ontology.pdf

El-Sherbini, Magda, and George Klim. (2004). "Metadata and Cataloging Practices." *The Electronic Library* 22 (3) [Online]: 238–48.

Encoded Archival Description (EAD): Official EAD Version 2002 Web Site [Online]. (2004). Available: http://lcweb.loc.gov/ead/

Encoded Archival Description (EAD): Official EAD Version 2002 Web Site. Tag Library Conventions [Online]. (2004). Available: http://www.loc.gov/ead/tglib/tlc.html

Final Glossary for IME ICC, 2 April 2004 [Online]. (2004). Available: http://www.ddb.de/news/ifla_conf_papers.htm

Functional Requirements for Bibliographic Records—Final Report [Online]. (2004). Available: http://www.ifla.org/VII/s13/frbr/frbr1.htm

The Future of Cataloging: Insights from the Lubetzky Symposium. (2000). Chicago: American Library Association.

Gonzalez, Linda. (2003). "Newly Published AACR2 Integrates All New Amendments." *BCR Online* (January) [Online]. Available: http://www.bcr.org/publications/afl/2003/january/aacr2-revised.html

Gonzalez, Linda. (2004). "2004 Update of AACR2 Released by ALA in August." *BCR Online* (October) [Online]. Available: http://www.bcr.org/publications/afl/2004/october/aacr2update.html

Gorman, Michael. (2003). "Cataloguing in an Electronic Age." *Cataloging & Classification Quarterly* 36 (3/4): 5–17.

Guenther, Rebecca S. (2003). "MODS: The Metadata Object Description Schema." *Portal: Libraries and the Academy* 3 (1): 137–50.

Hickey, Thomas B. (2002). "Experiments with the IFLA Functional Requirements for Bibliographic Records (FRBR)." *D-Lib Magazine* 8 (9) [Online]. Available: http://www.dlib.org/dlib/september02/hickey/09hickey.html

Hirons, Jean. (2003). "Seriality: What Have We Accomplished? What's Next?" *Cataloging & Classification Quarterly* 36 (3/4): 121–40.

Hostage, John. (2002). *Changes in AACR2, 2002 Revision* [Online]. Available: http://lacuny.cuny.edu/committees/changesinaacr2.html

Hudgins, Jean, Grace Agnew, and Elizabeth Brown. (1999). *Getting Mileage out of Metadata: Applications for the Library.* LITA Guides #5. Chicago: American Library Association.

Huthwaite, Ann. (2003). "AACR2 and Other Metadata Standards: The Way Forward." *Cataloging & Classification Quarterly* 36 (3/4): 87–100.

ICOM /CIDOC CRM Special Interest Group. (2003). *Definition of the CIDOC Conceptual Reference Model* [Online]. Available: http://cidoc.ics.forth.gr/docs/cidoc_crm_version_3.4.9.pdf

IFLA-CDNL Alliance for Bibliographic Standards (ICABS). Annual Report October 2003–2004 [Online]. (2004). Available: http://www.ifla.org/VI/7/annual/ar03-04.htm

IFLA Core Activity: IFLA-CDNL Alliance for Bibliographic Standards (ICABS) [Online]. (2004). Available: http://www.ifla.org/VI/7/icabs.htm

IFLA Study Group on the Functional Requirements for Bibliographic Records. (1998). *Functional Requirements for Bibliographic Records. Final Report* [Online] . Available: http://www.ifla.org/VI/7/annual/ar03-04.htm

Joint Steering Committee for Revision of *Anglo-American Cataloguing Rules.* (2004). *Current Activities* [Online]. Available: http://www.collectionscanada.ca/jsc/current.html

Joint Steering Committee for Revision of *Anglo-American Cataloguing Rules.* (2004). *Strategic Plan for AACR. Progress Report on Targets and Tasks: May 2004* [Online]. Available: http://www.collectionscanada.ca/jsc/stratplan1.html

Joint Steering Committee for Revision of *Anglo-American Cataloguing Rules.* (2005). *News & Announcements: Amendments 2005.* Available: http://www.collectionscanada.ca/jsc/2005amend.html

Joint Steering Committee for the Revision of *Anglo-American Cataloging Rules.* (2005b). RDA: Resource Description and Access. Available: http://www. collectionscanada.ca/jsc/rda.html

Jonsson, Gunilla. (2003). "The Basis for a Record: In the Light of *Functional Requirements for Bibliographic Records.*" *IFLA Journal* 29 (1):41–46.

Jul, Eric. (2003). "MARC and Mark-Up." *Cataloging & Classification Quarterly* 36 (3/4): 141–53.

Lagoze, Carl, and Jane Hunter. (2001). "The ABC Ontology and Model." *Journal of Digital Information* 2 (2) [Online]. Available: http://jodi.ecs.soton.ac.uk/ Articles/v02/i02/Lagoze/

Lazinger, Susan S. (2001). *Digital Preservation and Metadata: History, Theory, Practice.* Englewood, CO: Libraries Unlimited.

Le Boeuf, Patrick. (2004). "Brave New FRBR World." *First IFLA Meeting of Experts on an International Cataloguing Code / Papers* [Online]. Available: http://www. ddb.de/news/ifla_conf_papers.htm

MARC Content Designation Use." *2003 Dublin Core Conference: Supporting Communities of Discourse and Practice—Metadata Research & Applications,* 28 September–2 October 2003. Seattle, Washington[Online]. Available: http://www. siderean.com/dc2003/Paper58-abstract.pdf

Mapping ISBD Elements to FRBR Entity Attributes and Relationships [Online]. (2004). Available: http://www.ifla.org/VII/s13/pubs/ISBD-FRBR-mappingFinal.pdf

Martin, Ruth. (2002). "Schemas." *Metadata Watch Report* 8 and *Standards Framework Report* 4 [Online]. Available: http://www.schemas-forum.org/metadata-watch/ d29/d29.htm

McCallum, Sally (2004). "Metadata, Protocol, and Identifier Activities: Library of Congress IFLA/CDNL Alliance for Bibliographic Standards Report, 2004, Buenos Aires." *World Library and Information Congress: 70th IFLA General Conference and Council,* August 22–27, 2004, Buenos Aires, Argentina [Online]. Available: http://www.ifla.org/IV/ifla70/papers/024e-McCallum.pdf

Metadata Encoding and Transmission Standard Official Web Site (METS). (2003). *Mets: An Overview & Tutorial* [Online]. Available: http://www.loc.gov/standards/ mets/METSOverview.v2.html

Metadata Object Description Schema (MODS) Official Web Site. (2002). *Announcement: Metadata Object Description Schema (MODS) available for trial use* [Online]. Available: http://www.loc.gov/standards/mods/mods-announce.html

Metadata Object Description Schema (MODS) Official Web Site. (2003a). [*Revised MODS schema version 2.0*] [Online]. Available: http://www.loc.gov/standards/ mods/mods.xsd

Metadata Object Description Schema (MODS) Official Web Site. (2003b). *MODS to MARC 21 Mapping. Version 3.0. December 2003* [Online]. Available: http:// www.loc.gov/standards/mods/mods2marc-mapping.html

Metadata Object Description Schema (MODS) Official Web Site. (2003c). *MODS: Uses and Features* [Online]. Available: http://www.loc.gov/standards/mods/mods-overview.html

Metadata Object Description Schema (MODS) Official Web Site. (2003d). *Outline of Elements and Attributes in MODS Version 3.0* [Online]. Available: http://www.loc.gov/standards/mods/v3/mods-3-0-outline.html

Minutes of the 3rd DELOS Harmonization Working Group Meeting, ICS FORTH, June 3–5, 2002 [Online]. (2002). Available: http://metadata.net/harmony/3rdDelosHarmony_Minutes.doc

Moen, William E., and Penelope Bernardino. (2003). "Assessing Metadata Utilization: An Analysis of MARC Content Designation Use." *2003 Dublin Core Conference: Supporting Communities Discourse and Practice—Metadata Research and Applications,* September 28–October 2, 2003, Seattle, Washington, USA [Online]. Available: http://sidrean.com/dc2003/Paper58-abstract.pdf

Network Development and MARC Standards Office. (2004a). FRBR Display Tool. Version 2.0. [Online]. Available: http://www.loc.gov/marc/marc-functional-analysis/tool.html

Network Development and MARC Standards Office. (2004b). MARC Standards. [Online]. Available: http://www.loc.gov/marc/

Notice of AACR2 Revisions [Online]. (2002?). Available: http://www.sabinet.co.za/sabicatweb/aacr2_2002_revi.htm

Oliver, Chris. (2004). "FRBR Is Everywhere, But What Happened to the Format Variation Issue? Content versus Carrier in FRBR." *The Serials Librarian* 45(4): 27–36.

Oliver, Christine. (2004). Report of Activities From the Canadian Committee on Cataloguing for 2003/2004 [Online]. Available: http://www.fis.utoronto.ca/people/affiliated/tsig/ccc04.html

The Role of Classification Schemes in Internet Resource Description and Discovery: The Dewey Decimal System (DDC) [Online]. (1997). Work Package 3 of Telematics for Research Project DESIRE (RE 1004). Available: www.ukoln.ac.uk/metadata/desire/classification/class_2.htm

Schottlaender, Brian E.C. (2003). "Why Metadata? Why Me? Why Now?" *Cataloging & Classification Quarterly* 36 (3/4): 19–29.

St. Pierre, Margaret, and William P. LaPlant. (2004). *Issues in Crosswalking Content Metadata Standards* [Online]. Available: http://www.niso.org/press/whitepapers/crsswalk.html

Statement of International Cataloguing Principles. Draft Approved by the IFLA Meeting of Experts on an International Cataloguing Code, First Meeting, Frankfurt, Germany, 2003. First IFLA Meeting of Experts on an International Cataloguing Code / Papers [Online]. (2003). Available: http://www.ddb.de/news/ifla_conf_papers.htm

Subject Access to Digital Collections: Background and Rationale for UO Decisions [Online]. (2004).

Tillett, Barbara B. (2001). *Principles of AACR. Work in Progress* [Online]. Available: http://www.collectionscanada.ca/jsc/docs/prin2001.pdf

Tillett, Barbara B. (2003a). "AACR2 and Metadata: Library Opportunities in the Global Semantic Web." *Cataloging & Classification Quarterly* 36 (3/4): 101–19.

Tillett, Barbara B. (2003b). "FRBR: Bringing New Capabilities to the Catalog." *OCLC Newsletter* (Oct/Nov/Dec):13–15.

Tillett, Barbara B. (2004). *AACR3: Resource Description and Access.* Notes to Accompany PowerPoint Slides [Online]. Available: www.collectionscanada.ca/jsc/docs/aacr3ppttext.pdf

Van der Merwe, Ina. (2002). *The Impact of the AACR2 Amendments 2002 on the Cataloguing of Electronic Resources* [Online]. Available: http://www.sabinet.co.za/sabicatweb/iugsa2002ina1.pdf

Van der Walt, Anne. (2003). [Sabicat] *Changes to AACR2 and MARC21* [Online]. Available: http://mailman.sabinet.co.za/pipermail/sabicat/2003-January/000270.html

Vizine-Goetz, Diane. (1999). Using Library Classification Schemes for Internet Resources [Online]. Available: http://staff.oclc.org/~vizine/Intercat/vizine-goetz.htm

Vizine-Goetz, Diane. (2002). "Classification Schemes for Internet Resources Revisited." *Journal of Internet Cataloging* 5 (4): 5–18.

Wisser, Katherine M., and Jennifer O'Brien Roper. (2003). "Maximizing Metadata: Exploring the EAD-MARC Relationship." *LRTS* 47 (2): 71–76.

Chapter 4

Creating Library Metadata for Monographic Materials

Having surveyed library and information-related metadata schemas in Chapter 3, we turn now to putting these schemas to practical use in libraries. The model for creating library metadata for monographic materials in electronic form should be familiar to librarians who have cataloging responsibilities as well as to those who remember having cataloged in an earlier position or had academic courses in cataloging and classification. It is the standard library catalog record, such as one finds in the Library of Congress's MARC database, the Library and Archives of Canada's AMICUS, OCLC's WorldCat, and other library network databases. It consists of a standardized bibliographic description to which descriptive and subject-related access points under authority control are added, along with additional data, much of it in coded form, used to control and manipulate the information within the database. How this standardized model is applied to monographic electronic resources is explained and illustrated in this chapter.

The chapter is divided into sections beginning with subject analysis, in contrast to many cataloging manuals, which begin with the bibliographic description. Indeed, cataloging manuals often give much more attention and space to description than to subject analysis (some omit it altogether) for several reasons, among them the following:

- The rules for creating bibliographic descriptions are lengthy and complex, and some authors see their task as covering them alone.

- No uniform set of rules standardizes subject analysis, although there are tools (not rules) for creating subject headings and call numbers, and they have many similarities.

- An element of intuition is involved in analyzing the subject matter of items being cataloged and classified, which is difficult to reduce to hard and fast rules, so that it does not equate with the transcription process codified by descriptive cataloging rules.

◆ Some librarians believe that because electronic resources do not have physical manifestations and are not stored on library shelves, classifying them—the first step in creating call numbers—is not appropriate.

Contrary to the last-mentioned opinion, call numbers need not be linked solely to shelved objects. They can be used to gather resources on like topics in bibliographies, catalogs, and other listings and are, therefore, as appropriate for electronic resources as for any other kind of material. Call numbers have the advantage of avoiding linguistic problems, which suits them for use with resources having global distribution. Given that the Internet is available to be searched internationally, attention should be paid to overcoming barriers posed by subject matter expressed in the words of any one language. If all libraries were encouraged to assign classification numbers, a searcher could find a document on a foreign language Web site that is so pertinent that he or she would want to have it translated. For example, a document on AMICUS with French subject headings might not appear in an English-language search but would be retrieved by a Dewey call number search. The same thing applies to documents in nonroman and transliterated scripts.

Subject access is a crucial element in resource discovery and merits a reader's attention first and foremost, despite its difficulties.

Following subject analysis are sections covering bibliographic description, descriptive access points, and control data used in library cataloging. At the chapter's end are examples that readers may wish to try cataloging and classifying using all the forgoing information, with answers found in the "Answers to Exercises" at the back of the book. Bibliographic records were prepared for this book in March 2005 using the OCLC MARC-record style. At the time OCLC stated that the cataloging of these materials remains very much in flux (Weitz, n.d.).

Subject Analysis

Determining Subject Matter

One could say that determining the subject matter of an electronic resource is more of an art than a science. Titles, descriptive sections, indexes, and an author's own vocabulary provide catalogers with hints about the subject matter of a particular resource, but the cataloger must be able to take these hints, treat them in a systematic manner, and come up with an effective assessment.

Different library policies can direct catalogers to assess only the broadest subject contents or delve more deeply and identify detailed topics and subtopics. Moreover, each cataloger brings a unique background to the task. A person's individual knowledge, experience, and familiarity with a subject area and its topics and subtopics prompt one to perceive the subject content of a resource differently. Specialists in a subject area are likely to recognize very specific subtopics that a nonspecialist might miss and, as a result, perceive it as having many narrowly defined categories. True neophytes might have so little knowledge of a subject that they fail to identify it correctly or define it only in the broadest terms.

Problems arise if the subject matter of an electronic resource is not uniformly focused on one topical area or discipline. Some electronic resources cover a wide range of subjects, and when this occurs, it takes more than a simple count of pages, as is done for books, to decide whether any one of them is predominant. However, catalogers must try to estimate how much of the resource covers each topic to decide which topics should be represented and, when there is more than one, their relative importance.

The process of determining subject contents has three steps:

1. *Examine the subject rich areas of the resource.* Areas of the resource that are likely to have descriptions of its intellectual content include the title and subtitle, the "about" file, other introductory screens and files, and menu headers. If the item has an index, it can contain subject words revealing the topics covered in the resource. Although an experienced cataloger would not "read" every page of an item, scanning some of the material often helps to pin down the approach to the material and the intended audience for the resource (see Figure 4.1).

Figure 4.1. Subject rich home page.

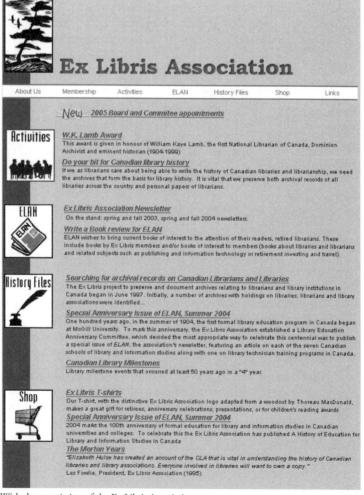

With the permission of the Ex Libris Association.

2. *Write down, in your own words, the topics you identify.* Catalogers may be tempted to echo the terminology of a Web site in identifying the topics it covers, but whether they use their own vocabulary or the resource author's terminology, topics need to be listed along with estimates of the amount of material devoted to them. This determines their relative priorities.

   Without pages to count, how does one go about estimating coverage? One way is to look at the number of menu headers relevant to a topic. Another is to see how many subtopics it has in the index of the item. A third is to click through the most relevant sections of the item to determine their length and the amount of detail they offer.

3. *Rearrange the list of topics in priority order.* Cataloging tradition dictates that the most important (read "largest") topic goes first. Moreover, the first subject heading becomes a guide to classifying the material. Electronic resource cataloging is unlikely to depart from this model.

Beyond the first, highest priority topic, other topics are ranked in descending order of importance, importance defined as containing measurable amounts of material; for example, the predominant topic might contain 50 percent of the material in the resource; the second ranked topic might contain 30 percent; the third ranked topic might contain the final 20 percent. One way of deciding whether an item has enough material on a topic to warrant making a subject heading is to ask, "If I were seeking material on this subject and was directed to this item, would it satisfy me?" An enthusiastic "yes" means it probably warrants a subject heading for the topic. A strong "no" means it probably does not. A lukewarm "maybe" indicates that one should consider it further in light of the total number of headings being assigned to the item as well as how the item compares to resources the library catalog has already listed under the subject heading for that topic.

If a topic that elicited a "maybe" follows five or six other topics with stronger, clearer priorities, one might choose to not to add it to the list and stop adding topics with even less coverage. If there are fewer than five headings and this test does not help with a decision, one might ask whether the library has assigned a subject heading for this topic to other items and, if so, compare those with the one being cataloged. One might consider how important the topic is to library users and what other materials on the topic are available in other formats. It also is reasonable to ask whether something unique in this item's coverage of the topic merits special consideration.

Eventually, one must make decisions. A practical rule of thumb is to exclude topics when all the evaluations just described still leave one uncertain about whether enough material about the topic is present to warrant a subject heading. When in doubt, don't make a heading.

When a resource devotes approximately the same amount of space to each of several topics, catalogers should list them in the order in which they appear. For books and other sequential works, a quick scan clarifies the sequence. In electronic resources that offer random access to their contents, sequence is irrelevant. One could take a list of numbered menu topics as indicating order of importance. Or, if the menu topics are not numbered, they can be read from top to bottom and left to right. When the usual observations are unclear, the topics can be given in any order.

Representing Subject Matter in Library Catalogs

Identifying the topic(s) of the contents of an electronic resource, writing them down in one's own words, and ranking them in order of importance is the first part of the process of making the intellectual content of the resource accessible to catalog users. The next part is equally important. It involves translating the list of topics into subject headings authorized for use in the library's catalog. For most North American libraries and increasing numbers of non-American libraries, this means selecting terms from *Library of Congress Subject Headings* (LCSH) that match the topics the cataloger has listed. LCSH headings are found in online subject authority files maintained jointly by the Library of Congress, Library and Archives of Canada, and cooperating members of the Subject Authorities Cooperative program (SACO), and are issued annually in book form as well. Librarians may decide not to use LCSH but choose instead to use other subject vocabularies (thesauri or subject heading lists) that serve their purposes more effectively.

Among the advantages of LCSH is that it covers all knowledge areas and is continuously maintained at high levels of quality. The importance of continuous maintenance cannot be overstated. It is an enormously costly effort. In addition, LCSH is widely used throughout North America, United Kingdom, and other English-speaking countries. Its headings are used most frequently in the catalog records of bibliographic networks. Among its disadvantages is that LCSH may lack the headings needed by some libraries, especially those outside North America or using languages other than English. LCSH's creators only establish English-language headings needed for the materials they collect. As a result, LCSH's vocabulary tends to exhibit a North American, English-language bias. Moreover, LCSH's headings do not follow simple, uniform rules either in their establishment or their application, nor can new headings be added officially without following a lengthy process dictated by the Library of Congress.

Why should a library bother with authorized subject headings and the complicated process of subject cataloging? Isn't one of the beauties of searching the Internet, in contrast to searching for information by subject in books, the ability to locate topical terms (keywords) simply by asking a search engine to find them? What are the advantages of continuing to assign subject headings from lists of approved terms?

The principal advantage of subject headings over keywords is the high level of precision they provide. A search engine matches the searcher's selected keywords to the words appearing in Internet resources. The words do not have to appear in meaningful relationships, nor do they have to identify a specified topic. A subject heading, on the other hand, not only requires that the words it matches appear in meaningful relationships and represent desired topics, but that a person who examined the item decided it had sufficient material on the topic to justify assigning that subject heading to it. At this writing, no computer program yet developed can perform this work as well as humans, despite the potential for human error in subject cataloging described earlier.

A detailed description of the process of converting one's list of topics into authorized subject headings is beyond the scope of this book, but there is no scarcity of helpful manuals that cover it. Several good ones are listed in the Bibliography at the end of this chapter, with titles that include the terms "subject headings" or "subject cataloging." These manuals describe assigning terms from LCSH or *Sears List of Subject Headings* (a smaller, simpler list intended for schools and small public libraries), but the process they teach could be applied to other lists.

Expressing Subject Matter in Classification— Shelving Arrangement

As mentioned earlier in this chapter, cataloging tradition dictates that the first subject heading guides the selection of a classification number for an item. To classify the item, the cataloger matches the first subject heading to an appropriate classification number from a list of authorized numbers (that is, a classification scheme that gives lists of approved numbers for specified topics). This process is similar to selecting authorized subject headings from a list of headings. Teaching the process goes beyond the scope of this manual, but manuals that do so are listed at the end of the chapter. Their titles include the word "classification." Generally, English-language manuals assume the Dewey Decimal Classification or the Library of Congress Classification are used.

In North American library practice, only one classification number is assigned to each item being cataloged no matter how many numbers might be relevant to its contents. As a result, classification reveals only the most important topic of a resource, which may not be all that it covers. In the case of books and other traditional materials stored on library shelves, the objective of classification is not only to identify materials having the same subject matter; it is also to gather them together in one place on the shelves. The shelving function limits classification to a linear sequence, because library shelves run in straight lines. Shelves do not branch off in multiple directions that would bring together the common parts of different topics. To visualize this concept, think about bringing together the "children" parts of "children's literature" and "diseases of children." The first topic is part of the broader subject "literature," and the second is part of the broader subject "disease." Yet both involve "children."

Should the same policies that govern book classification be applied to electronic resources, which do not require physical shelving? Might a different policy be more appropriate? Why not assign several classification numbers to each item, for example, one for each subject heading assigned to it, or one for each identifiable part of a subject? Applying such a policy to the previous example, two classification numbers would be assigned to each resource, the first number representing "literature" for one and "disease" for the other, and the second number representing "children" for both. A searcher asking for the classification number for "children" would retrieve both resources, whereas a searcher asking for "literature" or "disease" would retrieve only the relevant one. It is up to the searcher to decide which of the resources matches his or her information need.

The downside of such a policy is that it emulates the type of retrieval fostered by keywords and muddies the precision of subject headings. A compromise position might be to assign a classification number for each subject heading, but not for each part of a subject heading. Research into these and other alternatives can help catalogers decide the best policy for the future; meanwhile, conforming to traditional policies seems justified until all the consequences of making changes are explored.

As already mentioned, in North American libraries, the most popularly used classifications are the Dewey Decimal and the Library of Congress classifications. They differ in many respects, but both arrange materials by discipline and enumerate lists of classification numbers. Both result in a linear arrangement of materials. Libraries may choose other classification schemes that they believe are better suited their needs. Some schemes permit the representation of parts of topics (known as faceted schemes), such as the Universal Decimal Classification, and some provide greater depth in limited subject areas, such as the (U.S.) National Library of Medicine Classification. More detailed explanations of Dewey Decimal and Library of Congress classifications as well as advice on selecting an appropriate classification for one's library may be found in *Standard Cataloging for School and Public Libraries* or *Special Libraries: A Cataloging Guide* by Intner and Weihs, listed at the end of this chapter.

Creating a Call Number

Call numbers require more than a classification number. They include shelf marks (known as "book" marks even when applied to other materials) that complete the shelf address, which, depending on the policies of an individual library, can be unique for each item cataloged or shared by several items with similar characteristics. Typical shelf marks for traditional materials include cutter numbers, dates of publication, and volume and copy numbers. Libraries may divide their collections into branches, departments, or collections, and, when they do, shelf marks that relate to the location may precede the rest of the call number, including the classification number. For example, a library may assign R for "Reference Collection" or "B" for a Branch Collection. When collection marks are used, the call numbers of two copies of the same item purchased, say, both for the reference and circulating collections or the main library and branch collections will differ solely in the collection designation. This is common with children's, young adult, and adult collections in public libraries.

Cutter numbers used as shelf marks, first codified into published lists by Charles A. Cutter (1969a, 1969b; *Cutter-Sanborn Three-Figure Author Table*, 1969),[1] are alphanumerical codes intended to alphabetize the things to which they are assigned while keeping the number of characters involved to a minimum. Some published lists of Cutter numbers use an initial letter followed by two numbers; others use an initial letter followed by three numbers. (The Cutter numbers that appear in the examples in this book are taken from the Swanson-Swift revision of the Cutter-Sanborn three-figure author tables.) Small libraries may use an initial letter alone—a Cutter letter—or add just one number after the letter. Cutter numbers also can be used in classification, for example, they are frequently encountered in the Library of Congress scheme, where they may represent geographic locations, languages, or topics.

Once the classification number of an item has been determined, shelf marks are added to form a call number, which designates the place on the shelves where the item is stored. The exact location is not fixed, because, as new items are added to or removed from the shelves, other materials will shift to accommodate them. However, the relative positions of call numbers to one another remain fixed, following the plan of the classification scheme as implemented by an individual library.

Should shelf marks be assigned to electronic materials that do not require shelf addresses? If several resources share a classification number, shelf marks can distinguish them. This would enable a searcher who knows the entire call number to retrieve a single resource and not the others that share its classification number. Given the large number of online resources, it is reasonable to believe that even small libraries might need call numbers for them to facilitate efficient retrieval.

Bibliographic Description

Describing the Resource

The current version of the *Anglo-American Cataloguing Rules*, 2nd edition, 2002 revision, and updated in 2003, 2004, and 2005 (AACR2; updates to the rules are made continuously and published on an irregular basis), has special rules for describing Internet resources as part of the category it calls remote access electronic resources. In addition to the rules from chapter 1, which apply to all resources being described, special rules in chapter 9 (electronic resources) apply to monographic Internet resources.

The ISBD template mandated by AACR2[2] is modified for Internet resources, mainly by eliminating the physical description area, because Internet resources have no tangible physical substance that one can hold in one's hand or put on a shelf, as well as the material specific details area, which is no longer applicable although under earlier rules it was used to give information about file characteristics. The other six areas are used to give information that identifies resources and distinguishes them from one another.

One of the first differences in the rules for this chapter is that the entire resource (AACR2 says "the resource itself"; AACR2, p. 9–3) is the chief source of information, unlike other chapters where only selected parts of an item are given this designation (for example, for printed monographs, the title page or its equivalent is the chief source). Catalogers are given great latitude for selecting the chief source when the resource is in several parts.

In every area of description in this chapter, the initial instruction is to complete the area as directed in the relevant rule(s) in chapter 1. No departure from the pattern is made for this format; however, a number of the interpretations do differ. Following are a list of the principal differences for electronic resources.

1. The source of the title proper must be given in a note to inform those trying to match the data accessed in the resource with the catalog record.

2. The general material designation "electronic resource" is added in square brackets after the title proper.

3. The names of those "credited with a major role in creating the content of the resource" (AACR2, p. 9-6) are to be given in the statement of responsibility; other names may be given in the note area at the discretion of the cataloger.

4. The source of an edition statement must be noted if it differs from the source that was used for title proper.

5. Words indicating that an edition statement is appropriate include *release*, *level*, and *update* as well as the terms enumerated in chapter 1.

6. Material specific details are no longer given for monographic electronic resources.

7. All resources appearing on the Internet (i.e., available as "remote access" resources) are considered published.

8. The first note consists of three parts: nature and scope, system requirements, and mode of access.

9. Examples of the note for added information about the type and extent of the resource include statements such as "File size varies," "File size unknown," and several more useful possibilities (AACR2, p. 9-19).

10. The final note mandates giving the date on which the resource was viewed for cataloging purposes; thus, discrepancies between data in the catalog record and data in a resource being accessed can be attributed to changes in the file itself. In recent cataloging practice, this note is often combined with the source of title note.

11. URLs are not mentioned in AACR2. This is usually the last note in common cataloging practice.

Differences from other formats are not always easy to interpret for individual resources, but for the most part they are straightforward and do not assume catalogers have extensive technical knowledge of the computer systems through which electronic resources are accessed. Because descriptive data are either transcribed as given in the item being cataloged or constructed from data seen in the item, they should not require much technical knowledge. Still, lack of familiarity with the medium raises the risk of misinterpreting relevant information from the item or missing it even when it is present.

One piece of transcribed information that is difficult to interpret for electronic resources is the publication date. Finding original publication dates for resources that are frequently updated may be all but impossible, and the dates displayed will change every time the resources are edited, no matter how minor the changes made. Noting the date a resource was examined for cataloging purposes helps those who use the catalog record to be aware of the accuracy of the information it contains, including the date that appears in the publication, distribution area of bibliographic description.

Specialized practical manuals that teach and illustrate how to catalog Internet resources are beginning to be published and can be very helpful. Some are listed at the end of this chapter and include online tutorials as well as printed books. Most specialized manuals are aimed at catalogers who already understand and are comfortable cataloging traditional materials. They concentrate mainly on the differences for this medium. True neophytes will likely need to consult basic how-to-catalog manuals as well as the more specialized ones.

Selecting Descriptive Access Points

AACR2's chapter 21 offers rules for selecting the descriptive access points. Internet resources follow the same pattern as do all other materials: first, a main entry must be chosen. The main entry is the creator of the content of the resource—or, if there is more than one, the most important—although there are some exceptions that are discussed briefly in this section. Once the main entry has been chosen, the names of other creators, the title proper, variations of the title, titles of parts of the resource, and a series title if one is present may be selected as secondary access points deemed "added entries" if the cataloger believes they might be searched by people who use the catalog. Two critical factors govern the selection of added entries:

1. Information providing the basis for each added entry must appear somewhere in the bibliographic description—notes often are made for this purpose (see Figure 4.2).

2. The cataloger must believe someone will search for the resource using the added entry as a search term.

Figure 4.2. Access point derived from note area.

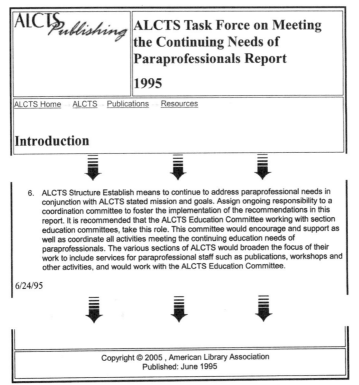

With the permission of ALCTS.

```
Type: a     Elvl: I     Srce: d     Audn:       Ctrl:        Lang: eng
BLvl: m     Form: s     Conf:       Biog:       MRec:        Ctry: ilu
            Cont:       GPub:       LitF:       Indx:
Desc: a     Ills:       Fest:       DtSt: s     Dates: 1995,
040     $c
020
050     4   Z682.4.L52 $b As78 1995
082
049
110 1   Association of Library Collections & Technical Services. $b
Task Force on Meeting the Continuing Needs of Paraprofessionals.
245 1 0 ALCTS Task Force on Meeting the Continuing Needs of
Paraprofessionals report $h [electronic resource].
260     Chicago : $b ALCTS Publishing, $c 1995.
538     Mode of access: World Wide Web.
530     "It is recommended that the ALCTS Education Committee ...
coordinate all activities meeting the continuing education needs of
paraprofessionals."
500     Title from title screen (viewed Mar. 11, 2005)
650   0 Library employees $z United States.
710 2   Association of Library Collections & Technical Services. $b
Education Committee.
856 4 0 $uhttp://www.ala.org/ala/alcts/alctscontent/alctsbucket/
alctssources/general/meetingthecontin/meetingcontinuing.html
```

The process of selecting the first and most important access point, the main entry, is illustrated in the following decision tree (see Figures 4.3–4.5):

1. Did the resource emanate from a corporate body? (Yes, go to question 2; No, go to question 3)

2. Is the resource one of the types eligible to be given a corporate body main entry (consult AACR2 rule 21.1B2 to find out)? (Yes, make the body *chiefly* responsible for the contents the main entry for the resource; No, treat the resource as if it didn't emanate and go on to question 3)

3. Is one person *chiefly* responsible for the resource's contents? (Yes, make that person the main entry; No, go on to question 4)

4. Did two or three persons share the same activity in creating the resource's contents? (Yes, consult the rules for shared responsibility; No, go on to question 5)

5. Did two or three persons contribute different kinds of activities in creating the resource's contents? (Yes, consult the rules for mixed responsibility; No, go on to question 6)

6. Are more than three persons responsible for the creation of the resource's contents? (Yes, make title proper the main entry; No, go on to question 7)

7. Is the person (or persons) responsible for creating the resource's contents unknown? (Make title proper the main entry.)

The decision tree does not treat instances in which a resource emanates from a corporate body and is eligible for corporate body main entry, but the body or bodies chiefly responsible for the contents either is unknown or exceeds three. In such instances, title proper main entry would be made, similar to the practices when a resource's personal authors are unknown or exceed three.

Formulating Descriptive Access Points in Authorized Form

AACR2's chapters 22 through 25 describe how to formulate names and titles in authorized forms: chapter 22 for personal names; chapter 23 for geographic names; chapter 24 for corporate body names; and chapter 25 for uniform titles. Titles proper and series titles proper, which AACR2 directs to transcribe as given on the item, do not require any changes to be used as access points.[3] The purpose of following a single set of rules for formulating name and uniform title headings is to ensure that all the works of an author and all editions/versions of a work will be brought together (that is, filed in the same place) in the catalog. Before turning to AACR2 to establish a name form, working catalogers typically consult existing files of names and titles already authorized for use in library catalogs. The LC/NACO Name Authority File,[4] established by the Library of Congress, the Library and Archives of Canada, and British Library, and augmented by contributions from trained catalogers participating in the Program for Cooperative Cataloging (PCC), is a valuable tool containing many thousands of authorized headings, cross references, and information sources. It can be accessed through a library's bibliographic network, or purchased as a separate reference tool.

The basic "rules of thumb" follow. For additional guidance, consult chapters 5 and 6 in *Standard Cataloging for School and Public Libraries,* or appropriate chapters in the cataloging manual of your choice.

Figure 4.3. Main entry under personal name.

Home | BISON Catalog | Databases by Title | Resources by Subject | Ask Us

What's New | Conferences | Newsletters | Useful Websites | Search | Home

General Material Designation in the Twenty-First Century: Results of a Survey by Jean Weihs

In April 2000 the Online Audiovisual Catalogers Inc. (OLAC) awarded its research grant to Jean Weihs for a study of general material designations (gmds) in the twenty-first century.

Last updated: June 29, 2001
http://www.olacinc.org/capc/gmd.html
Web page maintained by Sue Neumeister neumeist@buffalo.edu

With the permission of the author.

```
Type: a      ELvl: I     Srce: d     Audn:       Ctrl:       Lang: eng
BLvl: m      Form: s     Conf:       Biog:       MRec:       Ctry: xxu
             Cont:       GPub:       LitF:       Indx:
Desc: a      Ills:       Fest:       DtSt: s     Dates: 2001,
040       $c
020
050
082 0 4   025.3/44 $b W428 $2 22
049
100 1     Weihs, Jean.
245 1 0   General material designation in the twenty-first century $h
[electronic resource] : $b results of a survey / $c by Jean Weihs.
260       [United States] : $b Online Audiovisual Catalogers, $c 2001.
538       Mode of access: World Wide Web.
500       Title from title screen (viewed Mar. 10, 2005).
650     0 Descriptive cataloging $xRules.
856 4 0   $u http://www.olacinc.org/capc/gmd.html
```

Figure 4.4. Main entry under corporate body.

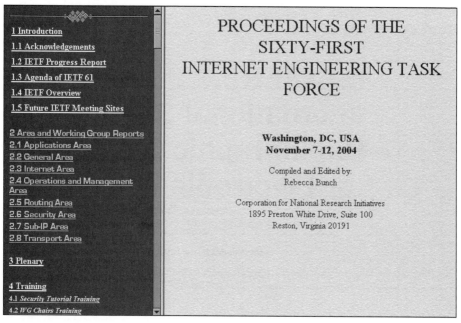

Reproduced by kind permission of the Internet Engineering Task Force.

```
Type: a      ELvl: I      Srce: d      Audn:        Ctrl:        Lang: eng
BLvl: m      Form: s      Conf: 1      Biog:        MRec:        Ctry: vau
             Cont:        GPub:        LitF: 0      Indx: 0
Desc: a      Ills:        Fest:        DtSt: s      Dates: 2004,
040     $c
020
050     4   TK5105.875 $b In8 2004
082
049
111 2       Internet Engineering Task Force $n (61st : $d 2004 : $c
Washington, D.C.).
245 1 0     Proceedings of the sixty-first Internet Engineering Task
Force, Washington DC, USA, November 7-12, 2004 $h [electronic resource]
/ $c compiled and edited by Rebecca Bunch.
260         Reston, Va. : $b Internet Engineering Task Force, $c 2004.
538         Mode of access: World Wide Web.
500         Title from title screen (viewed Mar. 14, 2005).
650   0     Internet $v Congresses.
650   0     Computer networks $v Congresses.
700 1       Bunch, Rebecca.
856 4 0     $u http://www1.ietf.org/proceedings_new/04nov/index.html
```

Authors' note: The IETF home page and associated pages states that IETF is "hosted by the
Corporation for National Initiatives" which presumably means that the corporation funds all or part
of the IETF. However, despite the fact that their addresses are identical, IETF has a separate
Web site and appears to be a separate organization.

Figure 4.5. Main entry under title.

With the permission of the International Federation of Library Associations and Institutions.

```
Type: a    ELvl: I    Srce: d    Audn:      Ctrl:      Lang: eng
BLvl: m    Form: s    Conf: 0    Biog:      MRec:      Ctry: ne
           Cont:      GPub:      LitF: 0    Indx: 1
Desc: a    Ills:      Fest: 0    DtSt: c    Dates: 1997,9999
$c
020
050
082 0 4   025.3/44 $b Is1 $2 22
049
245 0 0   ISBD(ER) : $h [electronic resource] $b international standard
bibliographic description for electronic resources : revised from the
International standard bibliographic description for computer files /
$c recommended by the ISBD(CF) Review Group.
246 3 0   International standard bibliographic description for
electronic resources
250       Rev.
260       The Hague : $b International Federation of Library
Associations and Institutions, $c 1997-.
538       Mode of access: World Wide Web.
500       Title from title screen (viewed Mar. 11, 2005).
530       "Originally issued by K.G. Saur, Muenchen, 1997 as vol. 17 in
the UBCIM Publications, New Series."
500       "Latest revision July 2, 1999".
504       Includes index.
650    0  International standard bibliographic description for
electronic resources.
650    0  Cataloging of computer files $x Standards.
650    0  Descriptive cataloging $x Standards.
710 2     ISBD(CF) Review Group.
710 2     International Federation of Library Associations and
Institutions.
856 4 0   $u http://www.ifla.org/VII/s13/pubs/isbd.htm
```

Headings for Persons: Headings for persons are made after examining the way their names appear in their published works. The form selected as the authorized form should be the one that appears most frequently. Because most authors publish only one work, the way it appears on that work is generally chosen. When catalogers select one name form from multiple possibilities appearing in publications, the forms not chosen become cross-references leading to the authorized form.

When a person's name includes a surname, that is generally selected as the first part of the heading, followed by a comma and the rest of the name. This means William Shakespeare would be established as Shakespeare, William. When a surname has several parts, the part chosen to go first in the heading depends on the person's country and language. Walter de la Mare, for example, could be established as follows:

1. Mare, Walter de la

2. La Mare, Walter de

3. De la Mare, Walter

Because Walter de la Mare was an English-speaking American, his heading begins with "De," as in number 3, above, which is the way we alphabetize the name. Non-English names are generally established the way they would appear in alphabetized listings in their home country and language. AACR2 includes special rules for Arabic, Burmese, Karen, Chinese, Indic, Indonesian, Malay, and Thai names as well as general rules for English names, exceptions for selected European languages, and for royalty and nobility.

Headings for Corporate Bodies: Headings for corporate bodies are made in the same way as headings for persons, by examining the way the names appear in items issued by the bodies themselves. Published works such as directories and bylaws, official stationery, and Web sites are all places where names of the bodies appear. If the name appears in more than one form, the most commonly used form is chosen, and cross-references are made from the other forms.

Having said that the most commonly used form of name of a corporate body is used as its heading, it should be recognized that corporate body names present unique problems—mainly that some corporate bodies consist of different units or parts and, when one of the parts issues a resource and is selected to be named as an access point, its name might not be understandable as a heading. For that reason, AACR2 has rules governing when a body is entered directly under its own name (for example, Canadian Library Association, Library of Congress, International Business Machines) and when it is entered subordinately under the name of another body (for example, the Cataloging and Classification Section of the Association for Library Collections & Technical Services is entered subordinately under its parent body as: Association for Library Collections & Technical Services. Cataloging and Classification Section). Rules for making these choices (24.12–24.14) identify sets of conditions that govern the decision.

A useful rule of thumb that works much of the time is to enter the name *directly* when it is unlikely to be confused with any other body (see Figure 4.2—multiple associations called "Association for Library Collections & Technical Services" are unlikely). Enter the name *subordinately* after the name of its parent body when other bodies might bear the same name without it (many universities have faculties, departments, or schools of arts and sciences, law, medicine, etc., and entering the name of a faculty, department, or school directly is likely to result in duplication; whereas, entering it after the name of its university is not; see Figure 5.7).

More special rules in AACR2 deal with corporate bodies whose names include the names of geographic entities, initials, or acronyms or that require the addition of terms to distinguish them from similar names. Prominent among this last type of problem are conference names, the names of rulers and other heads of state, and so on. The best way to approach establishing corporate body names is to search them, first of all, in the LC/NACO Name Authority File or, for Canadian corporate body names, the AMICUS file. If the name is not listed there, determine the type of name it is and then apply the rules in AACR2 for that type.

Uniform Title Headings: Uniform titles serve two distinct purposes: at times they are used to bring together resources that share the same content but are issued under different titles proper; at other times, they are used to distinguish resources that contain different content but share the same title proper. Because they do not always accomplish the same task, the rules of AACR2 for uniform titles appear to be complicated, but once the type of problem is identified, rules for it are clear.

Works that are issued again and again under different titles, are translated from one language to another, are parts of other titles, and so on fall into the first category. Their titles proper differ, but their contents are alike. Such resources qualify for the creation of uniform titles to bring them together under a single agreed-on title because their own titles proper do not do so. If there was a Web site titled "Alice online" containing the text of Lewis Carroll's "Alice in Wonderland," it would not file together with versions titled *Alice in Wonderland* or *Alice's Adventures in Wonderland,* or the film version of the story, or any of the other versions of this classic tale. If, however, it were given the uniform title "Alice in Wonderland," it would join its companions at the same filing point.

Different resources may also be issued that bear the same "generic" titles proper, such as "Symphony," or "Laws, etc." Such resources also qualify for the creation of uniform title headings, but this time they serve to distinguish the resources from one another. They share the same titles proper but have different contents. Creating uniform titles for these resources usually requires adding distinguishing terms to the common title. Each of the symphonies of Beethoven has the title proper "Symphony," but to separate them from one another, AACR2 instructs catalogers to add the serial number, opus number, and key signature. This results in a useful title file, as follows:

Symphony, no. 1, opus 21, C major

Symphony, no. 2, opus 36, D major

Symphony, no. 3, opus 55, E flat major, and so on

Even if one did not know the composer was Beethoven, it is unlikely other composers have written symphonies with identical serial numbers, opus numbers, and key signatures. The title heading for Beethoven's first symphony would stand out from, say, that for Brahms's first symphony or Mahler's first symphony.

Uniform titles constructed according to the rules of AACR2 make it possible to find different resources containing identical content under one title even when they are each issued under different titles proper as well as to find unique content that shares a title with other resources containing different content.

Referring to Related Materials

AACR2's chapter 26 describes three kinds of references:

1. *See* references, which lead from an unused form to the authorized form;

2. *See also* references, which lead from one authorized form to another, related, authorized form; and

3. *Explanatory* references, which give information about a particular authorized heading that searchers might find useful.

Each of the three types of reference can be applied to personal names, geographic and/or corporate body names, and uniform titles. AACR2 gives numerous examples for every reference and heading type. Catalogers of electronic resources will likely find plenty of guidance in its pages.

One type of reference helpful for catalogers of electronic resources is the name-title added entry, which links a resource being cataloged to a related work whose main entry differs. An example is a Web site devoted to Shakespeare's *Hamlet*. Shakespeare cannot be considered responsible for the Web site, yet his play is the reason for its existence. Should a cataloger working on the Web site want to include a reference to the original play, to be precise, he or she would make a name-title reference.

References cover instances in which added entries are not given, as for forms of names or titles that are not authorized for use in the catalog, when more information than a simple heading is desired, and when numerous added entries lead to the same heading, as with the *Hamlet* example above.

Control Data

Inventory Control Data

Many overlapping systems of inventory control are present in catalog records, including ISBNs and ISSNs, other types of publisher's numbers, Universal Product Codes, Library of Congress Control Numbers, and local library call numbers. Library policies guide catalogers to record most or all of them, either as part of the bibliographic description or in the control data portions of online cataloging worksheets, that is, in fields of the MARC format beginning with a zero, such as 010 (LCCN), 020 (ISBN), 050 (LC call number), 082 (Dewey call number), and so on. Except for the call numbers, the data generally do not display in the public catalog unless specifically requested by a searcher; sometimes, no provision to make such as request is available. Because inventory control data are thought to distract and confuse nonlibrarians, they are suppressed from public display.

In individual libraries, data about specific copies are added to catalog records, usually in a locally operated computer system designed to track and administer local resources but do not appear in the main catalog record. The inventory control data likely to be most helpful to individual libraries are local call numbers. At this time, few of the common identifiers are being assigned to electronic resources (ISBN, ISSN, UPC, LCCN), but if assigned, they should be included in catalog records.

Retrieval Data

Selected elements from eye-readable portions of bibliographic descriptions and subject heading fields may be given in coded form to facilitate retrieval. Using the codes simplifies programming and enables software developers to avoid having to account for variations in natural language terminology. In the MARC formats used by bibliographic networks such as OCLC and RLIN (Research Libraries Information Network), these fields are known as "fixed fields."

The three types of retrieval data with which librarians are most familiar are language, date of publication, and medium, but these are not the only elements that can be employed to enhance complex catalog searches. Existing fixed fields accommodate coding for elements such as fiction/nonfiction; the presence of illustrations, bibliographies, and indexes; selected literary genres such as biography and festschriften; country of publication; the presence of many types of accompanying materials; and more. Few automated catalogs take advantage of many of these elements, but the potential to do so exists.

Cost and Copyright Management Data

AACR2 accommodates data about the price of an item in its eighth area of bibliographic description. Price, along with other "terms of availability," can be entered into the catalog record in that area, along with the ISBN (standard number). However, librarians are reluctant to enter prices for books and other offline monographs, because they are subject to change over time as well as differences in actual prices paid by individual purchasers. Access to electronic resources presents another problem. Terms of access usually are negotiated as a contract between the owner of the resource and an individual library or consortium of libraries. Because the contracted cost is unlikely to be the same for all purchasers, no one figure is appropriate for use as a standard price along the lines of a "list price," or "manufacturer's suggested retail price," which is what is expected to be entered here for other types of material.

Electronic resources do not present the same problems of cost recovery for lost items that traditional kinds of library materials do. Putting the price of an item in its catalog record became something of an issue after library catalogs were computerized and borrowers could see the whole catalog record for an item, including its list price. Librarians discovered to their dismay that when a catalog record stated a price for an item that someone borrowed and lost, the borrower balked at being asked to pay anything more. It did not seem to matter that the price of the item might have risen or that the library had to pay more than the list price to acquire and process the item for use. As a result, libraries now typically omit price information from catalog records. Instead, they are likely to charge a flat fee or a sliding scale of fees that average the varying prices of and acquisitions and processing fees for specific types of items.

"Terms of availability," however, can be construed as including information about who can access electronic resources as well as what users can and cannot do with the material they access from a resource, and other information indicating copyright management specifications. Unfortunately, traditional cataloging practice discourages giving information such as this in area 8, because that practice was established when catalogs were in book or card form. Cards, in particular, furnished precious little space for long, complicated explanations. Thus, librarians working with electronic resources have not used area 8. They want to establish fields designed specifically to handle critical copyright management information. Such fields, while relating to terms of availability, have not yet been established by the authorities governing either cataloging rules or library encoding (MARC) formats.

Other Control Data

Traditional library cataloging tends to limit itself to the kinds of information described earlier, although there is no reason the list of available elements could not be expanded to accommodate other needs. Information about preservation and archiving, provenance, resource ownership, record derivation, sponsorship, funding, and other elements can be accommodated in traditional-style catalog records if librarians choose to take advantage of existing fields or create new ones.

Specialized communities such as art libraries and music libraries have already made use of existing opportunities to include information that might not be of use to outsiders, such as recording labels and numbers, composition types, and details of artistic mediums. At the same time, there has been some reluctance in the cataloging world to add elements such as grade levels and reading levels, which could be of use to elementary school teachers, in particular. The desire to minimize the complexity of catalog records must always be balanced with the need to accommodate an increasingly diverse set of people employing the traditional cataloging model.

Summary

The traditional cataloging model used for books and other monographic materials having a physical existence has been explored in this chapter. Exceptions and interpretations employed in applying standard descriptive cataloging, subject cataloging, and classification practices to electronic resources have been described and explained.

The advantage for library-based searchers of following the standard model and using standard procedures to provide access to electronic resources is the opportunity to integrate electronic resources into existing catalogs containing records for other library materials. This empowers searchers by enabling them to see a wider array of resources simultaneously. Searchers are not limited to a few kinds of materials or forced to repeat their searches in multiple catalogs. Following existing standards for electronic resources and integrating them into current catalogs increases the likelihood large numbers of diverse searchers can find the information they want in the form that is most effective for their individual needs.

Exercises

Figures 4.6 through 4.10 present examples of the sources of information that may be encountered in cataloging electronic resources. Try cataloging them according to the second level of description. Completed descriptions are given at the end of the book in "Answers to Exercises."

Figure 4.6. Picture of survey of audio collections in academic libraries.

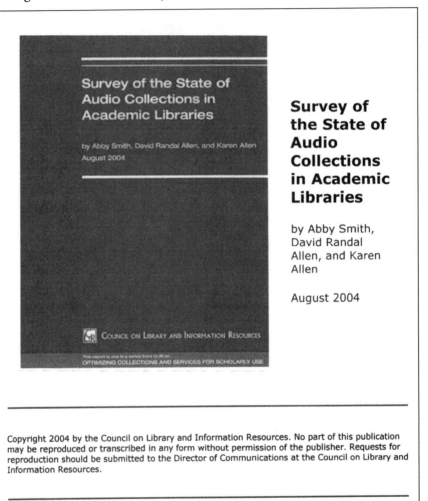

Survey of
the State of
Audio
Collections
in Academic
Libraries

by Abby Smith,
David Randal
Allen, and Karen
Allen

August 2004

With the permission of the Council on Library and Information Resources.

Figure 4.7. Picture of *Dictionary of Canadian Biography Online.*

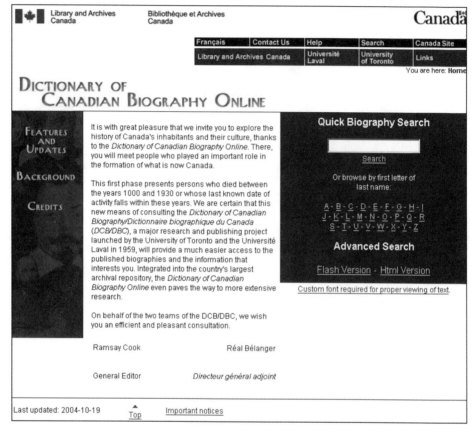

Figure 4.8. Picture of Universal Declaration of Human Rights title screen.

Figure 4.9. Picture of Library Education Chronologies title screen.

ELAN LIBRARY EDUCATION CHRONOLOGIES

Inside this Issue

Home

Dalhousie University

McGill University

Université de Montréal

University of Alberta

University of British Columbia

University of Toronto

University of Western Ontario

Library Technicians

Special Anniversary Issue of ELAN, Fall 2004
Library and Information Studies Education in Canada

One hundred years ago, in the summer of 1904, the first formal library education program in Canada began at McGill University. To mark this anniversary, the Ex Libris Association established a Library Education Anniversary Committee, which decided the most appropriate way to celebrate this centennial was to publish a special issue of *ELAN* , the association's newsletter, featuring an article on each of the seven Canadian schools of library and information studies along with one on library technician training programs in Canada.

Not since the *Encyclopedia of Library and Information Science* published historical articles in the 1970s and early 1980s on each Canadian school has there been a systematic review of their individual histories, programs, issues and trends. In his excellent survey article in 1993, Professor Peter McNally of McGill University lamented the fact that the anniversaries of a number of important events in graduate education in library and information studies in Canada have been largely ignored. In an effort to remedy this situation, our committee was fortunate in recruiting volunteer authors closely associated with their respective programs who generously donated their expertise and time to this project. To them we owe a debt of gratitude.

The authors are as follows:

Alberta: John Wright and others
British Columbia: Lois Bewley
Dalhousie: Norman Horrocks
McGill: Peter McNally
Montreal : Marcel Lajeunesse
Toronto: Diane Henderson
Western Ontario: Janette White
Library Technicians: Jean Weihs and Frances Davidson-Arnott

Published in September 2004, the Special Issue is free to ELA members. The sale price, including handling and mailing, is $7.00.

Chronologies on ELA Web Site

To complement the articles in ELAN, a chronology has been compiled for each institution summarizing the major events that have taken place over the years as well as listing the names of the deans, directors, or chairpersons who have served. For reasons of space, these chronologies and other summary data appear on this ELA Web site, not in the published volume. It is intended to keep these chronologies updated and appropriate additions are welcomed.

Brian Land, Chair, Library Education Anniversary Committee, Ex Libris Association.

Ex Libris Association gratefully acknowledges the ongoing support of the Faculty of Information Studies, University of Toronto. For suggestions, comments or questions about this Web page contact the Webmaster. For information about Ex Libris Association, contact the Secretary .

With the permission of the Ex Libris Association.

Figure 4.10. Picture of Introduction to HTML title screen.

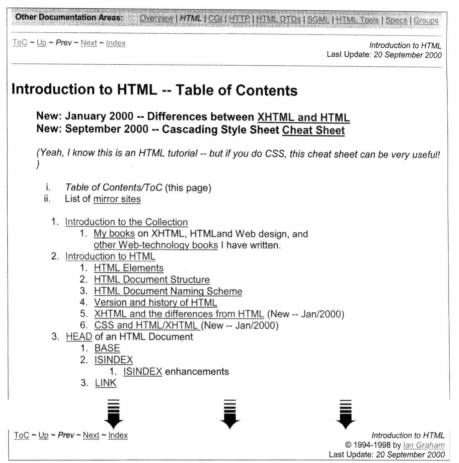

With permission of Dr. Ian Graham

Questions for Discussion

1. Name two places in an electronic resource that are likely to furnish useful information for subject cataloging.

2. What tools are used to assign subject headings and classification numbers to electronic resources?

3. Why should the same classification used for library materials in other physical formats be used for electronic resources?

4. Name three differences in the rules for bibliographic description that pertain to electronic resources and explain them briefly.

5. How can the eighth area of description, standard numbers and terms of availability, be useful for electronic resources?

Notes

1. The Cutter numbers that are part of the call numbers in the figures in this chapter were derived from *C.A. Cutter's Three-Figure Table* (Swanson-Swift Revision, 1969). This does not mean that the authors prefer this cuttering system to other schemes. Whatever shelf mark system is chosen by a library, it should be applied consistently to all materials.

2. This refers to areas of description: 1. title and statement of responsibility; 2. edition; 3. material specific details; 4. publication, distribution information; 5. physical description; 6. series; 7. notes; 8. standard numbers and terms of availability.

3. Because patrons are accustomed to them or changing them would require a great deal of updating work, long-established series title heading forms made using previous cataloging rules may continue to be preferred by some libraries. As a result, in practice, catalogers may opt *not* to use an item's series title proper as a heading and use a previously established form in its place. However, the series title proper will still be transcribed into area 6 of the bibliographic description. References are made to connect the different forms.

4. LC/NACO Name Authority File. Available at http://authorities.loc.gov. For Canadian name authorities, see www.collectionscanada.ca/amicus.

Bibliography

Ahronheim, Judith R., ed. (2002). *High-Level Subject Access: Tools and Techniques in Internet Cataloging.* New York: Haworth Information Press. [Also published as *Journal of Internet Cataloging*, 5, no. 4 (2002).]

Anglo-American Cataloguing Rules. (2002–2005). 2002 revision. Prepared under the direction of the Joint Steering Committee for Revision of AACR. Ottawa: Canadian Library Association; London: Chartered Institute of Library and Information Professionals; Chicago: American Library Association, 2002. Updates issued in 2003, 2004, and 2005.

Authority Tools for Audiovisual and Music Catalogers: An Annotated List of Useful Resources [Online]. Robert Bratton, ed. Available: http://www.olacinc.org/capc/authtools.html

Chan, Lois Mai. (1996). *Library of Congress Subject Headings.* 5th ed. Englewood, CO: Libraries Unlimited, 1996.

Chan, Lois Mai. (1998). *Immroth's Guide to the Library of Congress Classification.* 4th ed. Englewood, CO: Libraries Unlimited.

Cutter, Charles Ammi. (1969a). *Two-Figure Author Table.* Chicopee Falls, MA: H. R. Huntting; distr. Littleton, CO: Libraries Unlimited.

Cutter, Charles Ammi. (1969b). *Three-Figure Author Table.* Chicopee Falls, MA: H. R. Huntting; distr. Littleton, CO: Libraries Unlimited.

Cutter-Sanborn Three-Figure Author Table. (1969). Swanson-Swift revision. Littleton, CO: Libraries Unlimited. Also available on CD-ROM from Libraries Unlimited.

Fountain, Joanna G. (2001). *Subject Headings for School and Public Libraries: An LCSH/Sears Companion.* 3rd ed. Westport, CT: Libraries Unlimited.

Greenberg, Jane, ed. (2000). *Metadata and Organizing Educational Resources on the Internet.* New York: Haworth Press. [Also published as *Journal of Internet Cataloging* 3, nos. 1–3 (2000).]

Hsieh-Yee, Ingrid. (2000). *Organizing Audiovisual and Electronic Resources for Access: A Cataloging Guide.* Englewood, CO: Libraries Unlimited.

Intner, Sheila S., and Jean Weihs. (1998). *Special Libraries: A Cataloging Guide.* Englewood, CO: Libraries Unlimited.

Intner, Sheila S., and Jean Weihs. (2001). *Standard Cataloging for School and Public Libraries.* 3rd ed. Englewood, CO: Libraries Unlimited.

Intner, Sheila S., Sally C. Tseng, and Mary Lynette Larsgaard, eds. (2003). *Electronic Cataloging: AACR2 and Metadata for Serials and Monographs.* New York: Haworth Press. [Simultaneously published as *Cataloging & Classification Quarterly*, vol. 36, nos. 3–4 (2003).]

Journal of Internet Cataloging. (1998–). Binghamton, NY: Haworth Press.

Lehnus, Donald J. (1980). *Book Numbers: History, Principles, and Application.* Chicago: American Library Association.

Mitchell, Anne M., and Brian E. Surratt. (2005). *Cataloging and Organizing Digital Resources.* New York: Neal-Schuman.

Olson, Hope A., and John J. Boll. (2001). *Subject Analysis in Online Catalogs.* 2nd ed. Westport, CT: Libraries Unlimited.

Olson, Nancy B. (1998). *Cataloging of Audiovisual Materials and Other Special Materials.* 4th ed. Mankato, MN: Minnesota Scholarly Press.

Pattie, Ling-yuh (Miko), ed. (1996). "Electronic Resources: Selection and Bibliographic Control." *Cataloging & Classification Quarterly* 22, nos. 3 & 4.

"Principles of the *Sears List of Subject Headings*." (2004). In *Sears List of Subject Headings*, 18th ed., Joseph Miller and Joan Goodsell, eds. H. W. Wilson, p. xv–xxxix.

Roe, Sandra K., ed. *The Audiovisual Cataloging Current*. (2001). New York: Haworth Information Press. [Also published as *Cataloging & Classification Quarterly* 31, nos. 3 & 4 (2001).]

Sauperl, Alenka. (2002). *Subject Determination During the Cataloging Process*. Lanham, MD: Scarecrow Press.

Taylor, Arlene G. *The Organization of Information*. (2004). 2nd ed. Westport, CT: Libraries Unlimited/Greenwood.

Weber, Mary Beth. (2002). *Cataloging Nonprint and Internet Resources: A How-to-Do-It Manual for Librarians*. New York: Neal-Schuman Publishers.

Weihs, Jean. (1991). *The Integrated Library: Encouraging Access to Multimedia Materials*. 2nd ed. Phoenix, AZ: Oryx Press.

Weitz, Jay. (n.d.). *Cataloging Electronic Resources: OCLC-MARC Coding Guidelines*. Available: http//:www.oclc.org (accessed April 18, 2005).

Chapter 5

Creating Library Metadata for Continuing Resources

Many electronic resources are published on a continuing basis and cannot be categorized as monographic publications. Nevertheless, the model for creating library metadata for these materials is similar to the one for monographic materials in electronic form, discussed in Chapter 4, that is, it consists of a bibliographic description following the rules of the *Anglo-American Cataloguing Rules*, 2nd edition, 2002 revision (AACR2) and its updates, to which descriptive and subject-related access points under authority control are added, along with additional data mainly in coded form, used to control and manipulate selected pieces of information within the database. This chapter explains and illustrates how information is obtained from continuing electronic resources and recorded to create a standard bibliographic record. Some attention also is paid to CONSER guidelines for these materials, which specify particular interpretations of cataloging rules and are used by contributors to the CONSER database.[1]

This chapter begins with subject analysis. Following subject analysis are sections covering bibliographic description, descriptive access points, and control data used in library cataloging. At the chapter's end are examples that readers may wish to try cataloging and classifying using all the forgoing information, with answers at the back of the book in the "Answers to Exercises" section. Bibliographic records were prepared for this book in March 2005 using the OCLC MARC-record style. At the time OCLC stated that the cataloging of these materials remains very much in flux (Weitz, n.d.).

Subject Analysis

Determining Subject Matter

The discussion in Chapter 4 about determining the subject matter of an electronic resource applies also to subject analysis for continuing resources, but with some additional caveats. Unlike monographic materials, which are published only once and are thus unchanging, the topical interests of continuing resources tend to

135

evolve over time to match the ongoing evolution of the fields they cover. This makes it more difficult to pin down subject matter appropriate to represent in catalog records. In all cases, however, determining subject matter is more of an art than a science.

Catalogers will wish to examine all parts of the resource likely to contain subject information (known collectively as "subject-rich" parts): titles, descriptive sections about the resource in "about" files or "history" files, and statements intended to guide prospective subscribers and authors that describe the topical areas covered by the publication. In electronic journals as in printed ones, masthead pages and editorial policy statements (or their electronic counterparts) are likely to offer substantial guidance about subject matter. When these parts are not provided, instructions for authors may contain indications of subjects of interest. An examination of the subject matter of the articles in the issue of the resource used as the basis of cataloging and any other issues available may also be helpful.

As with monographic resources, library policies can direct catalogers to assess subject contents broadly or narrowly. Policies covering the subject analysis of continuing electronic resources may need to take both approaches, depending on how focused the publication is as well as whether there are alternatives to the library's catalog record immediately available to searchers. Publications with a general focus that aim to cover topics in many disciplinary areas, such as *ABC Online* (see Figure 5.3), need broad treatment. Publications with more specific subject interests, such as *Stem Cell Information* (see Figure 5.8) require narrower treatments, but not necessarily the narrowest analyses possible. Catalogers must assess whether the publication is indexed internally or in an external index and, if so, see what such indexing provides so as not to duplicate it in local records. Adding a link from the catalog records to the index(es) is a better choice than duplicating it (them).

At the same time, the perspective of the individual cataloger will affect how subject matter is perceived and interpreted. Subject specialists tend to recognize very specific subtopics that nonspecialists might miss; nonspecialists may lack sufficient knowledge to identify topics and subtopics correctly. At the least, catalogers should be prepared to give information about every topic or subtopic identified in the subject-rich parts of the publication (mentioned earlier), and more if the library catalog is the only place where subject information can be found.

Continuing electronic resources may be expected to cover wider ranges of subjects than monographic resources. Catalogers would do well to be flexible in regarding available subject information for inclusion in catalog records. Nevertheless, estimates of the relative importance of whatever subject areas are said to be covered need to be determined in order to rank them. Viewing one issue of a continuing resource is unlikely to reveal the true range of its subject matter. Instead, catalogers might begin by assigning subject headings for subject areas explicitly mentioned in the resource but follow up after several issues have appeared to see if additions or adjustments need to be made to the initial assignments. The first subject heading might be interpreted more broadly than would be done for a monographic resource, knowing that subsequent issues will depart to some degree from the initial contents.

The process of determining subject contents has three steps:

1. *Examine the subject-rich areas of the resource.* Areas of the resource that are likely to have descriptions of its intellectual content include the title and subtitle, the "about" file, other introductory screens and files, and menu

headers (see Figure 5.1). If the item has an index, it can contain subject words revealing the topics covered in the resource. Although an experienced cataloger would not "read" every page of an item, scanning some of the material often helps to pin down the approach to the material and intended audience for the resource.

Figure 5.1. Subject-rich home page.

With the permission of the Ontario Science Centre www.ontariosciencecentre.ca.

2. *Write down, in your own words, the topics you identify.* List the topics and estimates of the amount of material can be expected to be devoted to each one, such as the number of articles on the topic, the order of topics in menu listings, and/or the number of links related to each topical area. As previously stated, catalogers need to take a broader view of the topical areas they identify, knowing that subsequent issues of the resource are likely to contain articles covering a different mix of topics written by authors using different approaches than the ones being reviewed at the time of cataloging.

3. *Rearrange the list of topics in priority order.* Cataloging tradition dictates that the most important (read "largest") topic goes first. Every effort should be made to determine the predominant subject of the resource so it can be used as the basis for classification.

After the first priority topic, other topics are ranked in descending order of importance, similar to what one does in analyzing the topics of monographic resources. Importance can be defined as containing measurable amounts of material of sufficient size that someone searching for information on the topic would not be disappointed by the contents of the resource. However, taking a broad view allows catalogers to limit themselves to topics in which many articles are expected, not just an occasional article or a few articles of marginal interest. Taking an example from the professional literature with which readers should be familiar, librarians could readily list "cataloging" as a subject heading for *Cataloging & Classification Quarterly,* but not for *College & Research Libraries,* even though the latter journal often publishes outstanding articles about cataloging. Similarly, although *Cataloging & Classification Quarterly*'s articles often focus on cataloging in academic libraries, one would not list "academic libraries" for it as a subject heading, whereas that is the appropriate subject for *College & Research Libraries.*

If a resource devotes approximately the same amount of space to more than one topic, catalogers generally list them in the order in which they appear. In the example for *Cataloging & Classification Quarterly,* two separate headings for library cataloging and library classification could be assigned, in that order, because the order reflects that of the title.

In electronic resources that offer random access to their contents, sequence is irrelevant. One could take a list of numbered menu topics as indicating order of importance. Or, if the menu topics are not numbered, they can be read from top to bottom and left to right. When the usual observations are unclear, the topics can be given in any order. What is more important is that all the identified topics be listed and subject headings representing them assigned.

Representing Subject Matter in Library Catalogs

(*Authors' Note:* The three sections that follow are nearly identical to their counterparts in Chapter 4, pp. 113–116, because the processes are the same for all forms of material being cataloged.)

First, one identifies the topics of the contents of an electronic resource, writes them down in one's own words, and ranks them in order of importance. One must take a much broader view of subject coverage, because the focus of continuing resources tends to be broader than it is in monographs as well as changeable. Nevertheless, this process helps to make the intellectual content of the resource accessible to catalog users.

The next part is equally important. It involves translating the list of topics into subject headings authorized for use in the library's catalog. For most North American libraries and increasing numbers of non-American libraries, this means selecting terms from *Library of Congress Subject Headings* (LCSH) that match the topics the cataloger has listed. LCSH headings are found in online subject authority files maintained jointly by the Library of Congress, National Library of Canada, and cooperating members of the Subject Authorities Cooperative program (SACO) and are issued annually in book form as well. Librarians may decide not to use LCSH, but choose instead to use other subject vocabularies (thesauri or subject heading lists) that serve their purposes more effectively.

Among the advantages of LCSH is that it covers all knowledge areas and is continuously maintained at high levels of quality. The importance of continuous maintenance cannot be overstated. It is an enormously costly effort. In addition, LCSH is widely used throughout North America and other English-speaking countries. Its headings are used most frequently in the catalog records of bibliographic networks. Among its disadvantages is that LCSH may lack the headings needed by some libraries, especially those outside North America or using languages other than English. LCSH's creators only establish English-language headings needed for the materials they collect. As a result, LCSH's vocabulary tends to exhibit a North American, English-language bias. Moreover, LCSH's headings do not follow simple, uniform rules either in their establishment or their application, nor can new headings be added officially without following a lengthy process dictated by the Library of Congress.

Why should a library bother with authorized subject headings and the complicated process of subject cataloging? Isn't one of the beauties of searching the Internet, in contrast to searching for information by subject in printed resources, the ability to locate topical terms (keywords) simply by asking a search engine to find them? What are the advantages of continuing to assign subject headings from lists of approved terms?

The principal advantage of subject headings over keywords is the high level of precision they provide. A search engine matches the searcher's selected keywords to the words appearing in Internet resources. The words do not have to appear in meaningful relationships, nor do they have to identify a specified topic. A subject heading, on the other hand, not only requires that the words it matches appear in meaningful relationships and represent desired topics, but that a person who examined the item decided it had sufficient material on the topic to justify assigning that subject heading to it. At this writing, no computer program yet developed can perform this work as well as humans, despite the potential for human error in subject cataloging described earlier.

Another advantage of assigning subject headings from an authorized list is that it collocates all forms of material having relevant content. Searchers entering an LCSH term will retrieve both the continuing and monographic electronic resources on the subject as well as books, videos, printed journals, etc., that cover the same subject matter.

A detailed description of the process of converting one's list of topics into authorized subject headings is beyond the scope of this book, but there is no scarcity of helpful manuals that cover it thoroughly. Several good ones are listed in the Bibliography at the end of this chapter, with titles that include the terms "subject headings" or "subject cataloging." These manuals describe assigning terms from LCSH or *Sears List of Subject Headings* (a smaller, simpler list intended for schools and small public libraries), but the process they teach could be applied to other lists.

Expressing Subject Matter in Classification—Shelving Arrangement

Classification of printed periodicals (often the lion's share of printed continuing resources) has not had a strong tradition among some parts of the library and information community. Instead, they are shelved alphabetically by title. However, the authors believe classification should be considered for electronic resources even within agencies that do not classify their printed publications, in order to increase their accessibility to online searchers, who may browse call numbers as a search option.

As mentioned earlier in this chapter, cataloging tradition dictates that the first subject heading guides the selection of a classification number for an item. To classify the item, the cataloger matches the first subject heading to an appropriate classification number from a list of authorized numbers (that is, a classification scheme that gives lists of approved numbers for specified topics). This process is similar to selecting authorized subject headings from a list of headings. Teaching the process goes beyond the scope of this manual, but manuals that do so are listed at the end of the chapter. Their titles include the word "classification." Generally, English-language manuals assume the Dewey Decimal Classification or the Library of Congress Classification is used.

In North American library practice, only one classification number is assigned to each title being cataloged no matter how many numbers might be relevant to its contents. As a result, classification reveals only the most important topic of a resource, which may not be all that it covers. In the case of periodicals and other traditional materials stored on library shelves, the objective of classification is not only to identify materials having the same subject matter; it is also to gather them together in one place on the shelves. Serving the shelving function limits classification to a linear sequence, because library shelves run in straight lines. Shelves do not branch off in multiple directions that would bring together the common parts of different topics. To visualize this concept, think about bringing together the "children" parts of "children's literature" and "diseases of children." The first topic is part of the broader subject "literature," and the second is part of the broader subject "disease." Yet both involve "children."

Should the same policies that govern classification for printed materials be applied to electronic resources, which do not require physical shelving? Might a different policy be more appropriate? Why not assign several classification numbers to each item, for example, one for each subject heading assigned to it, or one for each identifiable part of a subject? Applying such a policy to the previous example, two classification numbers would be assigned to each resource, the first number representing "literature" for one and "disease" for the other, and the second number representing "children," for both. A searcher asking for the classification number for "children" would retrieve both resources, whereas a searcher asking for "literature" or "disease" would retrieve only the relevant one. It is up to the searcher to decide which of the resources matches his or her information need.

The downside of such a policy is that it emulates the type of retrieval fostered by keywords and muddies the precision of subject headings. A compromise position might be to assign a classification number for each subject heading, but not for each part of a subject heading. Research into these and other alternatives can help catalogers decide the best policy for the future; meanwhile, conforming to traditional policies seems justified until all the consequences of making changes are explored.

As already mentioned, in North American libraries the most popularly used classifications are the Dewey Decimal and the Library of Congress classifications. They differ in many respects, but both arrange materials by discipline and enumerate lists of classification numbers. Both result in a linear arrangement of materials. Libraries may choose other classification schemes that they believe are better suited their needs. Some schemes permit the representation of parts of topics (known as faceted schemes), such as the Universal Decimal Classification, and some provide greater depth in limited subject areas, such as the (U.S.) National Library of Medicine Classification. More detailed explanations of Dewey Decimal and Library of Congress classifications as well as advice on selecting an appropriate classification for one's library may be found in *Standard Cataloging for School and Public Libraries* or *Special Libraries: A Cataloging Guide* by Intner and Weihs, listed at the end of this chapter.

Creating a Call Number

Call numbers require more than a classification number. They include shelf marks (known as "book" marks even when applied to other materials) that complete the shelf address, which, depending on the policies of individual libraries, can be unique for each item cataloged or shared by several items with similar characteristics. Typical shelf marks for traditional materials include cutter numbers, dates of publication, and volume and copy numbers. Libraries may divide their collections into branches, departments, or subcollections, and when they do, shelf marks that relate to the location may precede the rest of the call number, including the classification number. For example, a library might assign R for "Reference Collection" and "B" for a Branch Collection. It might also assign BR to indicate a branch library reference collection. When collection marks are used, the call numbers of two copies of the same item purchased, say, both for the reference and circulating collections or the main library and branch collections will differ solely in the collection designation. This is typical for titles held in common by children's, young adult, and/or adult collections in public libraries, and with titles held in common by both reference and circulating collections in all types of libraries.

Cutter numbers used as shelf marks, first codified into published lists by Charles A. Cutter (1969a, 1969b; *Cutter-Sanborn Three-Figure Author Table,* 1969),[2] are alphanumerical codes intended to alphabetize the things to which they are assigned while keeping the number of characters involved to a minimum. Some published lists of Cutter numbers use an initial letter followed by two numbers; others use an initial letter followed by three numbers. Small libraries may use an initial letter alone—a Cutter letter—or add just one number after the letter. Cutter numbers also can be used in classification, for example, they are frequently encountered in the Library of Congress scheme, where they may represent geographical locations, languages, or topics.

Once the classification number of an item has been determined, shelf marks are added to form a call number, which designates the place on the shelves where the item is stored. The exact location is not fixed, because as new items are added to or removed from the shelves, other materials will shift to accommodate them. However, the relative positions of call numbers to one another remain fixed, following the plan of the classification scheme as implemented by an individual library.

Should shelf marks be assigned to electronic materials that do not require shelf addresses? If several resources share a classification number, shelf marks can distinguish them. This would enable a searcher who knows the entire call number to retrieve a single resource and not the others that share its classification number. Given the large number of online resources, it is reasonable to believe that even small libraries might benefit from assigning call numbers to them to facilitate efficient retrieval.

Bibliographic Description

Describing the Resource

The current version of the *Anglo-American Cataloguing Rules*, 2nd edition, issued in 2002 and updated in 2003, 2004, and 2005 (AACR2; updates to the rules are made continuously and published on a irregular basis), has a chapter of general rules applying to all materials being cataloged. In addition, it has a chapter of special rules in which Internet resources are described as part of the category it calls remote access electronic resources. A third chapter covers ongoing publications. Thus, to describe the materials covered in this chapter, rules from chapter 1, which apply to all resources being described, chapter 9 (electronic resources), which cover titles published on the Internet, and chapter 12 (continuing resources) must be combined.

The ISBD template mandated by AACR2[3] is modified for Internet resources, mainly by eliminating the physical description area, because these are remotely accessed resources having no tangible physical substance that one can hold in one's hand or place on a shelf. The other seven areas of description are used. In describing these materials, material specific details (area 3) covers chronological and numeric data identifying the publication pattern. Together, these descriptive elements give information that identifies resources precisely and distinguishes them from one another.

Two types of continuing resources are covered by AACR2's chapter 12: continuously issued titles, that is, those for which new issues appear over time and may be expected to continue appearing indefinitely; and integrating resources, that is, those for which the new issues that appear are incorporated into the whole of the resource and cease to exist as separate issues.[4] Both are found on the Internet, thus, the cataloger needs to decide at the start as to which type of continuing resource is being described, so the correct rules are applied.

The chief source of information for continuing Internet resources is the first or earliest issue available, similar to the practice for printed serials. When the first issue is not used, a note is made identifying the issue on which the cataloging was based.[5] Integrating resources differ, however, using the current iteration (i.e., the latest issue) of a title as chief source, except for the beginning date of publication, which comes from the first iteration. For all continuing Internet resources, no matter what issue is used as the basis for the catalog record, the date it was viewed is noted.[6] If a resource consists of several parts, catalogers may choose any formal statements that provide appropriate descriptive information as the chief source. Among the parts catalogers consider most often are the title's home page, publisher's statement page, and the contents page.

Title changes have always been a special problem for continuing resources in all formats, including Internet resources. Changes considered sufficiently significant to warrant making a new catalog record have been reinterpreted to minimize the times a new record must be created.[7] The AACR2 instruction for integrating Internet resources says: "If any change in the title proper occurs on a subsequent iteration, change the title and statement of responsibility area to reflect the current iteration and, in general, give the earlier title in a note."[8]

In every area of description in this chapter, the initial instruction is to complete the area as directed in the relevant rule(s) in Chapter 1. No departure from the pattern is made for this format; however, a number of the interpretations do differ. The principal variations that apply to continuing electronic resources are highlighted here.[9]

1. The source of title proper must be given in a note to inform those trying to match data accessed in the resource with that found in the catalog record.

2. Introductory words not intended to be interpreted as part of the main title should not be transcribed as title proper. This is similar to long-time practice in interpreting titles proper for moving image materials. It includes words such as "Welcome to ..." and "Disney presents ...." (see Figure 5.2).

3. The full form of a title name is preferred over an acronym when both are found on the chief source, even if the acronym is the sole form found elsewhere.

(*Text continues on page 146.*)

Figure 5.2. Resource title with introductory words.

Welcome to the new-look Heavens-Above!

If you're interested in satellites or astronomy, you've come to the right place! Our aim is to provide you with all the information you need to observe satellites such as the **International Space Station** and the **Space Shuttle**, spectacular events such as the dazzlingly bright **flares from Iridium satellites** as well as a wealth of other spaceflight and astronomical information.

We not only provide the times of visibility, but also detailed star charts showing the satellite's track through the heavens. All our pages, including the graphics, are **generated in real-time** and **customized** for your location and time zone. Frequent visitors will notice we have changed the appearance of the site somewhat and added the option of user registration. This has been done to open the door to a host of new, customisable features which will be appearing over the coming months.

Before we can generate the predictions for you, we need to know where you are, and there are several ways you can do this, depending on whether you are a registered user, want to become one, or prefer to use the site anonymously. For a discussion of the merits of registering, please click here. For some tips on how to get the best out of the site as an anonymous user, click here.

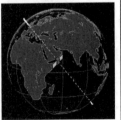

Current position of the ISS

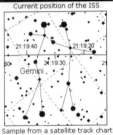

Sample from a satellite track chart

Registered Users
- Simply **log-on**. All your location details and preferences will be retrieved from our database.

Anonymous Users
- **Register** as a user with Heavens-Above. We encourage all our visitors to do so.
- **Select** your location from our huge database.
- **Enter** your coordinates manually.

Developed and maintained by Chris Peat, Heavens-Above GmbH
Please read the updated FAQ before sending e-mail.

Hosted by DLR/GSOC

With the permission of Chris Peat.

```
Type: p     ELvl: I    Srce: d    GPub: f    Ctrl:       Lang: eng
BLvl: i     Form: s    Conf: 0    Freq:      MRec:       Ctry: gw
S/L: 2      Orig:      EntW:      Regl: x    ISSN:       Alph: a
Desc: a     SrTp: w    Cont:      DtSt: c    Dates: 1997,9999
040        $c
020
050
082 0 4    523.80285 $b H352 $2 22
049
245 0 0    Heavens-above! $h [electronic resource].
260        Germany : $b DLR/GSOC.
362 1      Began in 1997.
538        Mode of access: World Wide Web.
500        Title from home page (viewed Mar. 18, 2005).
520        Web site developed and maintained by Chris Peat about
astronomical objects, artificial satellites, and objects visible in the
sky with resources provided by the U.S. Geological Survey and the U.S.
National Imaging and Mapping Agency.
650    0   Stars $v Databases.
650    0   Artificial satellites $v Databases.
700 1      Peat, Chris.
710 2      United States. $b Department of the Interior. $b Geological
Survey.
710 2      United States. $b National Imaging and Mapping Agency.
856 4 0    $u http://www.heavens-above.com.

Authors' note: Jay Weitz, "Cataloging Electronic Resources: OCLC-MARC
Coding Guidelines" (www.oclc.org) states "if the beginning date is not
explicitly stated in the resource, omit 260 subfield $c and give the
beginning date in 362/1 if ascertainable." This date was supplied by
Chris Peat.
```

Figure 5.3. Title screen with acronym and full form of name.

With the permission of the Australian Broadcasting Corporation.

```
Type: p      ELv1: I      Srce: d      GPub: f      Ctrl:        Lang: eng
BLv1: i      Form: s      Conf: 0      Freq: k      MRec:        Ctry: at
S/L:  2      Orig:        EntW:        Regl: r      ISSN:        Alph: a
Desc: a      SrTp: w      Cont:        DtSt: c      Dates: 1995,9999
040          $c
020
050
082 0 4      070.19/094 $b Au78 $2 22
049
245 0 0      Australian Broadcasting Corporation online $h [electronic
resource].
246 3 0      ABC online
260          Sydney, N.S.W. : $b Australian Broadcasting Corporation.
310          Frequently updated
362 1        Began in August 1995.
538          Mode of access: World Wide Web.
500          Title from home page (viewed Mar. 16, 2005).
500          Web site.
650    0     Television broadcasting $z Australia.
650    0     Television programs $z Australia.
650    0     Radio programs $z Australia.
710 2        Australian Broadcasting Corporation.
856 4 0      $u http://www.abc.net.au


Authors' note: See note at bottom of figure 5.2.  This date was
supplied by ABC.
```

4. The general material designation "electronic resource" is added in square brackets after the title proper.

5. Other title information is transcribed if it is an acronym not chosen for title proper, if it contains an embedded statement of responsibility, or if the title proper consists solely of the name of a corporate body; when none of these cases apply, catalogers may decide to include the data in area 1, give it as a quoted note in a note, or ignore it entirely.

6. Material specific details for continuing electronic resources are the dates of publication and/or sequential designation; innovative instructions clarify dates by converting hyphens separating a date span for a single issue to forward slashes (e.g., 2000–2001 becomes 2000/2001) (see Figure 5.5).

7. Data about the type and extent of the contents (computer programs, data, or both; numbers of files, records, and/or bytes, as appropriate) are given in a note.

8. Changes in numbering sequence do not prompt making new catalog records.

9. Publisher's names may not be abbreviated to "The Association ...," etc. (see Figures 5.5, 5.6, 5.7, etc.)

10. The dates associated with electronic resources, and continuing resources in particular, can be confusing. For example, in Figure 5.11 there are three dates:

    (a) 2002, the date on the document. Is this the date of publication? The preface tells us this is the first edition that has no print format, so can we assume that it was published electronically in 2002?

    (b) The copyright date. Is it a copyright date for the publication or for the Web site?

    (c) A "last revised" date. Does this date refer to the document or to the Web site?

    In these instances, catalogers must use their best judgment.

11. Notes for electronic resources follow the order set by chapter 12 and include some not made for monographic resources, such as frequency of issue as well as those relating to the electronic format, such as source of title and date viewed, nature of the work, system requirements, mode of access, and so on[10] (see Figures 5.6, 5.7, 5.10).

These interpretations are relatively straightforward and do not assume catalogers have extensive technical knowledge of the computer systems through which electronic resources are accessed. Because descriptive data are either transcribed as given in the item being cataloged or constructed from data seen in the item, they should not require sophisticated technical knowledge. Still, lack of familiarity with the medium raises the risk of misinterpreting relevant information from the item or missing it even when it is present.

Specialized manuals that teach and illustrate how to catalog Internet resources are beginning to be published and can be very helpful. Some, including printed books and online tutorials, are listed at the end of this chapter. Most specialized manuals are aimed at catalogers who understand and are comfortable cataloging traditional materials. They concentrate mainly on the differences for electronic and/or continuing resources. True neophytes will likely need to consult basic how-to-catalog manuals as well as the more specialized ones. The *CONSER Cataloging Manual* (n.d.) offers guidance for catalogers working with continuing Internet resources, although it sometimes departs from AACR2's interpretations and recommended practices. CONSER libraries must comply with CONSER practice. Others should comply with the source most appropriate to their individual institutional policies but attempt to maintain policies that are consistent and practical.

Selecting Descriptive Access Points

AACR2's chapter 21 offers rules for selecting descriptive access points. Continuing Internet resources follow the same procedure as all other materials: first, a main entry must be chosen. The main entry is the creator of the content of the resource—or, if there is more than one, the most important, although there are some exceptions. AACR2's guiding principle in selecting main entry is that an eligible creator must be responsible for the whole of the material, not solely a part. Applying the principle to continuing Internet resources, catalogers are limited to persons or bodies that do not change over time but that continue to be responsible for the entire content of the resource. This eliminates authors of articles or columnists who might be expected to write portions of content for one issue or, in the case of columnists, for a number of issues, but rarely for all of them. Editors of continuing publications, like editors of printed collections, are not considered the authors of the material they edit and are not eligible for main entry. As a result, many continuing resources are entered under their titles.

Similar to moving image materials, title main entry is the rule-of-thumb for continuing electronic resources. One group of exceptions, however, are those electronic publications of corporate bodies that qualify for corporate body main entry under the rules of 21.1B2, such as an organization's serially issued membership directory or annual report.

Once the main entry has been chosen, the following may be selected as secondary access points deemed "added entries":

1. Names of other creators responsible for the whole of the title

2. Title proper and/or uniform title (if not chosen as main entry)

3. Variations of the title appearing in the resource

4. Titles of parts of the resource

5. Series title, if one is present

Two critical factors govern the selection of added entries:

1. Information providing the basis for each added entry must appear somewhere in the bibliographic description—notes are often made for this purpose.

2. Catalogers must believe that someone will search for the resource using the added entry as a search term—no benefit results from access points no one is likely to use. However, AACR2 counsels being generous in making decisions about doubtful cases. When in doubt, make the added entry (see figure 5.6).

The process of selecting the first and most important access point, the main entry, is illustrated in the following decision tree:

1. Did the resource emanate from a corporate body? [Yes, go to question 2; No, go to question 3]

2. Is the resource one of the types eligible to be given a corporate body main entry (consult AACR2 rule 21.1B2 to find out)? [Yes, make the body *chiefly* responsible for the contents the main entry for the resource; No, treat the resource as if it didn't emanate and go on to question 3]

3. Is one person *chiefly* responsible for the resource's contents? [Yes, make that person the main entry; No, go on to question 4]

4. Did two or three persons share the same activity in creating the resource's contents? [Yes, consult the rules for shared responsibility; No, go on to question 5]

5. Did two or three persons contribute different kinds of activities in creating the resource's contents? [Yes, consult the rules for mixed responsibility; No, go on to question 6]

6. Are more than three persons responsible for the creation of the resource's contents? [Yes, make title the main entry; No, go on to question 7]

7. Is the person (or persons) responsible for creating the resource's contents unknown? [Make title the main entry.]

The decision tree does not treat two instances: first, when a resource emanates from a corporate body and is eligible for corporate body main entry but the body chiefly responsible for the contents is unknown; second, when a resource emanates from a corporate body and is eligible for corporate body main entry, but the number of eligible bodies exceeds three and all are equally responsible. In both of those instances, title main entry would be made, similar to what is done when a resource's personal authors are unknown or exceed three.

Figure 5.4. Internet resource entered under personal author.

Michael Friendly's Home Page

Welcome

Hi, and welcome to my home page. Most of the links here are to things I'm working on. A verbal welcome. (You need a sound card to hear my voice.)

Contents

- Statistical Graphics
- Graphical Methods for Categorical Data
    - Mosaic displays
    - Fourfold displays
    - Visual and Conceptual Models for Categorical Data
    - Other methods for categorical data
- SAS/GRAPH meets the Logo Turtle
- APL2STAT
- York Statistical Consulting Service
- Other links
- To contact me

Other pages | Visualizing Categorical Data ▾

With the permission of Michael Friendly.

```
Type: a      ELvl: I      Srce: d      GPub:        Ctrl:        Lang: eng
BLvl: i      Form: s      Conf: 0      Freq:        MRec:        Ctry: onc
S/L:  2      Orig:        EntW:        Regl: x      ISSN:        Alph: a
Desc: a      SrTp: w      Cont:        DtSt: c      Dates: 1996,9999
040       $c
020
050    4   QA276.3 $b F915
082
049
100 1      Friendly, Michael.
245 1 0    Michael Friendly's home page $h [electronic resource].
260        Toronto : $b York University.
538        Mode of access: World Wide Web.
538        System requirements: Sound card optional.
362 1      Began in 1996.
500        Title from home page (viewed Mar. 18, 2005).
650    0   Statistics $b Graphic methods.
856 4 0    $u http://www.math.yorku.ca/SCS/friendly.html

Authors' notes: Although this document was found on the York University
Web site, the university shares no responsibility for the content of
the document and, therefore, an added entry was not made for the
university.
        See note at bottom of figure 5.2.  This date was supplied by Dr.
Friendly.
```

Figure 5.5. Internet resource entered under corporate body.

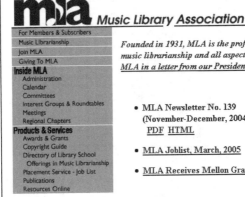

Reproduced with permission of the Music Library Association.

```
Type: a      ELvl: I     Srce: d     GPub: f     Ctrl:       Lang: eng
BLvl: s      Form: s     Conf: 0     Freq: a     MRec:       Ctry: wiu
S/L:         Orig:       EntW:       Regl: r     ISSN:       Alph: a
Desc: a      SrTp:       Cont:       DtSt: c     Dates: 2000, 1999,
040       $c
020
050
082       025.1782/021 M973 $2 22
049
110 1     Music Library Association. $b Statistics Subcommittee.
245 1 0   Annual survey of music collections in the United States $h
[electronic resource] / $c prepared by the Music Library Association
Statistics Subcommittee.
246 3 0   Survey of music collections in the United States
260       Middleton, Wis. : $b Music Library Association, $c 2000-
310       Annual
362 1     1998/99-
538       Mode of access: World Wide Web.
538       System requirement: Adobe Acrobat except for 1998/99 issue.
500       Title from title screen (viewed Mar. 17, 2005).
650    0  Libraries $x Special collections $x Sound recordings $x
Statistics $z United States.
650    0  Music libraries $x Statistics $z United States.
856 4 0   $u http://www.musiclibraryassoc.org
```

Figure 5.6. Internet resource entered under title.

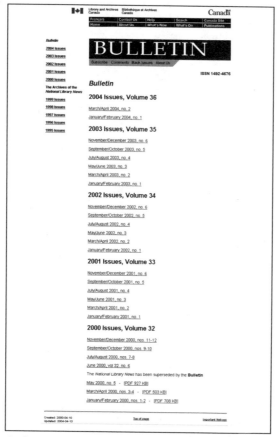

```
Type: a      ELvl: I     Srce: d     GPub: f     Ctrl:        Lang: eng
BLvl: s      Form: s     Conf: 0     Freq: b     MRec:        Ctry: onc
S/L:         Orig:       EntW:       Regl: r     ISSN: 4      Alph: a
Desc: a      SrTp: p     Cont:       DtSt: d     Dates: 2002, 2004,
040          $c
022          1713-0107 $y 1492-4676.
050
082 0 4      027.571/05 $b B874 $2 22
049
130 0        Bulletin (National Library of Canada). $l English.
245 1 0      Bulletin $h [electronic resource] / $c National Library of
Canada.
246 3 0      National Library of Canada bulletin
260          Ottawa : $b National Library of Canada, $c 2002-2004.
310          Bi-monthly
362          Vol. 27, no. 6 (June 1995)-vol. 36, no. 2 (Mar./Apr. 2004).
538          Mode of access: World Wide Web.
500          Title from contents page (viewed Mar. 17, 2005).
500          Issues from 1995 to May 2000 have title: National Library
News.
530          Also issued in print ed. previous to 2003.
530          Also issued in French-language ed.
500          Ceased publication.
610 2        National Library of Canada $v Periodicals.
650   0      Libraries $z Canada $v Periodicals.
710 2        National Library of Canada.
740 0        National Library news.
856 4 0      $u http://www.collectionscanada.ca/bulletin/index-e.html

Authors' note:  This publication was discontinued when the National
Library of Canada and the National Archives of Canada were merged into
the Library and Archives of Canada (LAC).  Therefore, LAC was not
responsible for this publication.  If a library believes that the
publication should also be accessed through LAC, a note can be made
that this publication is housed on the LAC Web site and an added entry
provided; or "see also" references could be made from one to the other
```

Serially issued continuing resources, taken as a whole, often are collections of articles, columns, editorials, letters, and other content created by numerous personal authors (or corporate bodies that do not qualify for corporate body main entry) and are entered under their titles. Integrating resources, on the other hand, exhibit different characteristics and should be treated accordingly.

Formulating Descriptive Access Points in Authorized Form

(*Authors' note:* This section is virtually identical to its counterpart in chapter 4, but it is repeated here so that readers focusing on continuing resources will not have to consult a different chapter for the information.)

AACR2's chapters 22 through 25 describe how to formulate names and titles in authorized forms: chapter 22 for personal names; chapter 23 for geographic names; chapter 24 for corporate body names; and chapter 25 for uniform titles. Titles proper and series titles proper, which AACR2 directs to transcribe as given on the item, do not require any changes to be used as access points.[11] The purpose of following a single set of rules for formulating name and uniform title headings is to ensure that all the works of an author and all editions/versions of a work will be brought together (that is, filed in the same place) in the catalog.

In cataloging monographs, when an item is entered under title, the title proper of the resource is most likely to be used for the main entry, although there are exceptions. When the title proper is such that it is not an appropriate choice,[12] a uniform title created for the resource serves the function instead. (In that case, the title proper could be selected as an added entry.) In cataloging continuing resources, however, instances often occur in which the resources are entered under their titles and also require uniform titles. Among them are the following:

1. The resource is issued in more than one format, generally, in both printed and electronic formats, in CD-ROM (direct access) and online (remote access) formats, or in all three formats

2. The resource emanates from a corporate body, but does not qualify for corporate body main entry under AACR2's rule 21.1B2 (AACR2, rule 21-7).

3. A person predominantly responsible for the content of the resource cannot be identified

For these reasons, uniform title main entries are not uncommon for continuing Internet resources and catalogers should be prepared to create them as needed. CONSER offers helpful guidelines on doing so.

Before turning to AACR2 to establish a name form or a uniform title, working catalogers typically consult existing files of names and titles already authorized for use in library catalogs. The LC/NACO Name Authority File,[13] established by the Library of Congress, the National Library of Canada, and the British Library, and augmented by contributions from trained catalogers participating in the Program for Cooperative Cataloging (PCC), is a valuable tool containing many thousands of authorized headings, cross references, and information sources. It can be accessed through a library's bibliographic network, or purchased as a separate reference tool.

The basic "rules of thumb" follow. For additional guidance, consult chapters 5 and 6 in *Standard Cataloging for School and Public Libraries*, the CONSER manual, or appropriate chapters in the cataloging manual of your choice.

Headings for Persons: Headings for persons are made after examining the way their names appear in their published works. The form of name to be selected as the authorized form should be that which appears most frequently. Because most authors publish only one work, the way the name appears on that work is generally chosen. If more than one name form appears in the publications, the forms not chosen become cross-references leading to the authorized form.

When a person's name includes a surname, it is generally selected as the first part of the heading, followed by a comma and the rest of the name. This means William Shakespeare would be established as Shakespeare, William. When a surname has several parts, the part chosen to go first in the heading depends on the person's country and language. Walter de la Mare, for example, could be established as follows:

1. Mare, Walter de la

2. La Mare, Walter de

3. De la Mare, Walter

Because Walter de la Mare was an English-speaking American, his heading begins with "De," as in number 3, which is the way we alphabetize the name. Non-English names are generally established the way they would appear in alphabetized listings in their home country and language. AACR2 includes special rules for Arabic, Burmese, Karen, Chinese, Indic, Indonesian, Malay, and Thai names as well as general rules for English names, exceptions for selected European languages, and for royalty and nobility.

Headings for Corporate Bodies: Headings for corporate bodies are made after examining the way their names appear on the items they issue themselves, such as official documents, stationery, and the like. Similar to personal names, the form chosen as the authoritative form is generally that which appears most frequently. Other forms of name found in the source materials but not chosen become cross-references leading to the authorized form.

The general rule is to enter a corporate body's name as found, but quite a few exceptions appear. AACR2 provides specialized rules for governmental and religious bodies and governmental and religious officials as well as for named events such as conferences, exhibitions, and so on. Generally, the authoritative names of national governments are the same as their English-language geographical place names[14] (for example, "Brazil," "Canada," "Sweden," "Malaysia") . The rules in AACR2's chapter 23 govern formulation of geographic names and must be applied to these corporate bodies.

Sometimes a corporate body name requires further qualification, as is the case with the separate governments known colloquially as East and West Germany from 1945 until the 1990s. In library catalogs they are known as Germany (Democratic Republic) and Germany (Federal Republic). Multiple names are assigned to the same geographic location when governments change, for example, depending on the timing, the same location is known as "Nyasaland" or "Malawi." Parenthetic qualifiers may include names, dates, or explanatory phrases so no mistake can be made about the government it represents.

Governments are not the only type of corporate body for which names may need further specification. Parenthetic qualifiers are also added to names that lack enough information to avoid misinterpretation (for example, "Who," the authorized form of name for the rock-and-roll group The Who, is qualified to "Who (Musical group)") and to identical names shared by different bodies. AACR2 can be consulted for these rules (AACR2, rules 24-12 to 24-14).

Some corporate bodies do not exist independently but are part of one or more larger bodies. In such cases, catalogers must decide whether to enter the name of the part directly as found or subordinately, after first naming the larger body or bodies. There is no easy, hard-and-fast rule for making the choice. Two examples follow that show one corporate body named directly even though it is part of a larger body (Association for Library Collections and Technical Services, a division of the American Library Association) and another named subordinately after first naming its parent body (Faculty of Information Studies of the University of Toronto). Rules for making these choices (24.12–24.14) identify sets of conditions that govern the decision.

A useful rule of thumb that works much of the time is to enter the name *directly* when it is unlikely to be confused with any other body (see Figure 4.2—multiple associations called "Association for Library Collections & Technical Services" are unlikely). Enter the name *subordinately* after the name of its parent body when other bodies might bear the same name without it (many universities have faculties, departments, or schools of arts and sciences, law, medicine, etc., and entering the name of a faculty, department, or school directly is likely to result in duplication; whereas, entering it after the name of its university is not).

Uniform Title Headings: Uniform titles are established for continuously issued Internet resources that bear the same title proper as another resource, appear in other formats (an instance of bearing the same title proper as another resource), or are translations from other languages in which they were originally published. Theoretically speaking, uniform titles play a dual role, differentiating among multiple resources that share a single title proper and bringing together a single resource that appears under multiple titles proper.

Chapter 25 of AACR2 does not have special rules for continuing resources but treats both monographic and continuing resources under one set of rules. Rule 25.5B covers creating uniform titles by adding parenthetic qualifiers to identify individual resources when different resources share a single title. Rule 25.5C covers creating uniform titles for a single resource when it is issued in multiple languages that do not file together in the catalog. An optional rule, 25.5D, instructs adding general material designations if they are used. This permits catalogers to distinguish the same title issued as a print resource, CD-ROM resource, and/or Internet resource.

Figure 5.7. Corporate body entered subordinately.

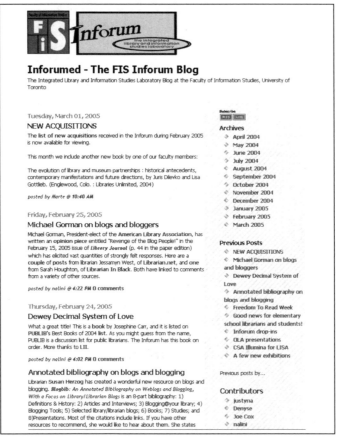

With the permission of the University of Toronto Faculty of Information Studies Inforum

```
Type: p     ELvl: I      Srce: d     GPub:        Ctrl:        Lang: eng
BLvl: i     Form: s      Conf: 0     Freq:        MRec:        Ctry: onc
S/L: 2      Orig:        EntW:       Regl: x      ISSN:        Alph: a
Desc: a     SrTp: w      Cont:       DtSt: c      Dates: 2004,9999

040         $c
020
050    4    Z674 $b Un3
082
049
110 2       University of Toronto. $b Faculty of Library and Information
Studies. $b Inforum.
245 1 0     Informed $h [electronic resource]  : $b the FIS Inforum blog.
246 3 0     FIS Inforum blog
246 3 0     Inforum blog
260         Toronto    $b University of Toronto.
362 1       Began in April 2004.
538         Mode of access: World Wide Web.
500         Title from home page (viewed Mar. 21, 2005).
650    0    Library science.
650    0    Information science.
650    0    Librarians.
856 4 0     $u http://www.fis.utoronto.ca/inforum/blog

Authors' note: See note at bottom of figure 5.2.  This date was
supplied by the Inform Director.
```

Simply put, rules-of-thumb for current practice in formulating uniform titles include the following:

1. Use the title wording by which the resource has become known (this follows the principle of selecting the wording most likely to be sought by searchers).

2. Use the original language for the uniform title; add the language of the translation being cataloged. (This is logical, but English speakers lacking knowledge of foreign languages sometimes have difficulty with it and titles in nonroman characters require transliteration.)

3. Omit initial articles.

4. Enclose the uniform title in brackets unless it is the main entry. If the uniform title is the main entry, do not enclose it in brackets. (The latter is an AACR2 option followed in North American practice.)

5. Add place(s) of publication as a parenthetic qualifier to distinguish two (or more) continuing Internet resources having the same uniform title. If this does not distinguish them, add both the place of publication and the initial year of issue.

6. Add "(Online)" to the uniform title to identify continuing resources available via the Internet. (This follows CONSER practice.)

Referring to Related Materials

AACR2's chapter 26 describes three kinds of references:

1. *See* references, which lead from an unused form to the authorized form;

2. *See also* references, which lead from one authorized form to another, related, authorized form; and,

3. *Explanatory* references, which give information about a particular authorized heading that searchers might find useful.

Each of the three types of reference can be applied to personal names, geographic and/or corporate body names, and uniform titles. AACR2 gives numerous examples for every reference and heading type. Catalogers of continuing Internet resources will likely find plenty of guidance in its pages. Among the cross-references frequently made for these materials are those from acronymic forms to the full form of a corporate body or title proper name, such as *JAMA* for *Journal of the American Medical Association.*

References cover instances in which added entries are not given, as for forms of names or titles that are not authorized for use in the catalog, when more information than a simple heading is desired, and when numerous added entries lead to the same heading.

Control Data

Inventory Control Data

Many overlapping systems of inventory control are present in catalog records, including ISSNs, key titles, codens, Universal Product Codes, Library of Congress Control Numbers, and local library call numbers. Library policies guide catalogers to record most or all of them, either as part of the bibliographic description or in the control data portions of online cataloging worksheets, that is, in fields of the MARC format beginning with a zero, such as 010 (LCCN), 022 (ISSN and key title), 024 (Universal Product Codes and a selection of other standard indentifiers), 030 (coden), 050 (LC call number), 082 (Dewey call number), and so on. Except for call numbers, these data generally do not display in the public catalog unless specifically requested by a searcher; sometimes, no provision to make such as request is available. Because inventory control data are thought to distract and confuse nonlibrarians, they are suppressed from public display.

In individual libraries, data about specific issues are linked to catalog records, usually in a locally operated computer system designed to track and administer local resources but do not appear in the main catalog record. The inventory control data likely to be most helpful to individual libraries are local call numbers. At this time, only a few identifiers are being assigned to electronic resources (ISSN, UPC, LCCN), but if assigned, they should be included in catalog records.

Retrieval Data

Selected elements from eye-readable portions of bibliographic descriptions and subject heading fields may be given in coded form to facilitate retrieval. Using the codes simplifies programming and enables software developers to avoid having to account for variations in natural language terminology. In the MARC formats used by bibliographic networks such as OCLC and RLIN (Research Libraries Information Network), these fields are known as "fixed fields."

Catalogers using the MARC format for continuing Internet resources will employ the 006 fields to identify the twin aspects of seriality (frequency, regularity, ISSN, etc.) and electronic format (type of file, etc.). At this writing, new codes to identify the integrating aspect of continuing resources have not been implemented in network coding systems. The serial 006 is coded instead.

The three types of retrieval data with which librarians are most familiar are language, date of publication, and medium, but these are not the only elements that can be employed to enhance complex catalog searches. Existing fixed fields accommodate coding for features such as fiction/nonfiction; illustrations, bibliographies, and indexes; selected literary genres such as biography and festschriften; country of publication; the presence of many types of accompanying materials; and more. Few automated catalogs take advantage of all of these elements, but the potential to do so exists.

Cost and Copyright Management Data

AACR2 accommodates data about the price of an item in its eighth area of bibliographic description. Price, along with other "terms of availability," can be entered into the catalog record in that area, along with the ISBN (standard number). However, librarians are reluctant to enter prices for books and other offline monographs, because they are subject to change over time as well as differences in actual prices paid by individual purchasers. Access to electronic resources presents another problem. Terms of access usually are negotiated as a contract between the owner of the resource and an individual library or consortium of libraries. Because the contracted cost is unlikely to be the same for all purchasers, no one figure is appropriate for use as a standard price along the lines of a "list price," or "manufacturer's suggested retail price," which is what is expected to be entered here for other types of material.

Electronic resources do not present the same problems of cost recovery for lost items that traditional kinds of library materials do. Putting the price of an item in its catalog record became something of an issue after library catalogs were computerized and borrowers could see the whole catalog record for an item, including its list price. Librarians discovered to their dismay that when a catalog record stated a price for an item that someone borrowed and lost, the borrower balked at being asked to pay anything more. It did not seem to matter that the price of the item might have risen or that the library had to pay more than the list price to acquire and process the item for use. As a result, libraries now typically omit price information from catalog records. Instead, they are likely to charge a flat fee or a sliding scale of fees that average the varying prices of and acquisitions and processing fees for specific types of items.

"Terms of availability," however, can be construed as including information about who can access electronic resources as well as what users can and cannot do with the material they access from a resource, and other information indicating copyright management specifications. Unfortunately, traditional cataloging practice discourages giving information such as this in area 8, because that practice was established when catalogs were in book or card form. Cards, in particular, furnished precious little space for long, complicated explanations. Thus, librarians working with electronic resources have not used area 8. They want to establish fields designed specifically to handle critical copyright management information. Such fields, while relating to terms of availability, have not yet been established by the authorities governing either cataloging rules or library encoding (MARC) formats.

Other Control Data

Traditional library cataloging tends to limit itself to the kinds of information described earlier, although there is no reason the list of available elements could not be expanded to accommodate other needs. Information about preservation and archiving, provenance, resource ownership, record derivation, sponsorship, funding, and other elements can be accommodated in traditional-style catalog records if librarians choose to take advantage of existing fields or create new ones.

Specialized communities (such as art libraries and music libraries) have already made use of existing opportunities to include information that might not be of use to outsiders, such as recording labels and numbers, composition types, and details of artistic mediums. At the same time, there has been some reluctance in the cataloging world to add elements such as grade levels and reading levels, which could be of use to elementary school teachers, in particular. The desire to minimize the complexity of catalog records must always be balanced with the need to accommodate an increasingly diverse set of people employing the traditional cataloging model.

Summary

The cataloging model used for serially issued materials has been explored in this chapter, as has a new set of interpretations in AACR2 for integrating resources. Exceptions and interpretations employed in applying standard descriptive cataloging, subject cataloging, and classification practices to Internet resources have been described and explained.

The advantage for library-based searchers of following the standard model and using standard procedures to provide access to continuing electronic resources is the opportunity to integrate them into existing catalogs containing records for other library materials. This empowers searchers by enabling them to see a wider array of resources simultaneously. Searchers are not limited to a few kinds of materials or forced to repeat their searches in multiple catalogs. Following existing standards for continuing electronic resources and integrating them into current catalogs increases the likelihood large numbers of diverse searchers can find the information they want in the form that is most effective for their individual needs.

Questions for Discussion

1. How does the process of identifying subject matter in continuing electronic resources differ from that for monographic electronic resources?

2. Are any of the basic tools used to provide bibliographic description for continuing electronic resources different than for monographic electronic resources? If so, identify them and what they cover.

3. Name three kinds of dates that appear in continuing electronic resources and briefly explain the problems of determining what they represent.

4. Why do continuing electronic resources often require the use of uniform titles?

Examples

Following are several examples of continuing resources opening screens. Try your hand at cataloging them. Answers are found at the back of the book in the "Answers to Exercises" section.

Figure 5.8. Home page of stem cell information Web site.

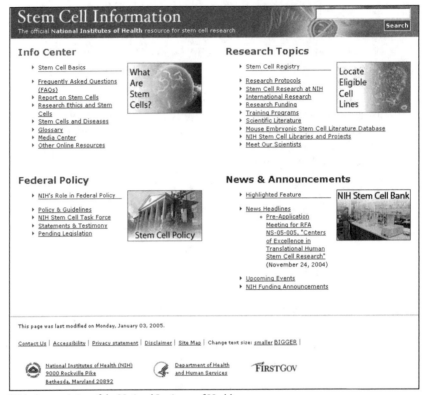

With the permission of the National Institutes of Health

Figure 5.9. Home page of a newsletter.

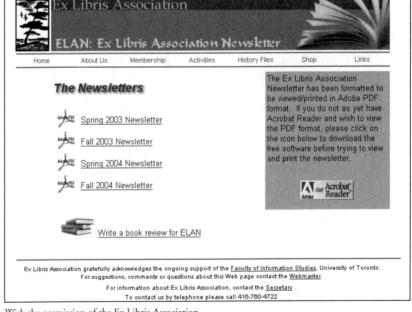

With the permission of the Ex Libris Association

Figure 5.10. Home page of a government organization.

Figure 5.11. Home page of a resource that can be cataloged as a monograph or as a serial.

With the permission of ALCTS

The print editions of this work have been catalogued as a continuing resource (e.g., by the Library of Congress) and the various editions as monographs (e.g., by the University of Toronto). Make a bibliographic record for the above as an electronic continuing resource and as an electronic monograph.

Notes

1. CONSER, which began in the 1970s as an effort to convert cataloging data for serial titles into a computerized database (CONversion of SERials), now stands for Cooperative ONline SERials program. It is a component of the Program for Cooperative Cataloging that also includes SACO, NACO, and the Core Record program. Its database is part of the OCLC shared cataloging database and provides standard, high-quality cataloging records for serial titles.

2. This does not mean that the authors prefer this cuttering system to other schemes. Whatever shelf mark system is chosen by a library, it should be applied consistently to all materials.

3. This refers to areas of description: 1: title and statement of responsibility; 2: edition; 3: material-specific details; 4: publication, distribution information; 5: physical description; 6: series; 7: notes; 8: standard numbers and terms of availability.

4. "Continuously issued" is what used to be called "serial" publications; "integrating" is what used to be called "loose-leaf" publications.

5. This should be a formal note, preceded by the phrase "Description based on:".

6. The date viewed note may be incorporated into the source of title note, for example, "Title from home page (viewed Dec. 1, 2004)."

7. For an excellent discussion of the new interpretations of major and minor title changes, see Jean Hirons, "Seriality: What Have We Accomplished? What's Next?" in *Electronic Cataloging: AACR2 and Metadata for Serials and Monographs,* Sheila S. Intner, et al., eds. (New York: Haworth Press, 2003), 134–39. In it, the author describes three occurrences now considered minor changes not warranting a new cataloging record: addition or deletion of words representing the type of publication; a difference in the name of the same corporate body; and changes in a serial listing.

8. AACR2, rule 12-8. The principle of updating catalog records to reflect data in current iterations and giving data from earlier iterations in notes is followed for many of the bibliographic elements.

9. Catalogers working with continuing electronic resources should consult the *CONSER Cataloging Manual* for remotely accessed electronic resources (available at www.loc.gov/acq/conser/Module31.pdf) as well as AACR2 chapter 12 and comply with the source most appropriate to their individual institutional policies.

10. Notes important for continuing resources, such as the bibliographic history note, which records name changes, mergers, splits, and other commonly encountered matters, are also made for continuing Internet resources but are not highlighted here, because they are also made, if appropriate, for monographs.

11. Because patrons are accustomed to them or because changing them would require a great deal of updating work, some libraries may continue to prefer long-established series title heading forms made using previous cataloging rules. As a result, in practice, catalogers may opt *not* to use an item's series title proper as a heading and use a previously established form in its place. However, the series title proper will still be transcribed into area 6 of the bibliographic description. References are made to connect the different forms.

12. For example, in cataloging a translation, its title proper would not collocate with the original title proper, but a uniform title is created that achieves the desired collocation.

13. Available at http://authorities.loc.gov/. For Canadian headings, see http://www.collectionscanada.ca/amicus.

14. Mandating use of English-language place names is a function of AACR2 being an "Anglo-American" code. This might well mean extra work for non-English-speaking catalogers, but the benefits of being compatible with internationally maintained Name Authority Files may help make up for it.

Bibliography

Anglo-American Cataloguing Rules. (2002). 2nd ed., revised. Prepared under the direction of the Joint Steering Committee for Revision of AACR. Ottawa: Canadian Library Association; London: Chartered Institute of Library and Information Professionals; Chicago: American Library Association, 2002. Updates issued in 2003 and 2004.

Bratton, Robert, ed. (n.d.). *Authority Tools for Audiovisual and Music Catalogers: An Annotated List of Useful Resources* [online]. Available: http://www.olacinc.org/capc/authtools.html

Chan, Lois Mai. (1998). *Immroth's Guide to the Library of Congress Classification.* 4th ed. Englewood, CO: Libraries Unlimited.

Chan, Lois Mai. (1996). *Library of Congress Subject Headings.* 5th ed. Englewood, CO: Libraries Unlimited.

CONSER Cataloging Manual. (n.d.). Available: http://www.loc.gov/acq/conser/Module31.pdf.

Cutter, Charles Ammi. (1969a). *Two-Figure Author Table.* Chicopee Falls, MA: H. R. Huntting; distr. Littleton, CO: Libraries Unlimited.

Cutter, Charles Ammi. (1969b). *Three-Figure Author Table.* Chicopee Falls, MA: H. R. Huntting; distr. Littleton, CO: Libraries Unlimited.

Cutter-Sanborn Three-Figure Author Table. (1969). Swanson-Swift revision. Littleton, CO: Libraries Unlimited. Also available on CD-ROM from Libraries Unlimited.

Fountain, Joanna G. (2001). *Subject Headings for School and Public Libraries: An LCSH/Sears Companion.* 3rd ed. Westport, CT: Libraries Unlimited.

Greenberg, Jane, ed. *Metadata and Organizing Educational Resources on the Internet.* New York: Haworth Press, 2000. [Also published as *Journal of Internet Cataloging* 3, nos. 1–3 (2000).]

Hsieh-Yee, Ingrid. (2000). *Organizing Audiovisual and Electronic Resources for Access: A Cataloging Guide.* Westport, CT: Libraries Unlimited.

Intner, Sheila S., and Jean Weihs. (1998). *Special Libraries: A Cataloging Guide.* Englewood, CO: Libraries Unlimited.

Intner, Sheila S., and Jean Weihs. (2001). *Standard Cataloging for School and Public Libraries.* 3rd ed. Englewood, CO: Libraries Unlimited.

Journal of Internet Cataloging. Binghamton, NY: Haworth Press, 1998–.

Lehnus, Donald J. (1980). *Book Numbers: History, Principles, and Application.* Chicago: American Library Association.

Liheng, Carol, and Winnie S. Chan. (1998). *Serials Cataloging Handbook: An Illustrative Guide to the Use of AACR2R and LC Rule Interpretations.* 2nd ed. Chicago: American Library Association.

Olson, Hope A., and John J. Boll. (2001). *Subject Analysis in Online Catalogs.* 2nd ed. Westport, CT: Libraries Unlimited.

Olson, Nancy B. (1998). *Cataloging of Audiovisual Materials and Other Special Materials.* 4th ed. Mankato, MN; DeKalb, IL: Minnesota Scholarly Press.

Pattie, Ling-yuh (Miko), ed. (1996). "Electronic Resources: Selection and Bibliographic Control." *Cataloging & Classification Quarterly* 22, nos. 3 & 4.

Roe, Sandra K., ed. *The Audiovisual Cataloging Current.* New York: Haworth Information Press, 2001. [Also published as *Cataloging & Classification Quarterly* 31, nos. 3 & 4 (2001).]

Sauperl, Alenka. *Subject Determination During the Cataloging Process.* Lanham, MD: Scarecrow Press, 2002.

Taylor, Arlene G. (2004). *The Organization of Information.* 2nd ed. Westport, CT: Libraries Unlimited/Greenwood.

Weber, Mary Beth. (2002). *Cataloging Nonprint and Internet Resources: A How-to-Do-It Manual for Librarians.* New York: Neal-Schuman.

Weihs, Jean. (1991). *The Integrated Library: Encouraging Access to Multimedia Materials.* 2nd ed. Phoenix, AZ: Oryx Press.

Weitz, Jay. (n.d.). *Cataloging Electronic Resources: OCLC-MARC Coding Guidelines.* Available: http//:www.oclc.org (accessed April 18, 2005).

Chapter 6

Integrating Library Metadata into Local Catalogs and Databases

One would think that completing the cataloging for Internet resources is all that has to happen to make them accessible through the library's public catalog, but that is not always the case. If the data are in the standard forms outlined in Chapters 4 and 5, they could simply be added to the catalog in the same manner as all other original cataloging in the institution. However, there are both practical and political problems involved in integrating data for electronically accessed materials with data for traditional materials in local search tools. This chapter explores the problems and suggests how they might be solved.

Practical Problems

Computers have helped librarians overcome many of the problems that plagued library catalogs in previous times. These problems include the monolithic and immobile nature of the card catalog, which, in large libraries, took up huge amounts of valuable floor space and was not easily replicated, and the perpetually out-of-date contents of the printed catalog, which required new editions to accommodate titles acquired after an edition went to press. Nevertheless, catalog problems still exist and bear examination and discussion before one can conclude with confidence that all one needs to do to supply information about electronic resources is to add them to a library's public catalog. The following matters are considered in the sections that follow:

1. Size of the database

2. Ability of the software to handle cataloging for nonbook formats, especially serially issued materials

3. Identification issues

4. Alternatives to one integrated public catalog

5. Unstable URLs—keeping the catalog current and accurate

165

Size of the Database

Computers succeed admirably in handling many thousands more entries than card catalogs did. Updating is easy. Computers can automatically file new entries in their proper places and, with proper programming, allow changes to be made to subject words, classification numbers, or names everywhere they appear in the catalog with a single set of keystrokes. Computers are economical with physical space and almost infinitely replicable. All the entries are available from any computer with a relatively tiny footprint, whether the database contains ten thousand or ten million titles. With an appropriate telecommunications network in place, the public catalog database can be accessed from any computer that is part of the network. Why, then, is the size of the database an issue to be considered? The answer is, because the larger the database, the greater the likelihood that a search request will retrieve a very large set of responses and many of the entries will appear to be similar.

Why should larger numbers of retrievals be a problem? The answer to this question is that larger the number of retrievals make it more difficult to determine which entries are relevant and desired and which are not, because they represent unwanted materials. Do a Google search on "Shakespeare" and see what happens. During the writing of this book, such a search retrieved close to 300,000 matching sites from the World Wide Web, many of which had nothing to do with the "Shakespeare" the authors had in mind. True, if Google were a library-style catalog, a searcher could cut down the number of retrievals significantly by asking for Shakespeare solely as an author, a title, or a subject, but the resulting number of retrievals would undoubtedly still exceed the patience of the average searcher to review them all. At the end of the day, size remains an issue of some importance, although the order of magnitude for what is considered a "large" catalog has increased importantly since libraries abandoned card catalogs.

One way for catalog searchers to exclude groups of unwanted material from the universe of entries from which retrievals are made is to permit limiting searches by medium. Nevertheless, the sheer size of the potential universe of metadata entries makes this strategy, by itself, unlikely to solve the problem. For that matter, adding large numbers of metadata entries to the catalog means that failing to limit by medium can make searches for all titles in all media other than electronic resources unnecessarily unwieldy. Making finer distinctions, such as limiting a search by the type of resource site being requested (e.g., by the extensions, .com, .edu, .org, .net, etc., in the URL) adds precision, but it also adds a layer of complexity to the search request.

If metadata were to be added automatically to library catalogs, the size of the catalogs would increase a great deal. The issue to be faced is whether the advantages of retrieving more material, a greater proportion of which may be unwanted, outweigh the disadvantages of increasing both the complexity of the search process and the need to assess a larger set of results carefully. At the same time, the very size of current library catalogs makes it more likely that casual searchers believe the catalog contains all the material there is to find on the subjects, authors, and titles they search. Omitting an entire category of material—even, or, perhaps, especially, if it is a huge category—does a disservice to them. Moreover, if searchers prefer using digital materials, as articles seem to suggest,[1] omitting metadata will degrade the value of library catalogs as primary tools.

Software Capabilities

Library software has developed incrementally over the decades since computers were first applied to bibliographic information in the second half of the twentieth century. It should come as no surprise that the earliest software was designed solely to handle information representing printed monographs (that is, books), and that, only in abbreviated form. By the end of the 1970s, enhancements ended the need to abbreviate data fields so severely—in some early library automation systems, personal names could not exceed 20 characters and titles could not exceed 30)—and enabled more kinds of data to be entered, successfully accommodating cataloging for printed serials, music, and maps. Still later, improvements accommodated specialized data needed to represent titles in more kinds of physical formats, connect records for whole titles and their parts, and link data for bibliographic, authority, acquisitions, and circulation functions.

Identification Issues

A glance through the literature of cataloging history can attest to the thorny problems concerning identification that emerged after 1978 when titles in formats other than printed books (videorecordings, visual images, music, and the like) were added to the library catalog. How to identify the format of a title and which terms to use in naming the formats were two principal issues. After much debate, the first issue was resolved by agreement to place an authorized keyword called a "general material designation" indicating the generic physical form in which a work appeared immediately following the title proper in the first area of description. In this way, catalogers created an early-warning system unlikely to be overlooked. If a retrieved entry for a video of Shakespeare's *Othello* displayed the line "*Othello* [videorecording] / by William Shakespeare," one could reasonably expect the searcher to notice that this version of *Othello* was not a book. General material designations did not give specific information about the type of videorecording, running time, recording medium, size, and so on. Those details were given in area 5, the physical description area, which began by giving the extent and a specific material designation for the item.

On the losing side of the debate were those who believed that information about the manifestation should appear only in the physical description area. Doing so, they argued, not only was sufficient to give searchers all the information they needed but did not interpose cataloger-constructed data within the sacrosanct territory of area 1 (title and statement of responsibility), which AACR2's rules required to be transcribed from the item being cataloged exactly as to wording, order, and spelling. The winning side agreed that disturbing area 1 by inserting something other than transcribed data was unfortunate but necessary, because searchers might not read all the way down to area 5 to discover that the item represented by the retrieved entry was a videorecording, not a book.

Disagreement ensued over the words to be used for general material designations. Eventually, two lists were developed, one for use by North Americans, the other for use by the British (AACR2, 1978).[2] The divergent lists have persisted to the time of this writing, with each side mostly satisfied with its choices. The British list contains fewer, more generic terms than the American list; for example, the British use only "graphic" whereas the North Americans use numerous terms including "art original," "art reproduction," "picture," and "technical drawing," among others. In recent years, tiny rumbles of dissatisfaction with the North American list have been heard in cataloging circles, not only because its terms are not as general as some prefer, but because terms have had to be added to represent physical manifestations that the existing terminology did not do an adequate job of representing.

Alternatives to One Integrated Catalog

One strategy for accommodating metadata is to offer it as a separate file within the catalog. This has the advantage of enabling those who prefer digital resources to search solely for that type of material in the most economical manner. Having a separate file for metadata also avoids adding large numbers of entries to catalogs that are already very large and mixing metadata up with cataloging for nondigital resources. These advantages are offset by the inability of searchers to find all the materials offered by the library by an author or on a subject as well as all the versions of a title. The main objective of the catalog to serve as an all-inclusive finding list, mandated in the nineteenth century by Charles Ammi Cutter,[3] is, thus, confounded. Searchers are obliged to conduct two (or more) searches just to examine a complete list of holdings matching their search term, no matter what kind of search it is.

No matter what arguments are mustered for and against an integrated catalog, the fact is that some searchers prefer it, while others do not. For some searchers, the integrated catalog offers the widest range of options in answer to their request and helps them discover unknown possibilities in their areas of interest. Similar to browsers who scan the shelves of a library for a likely book or video, these searchers are not bothered by long lists of titles in media or languages that they do not want, by having publication dates going back many years, and so on. For other searchers, the integrated catalog contains a host of things in which they are not interested and search requests retrieve more material than they wish to examine. They want to be able to exclude all types of titles in which they are not interested and concentrate their searches on the smallest number of titles that could fit their requests.

Fortunately, computerized catalogs can be created that allow both kinds of searchers to have their heart's desire, but only if their databases contain *all* the records for *all* the titles in the library's collections. Searchers who want only books, or only videos or, for that matter, only electronic resources, can narrow the range of retrievals by limiting their requests to their chosen medium. But if the catalog does not contain all the records and limits its database to selected media, searchers who want to see everything cannot satisfy their wishes with one search. The group of searchers who want smaller catalogs containing only the kinds of materials in which they are interested do not need to exclude titles from the catalog in media they wish to avoid; they need only frame their search requests in terms that do the excluding automatically as part of the search process. Technically speaking, the reverse could also be done—that is, searchers who want to see everything might frame their requests in terms of several databases that are wholly separate from one another—but at the time of this writing, it is more complicated and costly to do it this way.

Unstable URLs

Complicating the whole matter of incorporating metadata into existing public catalogs is the issue of unstable identifiers for electronic resources. Anyone who uses the Internet frequently is likely to encounter uniform resource locators (URLs, that is, addresses for electronic resources) taken from published directories, webliographies, research reports, conference handouts, and other sources that fail to respond as expected when searched. Instead, searchers may receive error messages stating that the addresses cannot be found or, sometimes, when they are lucky, a message explaining that the address has changed, with or without the new one. How can libraries plan to maintain high-quality catalogs if the addition of metadata is going to require so much updating? Which is better for patrons of the library—having no metadata or having a relatively high level of incorrect or useless metadata in the form of records that cannot be retrieved? Is there some middle ground in which librarians can be confident they are adding only "good" metadata to their catalogs, with "good" defined as information that will continue, at least for a reasonable period of time, to produce the expected results?

Political Problems

In any workplace, things get done through the efforts of the people who work there, and the policies and procedures accepted and understood by those people as governing their work activities. Together, the policies governing an activity, the procedures designed to accomplish the activity, and the people who do the work constitute the "politics" of the activity. Institutional policies about the creation and disposition of metadata are part of the politics of metadata. Added to the policies are the procedures designed to implement them and the people charged with doing the job. Political problems may affect any of these three components and include the following:

1. The need to coordinate work with multiple computer/OPAC suppliers or in-house computer support units

2. Perceptions on the part of members of cataloging units that metadata is inferior to their products and, therefore, cannot be coordinated with them

3. Perceptions of administrators that metadata is, essentially, a service matter, not a collection-related, bibliographic access, search and retrieval matter

4. Belief that different standards must be promulgated for online resources

Coordinating Work with Outside Suppliers and In-House Computer Support Units

Experience with computerizing circulation, cataloging, and other library functions has taught librarians something about the complexities of having to coordinate the work of more than one entity—vendors of hardware and software, institutional and/or library computer support units, and/or multiple internal departments—to complete tasks that, in the precomputer world, were the province of a single unit, vendor, or department. Metadata, by definition a computer-based product, involves the smooth coordination of a number of disparate entities in its creation and disposition.

Depending on the existing computer infrastructure within an individual library, metadata librarians might be expected to coordinate their activities with one or more outside suppliers of hardware, software, data, database management, and/or network services to the library as well as one or more internal units or departments in charge of local hardware, software, network, and/or data management systems. Understanding how each local system operates and negotiating paths that succeed in obtaining what is needed from each of the players may be no easy task, particularly if the metadata librarian's job description is new to the library and vaguely defined.

Perceptions of Metadata as Inferior to Traditional Cataloging

As was evident in earlier chapters in which various standards are described, metadata standards do not always address both the content and packaging of documents (as used here, the word "documents" means "items of library material") as specifically and precisely as library cataloging standards do. Because some metadata standards do not address all the elements and others address them in more general terms than library cataloging, librarians have tended to believe these standards necessarily produce inferior products.

If there are no rules, for example, about where to obtain the title of a document, it is possible that two people using a metadata standard might choose differing title wordings appearing in different parts of the document as the title for the document. Both would be following the "rules" of the metadata standard to give a title, but with no reason to prefer one wording instead of another, the results could differ. Two catalogers using AACR2, on the other hand, which directs them to prefer the title page wording over all other possibilities (with a few exceptions), can be expected to select the same title wording almost every time. If several wordings appear, library catalogers are directed to add notes and added entries for each variant wording, ensuring that searchers using any of the titles can succeed in locating the document.

Library cataloging also mandates authority control for name and subject term retrieval points, which results in the collocation of documents by or about a person and about a subject regardless of the words or spellings for them used by authors. Metadata standards do not always address the issue of authority control either for names or subject terms and, thus, permit using different words and/or different spellings for the same names or subjects. Failing to collocate items that were written by the same author or that cover the same subject is perceived by librarians as a poorer result for searchers, leading librarians to believe standards permitting such results are inferior to library standards. For the record, however, librarians ought to acknowledge that keyword access, which uses the language of documents being cataloged in preference to words from a controlled vocabulary, is a powerful search tool that gives important results, even if they are not the same results retrieved by authorized subject terms.

Why is all this a matter of concern? Because certain metadata standards may be applied to a great many more documents with less effort, time, and specialized knowledge than it takes to apply library standards to the same documents, leading bottom-line-oriented administrators to think that metadata standards are an attractive alternative to library cataloging, despite their drawbacks. Fearing the worst, library catalogers may leap to defend the high cost in time, labor, and expertise of their work by dismissing metadata as inferior, without discriminating among the array of available metadata standards or objectively evaluating metadata's real value.

Perceptions of Metadata as a Service Matter

Library cataloging relates to materials in the library's collection. Each catalog record usually describes a title owned by the library. In contrast, metadata relates to electronic resources to which a library buys a limited kind of access, but does not actually own. This difference is sometimes interpreted as making electronic resources a part of an electronic service rather than part of the library's collection. This interpretation subtly shifts the responsibility of providing bibliographic and intellectual access to electronic resources away from the library toward some other entity— perhaps, to the owner of the service, who is likely to be a distributor, or, perhaps, to the legal owner of the material, usually its publisher or creator.

Should differences in the details of ownership dictate how patrons obtain bibliographic and intellectual access, that is, the information they need to identify wanted electronic titles? Patrons might be quick to answer that if the material comes from the library—no matter how it gets there or in what form it appears—the library is responsible for providing bibliographic and intellectual access to it. As far as many patrons are concerned, electronic library materials are still library materials first and someone else's intellectual property second. After all, a book owned by a library does not become the library's intellectual property either, but in the case of books, there is no hesitation about providing a catalog record to make it possible for patrons to find the book in the library's collection. Why not do the same for an analogous item in electronic form?

A different conclusion can be drawn if one examines the difference in the cataloging libraries provide for books and for periodical articles. Libraries typically bear the full responsibility for providing the entire range of cataloging—description, access points, subject terms, classification numbers—for each book in their collections as well as for each periodical title, taken as a whole, but not for the articles that appear within the issues of the periodicals they buy. Instead, commercially produced indexing services traditionally have provided the bibliographic and intellectual access (that is, the "cataloging") for periodical articles—at least, for a selected group of titles chosen by the commercial producer. One of the problems libraries have had with access to periodical literature is that they cannot buy indexing solely for the periodical titles they purchase. They must buy what the commercial producer offers, which almost always includes some titles the library does not buy and does not include other titles it does buy. The library buys the indexing service. The producer of the service does the cataloging.

Some of the library's most prized electronic titles developed from yesterday's traditional indexing services. These services first were converted into digitized bibliographic databases. Later, the texts to which the bibliographic data related were added, creating "full-text" databases. Still later, distributors of the databases found it profitable to sell access to groups of databases, creating large aggregations that could be marketed to many kinds of information consumers, including libraries. Librarians have seemed reluctant to make the psychological leap from perceiving full-text databases as enhanced indexing services to accepting that they now function exactly like library materials. This begs another question: if electronic resources are library materials, why would libraries *not* be obligated to catalog them?

Perceptions of Metadata as Requiring Different Standards

Some librarians believe that metadata must be created using different standards than other types of library materials. In Chapters 4 and 5, however, we have shown how metadata compatible with current library standards is created. Such data can be integrated into the traditional cataloging workflow and displayed in the traditional public catalog without too much trouble. Gorman (2003) suggests that metadata will naturally evolve into something close to library standards and, besides, that librarians would not want to catalog everything on the Internet, only worthwhile titles selected specifically for their collections, much as they have always chosen small numbers of traditional titles from the universe of available publications.

Some librarians may have feared they would be overwhelmed by having to learn new and different methods for creating metadata. However, if previous experience with videorecordings, CD-ROMs, and other types of materials introduced in the last several decades is any indicator, no matter how strange the material may have first seemed and no matter how odd the rules pertaining to it may have appeared, once the decision was made to integrate it into the normal cataloging workflow, the rules were learned, and the material was quickly absorbed into the normal workflow. The key to success has always seemed to be the policy decision, not the type of material involved or the rules needed for cataloging the material. Nevertheless, in libraries that chose to take a different path, everything other than books was handled outside the normal cataloging workflow.

Recommendations and Conclusion

Without question, both the practical and the political problems must be overcome before a library can succeed in dealing with electronic resources. Either choice—to include metadata creation (that is, cataloging for electronic resources) with standard cataloging workflow or to bypass standard workflow and shift metadata creation to a different workflow—has some advantages and some disadvantages. In the paragraphs that follow, these are explored.

Possible Advantages to Bypassing the OPAC Workflow

Avoiding the existing cataloging unit and establishing a new and different unit to handle metadata creation gives an organization with a desire to do so a reason to enlarge its cataloging operations, expand its budget for metadata creation, hire new people—presumably with expert knowledge of electronic resources and metadata systems—and create a system that optimizes the workflow for this type of material. At the same time, it permits existing catalog operations to continue without being disturbed and without forcing the existing staff to go through a stressful, turbulent period of adjustment to new materials, new procedures, new methods, and new products. Bypassing the OPAC workflow makes it possible to place the metadata unit, organizationally, under a different umbrella, taking it away from those who focus on the catalog and bibliographic issues. Instead, the new unit might be placed in the hands of those who focus on service to end users, or, perhaps, those who deal with other automated systems, databases, networks, and similar kinds of high-tech matters.

Possible Disadvantages to Bypassing the OPAC Workflow

A key phrase in the previous paragraph is "an organization with a desire to do so...." Organizations that cannot or do not wish to enlarge their cataloging (or any other) operations will consider it a disadvantage to be required to have a separate unit for metadata. Instead, they will want to use existing staff, space, and workflow streams to accommodate the need for this new kind of cataloging, perhaps to save the cost of hiring new staff or, even if they do hire new people, having to revise their organizational chart, find space for the new unit, and accommodate all the day-to-day needs of a separate unit. Libraries that wish to integrate metadata into existing OPACs are also likely to find it desirable to keep all cataloging operations together in one unit to promote consistent decision making and uniform standards. Furthermore, those staff members in the library who possess the greatest expertise in cataloging would be put in charge of cataloging electronic resources, just as they are for all the other materials their library includes in its collections.

Suggested Recommendations

Whether or not a new administrative unit is formed for creating library metadata, certain issues need to be addressed, the most important of which is obtaining staff members who have the requisite knowledge. If a new staff member is hired, knowledge of electronic resources and metadata standards can be a required qualification for the job. If members already part of the cataloging staff are expected to handle the work, they need to acquire the knowledge needed to do it. Although it is possible for every member of a catalog department to know how to work with every type of material, more often individuals specialize in working with particular kinds of material, paying attention to and keeping up with nothing but the rules and tools applying to that material. In this situation, it might be easiest and most effective to hire someone new to work with metadata, unless a member of the staff expresses the desire to expand the scope of his or her job and obtain the needed knowledge.

Recommendation 1: Make certain the library has staff members available with knowledge of electronic resources, metadata, standards and systems, and so on, whether by hiring someone new with the appropriate qualifications or by enabling a current staff member to acquire the requisite knowledge.

Recommendation 2: Make certain the library has the budget to provide adequate equipment and supplies to support metadata operations.

No matter who handles the creation of metadata for a library and in what sort of administrative unit the work is done, needed equipment, tools, and supplies must be made available. At the least, a workstation with sufficient power, speed, and memory is needed, along with the online and offline source materials, which might involve obtaining access to new databases. In addition, ancillary supplies, such as those for printing, must be provided.

At this writing, if advertisements for metadata librarians are any indication, there is a great deal of mystery surrounding the future of metadata units, metadata products, and their disposition and use. Some advertisements have said explicitly that the metadata librarian is expected to create his or her own job description, be prepared to work independently, and be qualified to be entrepreneurial regarding metadata products. This last qualification is one that is not frequently requested for successful employment, at least not in the nonprofit library world. Several advertisements stated that the metadata librarian would begin working as part of a cataloging or technical services unit of the library but was expected to branch out and, possibly, establish a separate metadata unit if it seemed warranted. Thus, it appears unlikely that libraries are clear about their vision of the boundaries of the job or its outcomes.

Recommendation 3: Take a flexible approach to the place of metadata in the library and be prepared to accommodate administrative changes that emerge, as appropriate to the institution, its setting, and its mission.

To conclude, this chapter has explored some of the practical and political problems of incorporating metadata into the library's workflow and output. Issues that a library needs to consider and make decisions about relate to administrative placement, staffing, workflow, products or output, and the dissemination of metadata products. Although the traditions of each individual library may dictate the decisions to some degree, it would not be wise to allow tradition alone to rule. Too much is yet to be discovered about the creation and uses of metadata to permit traditional attitudes to close doors that might lead to innovative systems and services based on this exciting intellectual product.

Notes

1. In an assessment of undergraduate preferences for electronic resources titled "Cultivating Our Garden: The Impact of Digital Full Text Periodicals on the Liberal Arts College Library," Barbara Doyle-Wilch and Carla Tracy (2000, pp. 3–4) observe, plaintively: "Now, any article that is instantly available in electronic full text—regardless of its appropriateness—is nearly irresistible to the busy undergraduate." Many authors echo Doyle-Wilch and Tracy's sentiments since the chapter appeared.

2. The principal difference between the lists is that the British terms are fewer and more general; the North American list is more than twice as long and uses more specific terminology, particularly for visual images (Gorman and Winkler, 1978, p. 21).

3. Cutter (1904, p. 12) said the purposes (or "objects") of a library catalog are "1. To enable a person to find a book when one of the following is known: the author; the title; the subject; 2. To show what the library has: by a given author; on a given subject; in a given kind of literature; 3. To assist in the choice of a book: as to the edition (bibliographically); as to its character (literary or topical)."

Bibliography

Cutter, Charles A. (1904). *Rules for a Dictionary Catalog.* 4th ed. Washington, DC: Government Printing Office.

Doyle-Wilch, Barbara, and Carla Tracy (2000). "Cultivating Our Garden: The Impact of Digital Full Text Periodicals on the Liberal Arts College Library." In Susan D. McGinnis, ed. *Electronic Collection Management* (pp. [1]–16). New York: Haworth Information Press.

Gorman, Michael. (2003). "Cataloguing in an Electronic Age." In *Electronic Cataloging: AACR2 and Metadata for Serials and Monographs,* pp. 10–15. Edited by Sheila S. Intner, et al. New York: Haworth Information Press.

Edited by Michael Gorman and Paul Winkler. *Anglo-American Cataloguing Rules.* 2nd ed. (1987). Chicago: American Library Association.

Part 2

**Impact on Current and Future
Collections and Services**

Chapter 7

Digital Collections and Digital Libraries

Any review of "current" digital library projects is likely to become outdated very quickly, but today's innovative projects are also likely to become tomorrow's pioneering models, and knowledge of these endeavors always has historic interest. With those things in mind, this chapter reviews a small selection of the growing number of existing projects in which metadata is being employed to create digital collections and libraries, and then analyzes the elements these potential models exhibit.

A Selection of Current Digital Projects

The Colorado Digitization Project

Spearheaded by a one-year federal Library Services and Technology Act grant administered through the Colorado State Library, the Colorado Digitization Project (CDP; http://www.cdpheritage.org, accessed January 20, 2005) started in 1998. The project's first Web site was mounted a year later, funded by a second grant, this one from the Institute of Museum and Library Services. CDP is, at this writing, in the middle of its second strategic plan, a plan that began in 2003 and ends in 2006. No longer dependent entirely on federal grants, CDP has expanded its funding sources to include state grants as well.

The project's Web site has been redesigned several times, each time increasing the number and range of its offerings. At this writing, the homepage features several basic sets of links:

1. Links to databases of historic scenes ("Colorado's Main Streets" and "Western Trails")

2. Links to early newspapers ("Colorado's Historic Newspaper Collection")

3. Links to resources for educators and other people interested in learning about digitization

4. Links to partner organizations, including the Colorado State Library, the Colorado Virtual Library, Rocky Mountain Public Broadcasting System (PBS), and the Bibliographic Center for Research (BCR)

In addition, news and information about the CDP itself can be accessed through links from the homepage.

CDP operates by means of a working group infrastructure involving representatives from many communities within Colorado, including archives, libraries, museums, and historical societies. As a result of this collaboration, choices made for metadata and scanning standards and the collection development policies for the Web site satisfy a great many people and answer a wide variety of needs. Among the offerings are links to all Colorado cultural heritage institutions with Web access; workshops and guidelines to assist cultural heritage organizations in planning digital resource projects and managing digital assets; and resources to assist elementary and secondary school teachers in teaching about cultural heritage. CDP maintains four regional scanning centers and encourages local participation; with the Colorado Alliance of Research Libraries, it established and continues to develop the Heritage Colorado database, which, it says, "provides a single point of access to the digital collections of Colorado's cultural heritage institutions" ("Colorado Digitization Plan Program," n.d.). A developing initiative involves collaboration with four other western states—Kansas, Nebraska, Wyoming, and Utah—to expand access to digital content about the West beyond Colorado's borders.

CDP's metadata standard is the Dublin Core. The project's mission incorporates teaching Coloradoans about the application of Dublin Core and managing local digital projects. Without a doubt, the commitment to develop metadata and digitization expertise as widely as possible among members of the staffs of libraries, museums, historical societies, and archives, so all these communities within the state can share one metadata standard successfully, has been an important part of its program. The strategy not only facilitated CDP's growth but also avoided having to cope at some future date with many different local metadata schemes adopted without regard for uniformity in the choice of standards. Along with training, CDP's commitment to broad collaboration and its decision to be inclusive right from the start appears to have had a positive impact.

CORC (Cooperative Online Resource Catalog)

Initiated in 1998 as an Office of Research project by OCLC, Inc., the bibliographic network, the Cooperative Online Resource Catalog (CORC) responded to member libraries' tentative experiments in cataloging electronic resources with what has since become a valuable service. Early goals of the project were to harvest Web resources, create metadata for them, and support automated compilations of the resources by subject into "pathfinders" ("OCLC Cooperative Online Resource Catalog," n.d.). (Pathfinders in libraries are, typically, guides written by reference librarians that help searchers get started in a subject field and find material on desired topics, without covering the field exhaustively. The name seems apt for CORC compilations. They are not exhaustive either but help get a searcher started searching the Web in a subject area by listing preselected sites that contain accurate, pertinent information.) Aggregation of sites on similar subject matter was accomplished with relative ease by means of subject headings and/or classification numbers assigned to the resources when they were cataloged.[1]

At its inception, CORC supported only Dublin Core and MARC records but planned to add more metadata options, naming the TEI Header and Encoded Archival Description (EAD) schemas on its immediate agenda ("OCLC Cooperative Online Resource Catalog," n.d.). In 1999, the experimental phase of the project ended and CORC was "transitioned" into a regular service. The OCLC Web site says: "All features of the CORC service were incorporated into the new integrated cataloging service, *OCLC Connexion*, in 2002."

If a library wishes to create a digital archive of Web sites it has selected for its collections, OCLC can provide it. The network conforms to the Open Archival Information System (OAIS) and other international standards and uses the Metadata Encoding and Transmission Standard (METS). OCLC's commitment to maintaining standards is predictable and understandable because the network has long played a leadership role in information-related standards making bodies, both nationally and internationally.

Features of OCLC's Digital Archive service include using one familiar interface for cataloging and archiving; locating and archiving all or part of selected Web sites automatically (i.e., harvesting by predetermined parameters); grabbing the existing metadata automatically and using it to create a standard catalog record; and choosing to store selected and cataloged material either locally or in OCLC's network repository. The name "CORC" has disappeared as a separate entity from the OCLC Web site (when searching "CORC" at the site, one is led either to *Connexion* or the original Office of Research project blurb), but the program it represents presumably continues to grow as network members add new cataloging for the electronic material they have selected for their collections.

The California Digital Library

Initiated in 1997, the California Digital Library (CDL; http://www.cdlib.org, accessed January 31, 2005) may be seen as a natural outgrowth of long-established cooperative efforts by the University of California to share resources among its campuses effectively, particularly by means of computer technology.[2] According to its Web site, CDL's mission is as follows: "Harnessing technology and innovation, and leveraging the intellectual and cultural resources of the UC, the CDL supports the assembly and creative use of the world's scholarship and knowledge for the UC libraries and the communities they serve" ("California Digital Library, Mission," n.d.). Given the resources of the University of California, which is the largest multicampus university in the United States (and perhaps the world), it is no surprise that at this writing, the CDL deemed itself one of the largest digital libraries in the world (California Digital Library, n.d.). In January 2005, however, a group of research libraries that announced the intention of developing a global digital library partnership with Google (see, e.g., Fialkoff, 2005). Upon its establishment, this new venture will likely be the world's largest scholarly resource.

The CDL Web site offers links to seven programs' information in addition to the basic homepage links to descriptions and news about the CDL itself, advice for potential vendors, and advice for internal users (i.e., UC library staff):

    1.   *CaliforniaDigitalLibrary.org*—an aggregation of scholarly Web sites

2. *Counting California*—information, including images and statistics, about the State of California that users can search and browse by topic

3. *eScholarship Editions*—a database of approximately 1,400 e-books from academic presses, mainly scholarly treatises on a broad range of subjects; under some subject headings, for example, Jewish Studies, only one title is available, whereas under others, more than a hundred titles are available; searchable by a variety of bibliographic elements and keywords; indexes can be browsed; titles are displayed in much the same manner that amazon.com displays its offerings, with photographs of the covers and bibliographic information displaying first, followed by the pages of the book in sequence

4. *eScholarship Repository*—a browsable aggregation of approximately 5,800 research papers

5. *Melvyl Catalog*—the combined library catalog of all the UC campus libraries, which, as of 2005, included 32 million items (note: the term "items" does not mean discrete titles and may include many duplicate copies of a title)

6. *Online Archive of California (OAC)*—historical material from California's historical societies, museums, and archives, including textual matter and visual images

7. *SearchLight*—an aggregation of publicly available databases; divided into two parts, one for science and technology, and one for social sciences and humanities

CDL, which uses XML as its markup language, is in the forefront of standards development, with memberships in the Coalition for Networked Information (CNI), the Digital Library Federation (DLF), the National Information Standards Organization (NISO, the U.S. national standards-making organization for all library and information related standards), and the Scholarly Publishing Academic Resources Coalition (SPARC), among others. CDL staff members participate on relevant committees and advisory boards, including the Metadata Encoding and Transmission Standard (METS), Open Archives Initiative (OAI), OpenURL, and so on. Thus, it is not surprising that CDL is committed to consistency with standard metadata encoding, although it does not require others adopt particular metadata schemas, only that those used be consistent with recognized standards or, if they are customized or proprietary, that they be made available to CDL users without charge. For example, in its advice to vendors, it says: "Access to the resource must be simple, and should involve standard formats, protocols, and applications already in widespread use (e.g., HTTP, HTML, PDF, GIF, XML, etc.). We discourage specialized client applications, but, when required for access to the resources they should be available at no charge, be available for multiple platforms, and be easily acquired and implemented" ("Technical Requirements," n.d.).

CDL's scholarly focus is not unusual among library-initiated digital libraries, but its huge size is. Although CDL's mission is focused primarily on the needs of its own community members, primarily academic scholarship and curriculum support, its resources also satisfy the informational needs of members of the general public, even if they are not studying or teaching at UC. For people who can employ the kinds of information CDL provides in their daily work, such as teachers and community activists; people who seek information for personal projects, such as history buffs and art collectors; and all sorts of others interested solely in adding to their store of knowledge, CDL offers a wealth of valuable, well-organized, easily searched material.

JSTOR (Journal Storage)

JSTOR was initially funded by the Andrew W. Mellon Foundation as a pilot project intended to help struggling research university libraries resolve problems concerning scholarly journals. Among the problems JSTOR addressed were difficulties maintaining paper copies of the journals in good condition—both providing the increasing amounts of shelf space the materials consumed and protecting the paper on which they were printed; the high cost of buying burgeoning numbers of available titles; and difficulties, such as the mounting costs and legal and logistical issues in giving interlibrary loans for journal articles to growing numbers of scholars. The project began by providing electronic access to backfiles of ten journals in the fields of economics and history. It met with such enthusiastic success that JSTOR was officially established as an independent organization in August 1995 ("The History of JSTOR," n.d.).

At this writing, JSTOR lists the participation of 1,332 U.S. institutions and 965 international institutions located in 86 countries as well as of 280 publishers, mostly university presses and scholarly societies. More than 450 journal titles are accessible online, containing nearly 4,000,000 articles. Approximately 25% of the articles are available in full-text versions complete with graphics, equations, charts, and all the other nontextual accompaniments typically lost in ordinary preservation microfilming projects ("Facts and Figures," n.d.). To accomplish this, JSTOR uses OCR (Optical Character Recognition) scanning technology, which is more costly than ordinary text scanning. The benefit of sustaining the higher cost is that using OCR does more than reproduce the text of the material, which can be discarded safely afterward, it enhances access to the texts by making them fully searchable as well as retaining the visuals authors added to illustrate them ("The History of JSTOR," n.d.).

According to Guthrie (2000), "In JSTOR's early days, much of the infrastructure developed to support the resource was built locally by technical staff at the University of Michigan and Princeton University. As the organization has matured and the importance of the resource has increased, we have begun to migrate that technological infrastructure to more open standards. For example, the original bibliographic metadata for articles was stored according to the specification developed for the TULIP project [i.e., a local university library program]. We are now in the process of migrating that data to XML with a specific DTD." Presumably, that conversion is now completed, and XML is the markup language of choice for the project.

LC's National Digital Library Program

The Library of Congress has always played a leadership role in important areas related to digital library development. It focuses on standards—setting and promulgating them. Its mission includes exploring new ways to make information readily accessible through cataloging, indexing, and classification, to which metadata is closely related. It is the largest and richest repository of materials on and about American history and culture. It has a long history of cooperating both with American libraries and its foreign peers—the national libraries of other countries—working with all of them in numerous ways to build better collections and utilize information technologies effectively. Together with its U.S. peers, the National Library of Medicine, the National Agricultural Library, and National Archives and Records Administration, the Library of Congress contributes to and benefits from the use of digital technologies.

Foremost among the Library of Congress's initiatives is the American Memory Project. It began as a pilot project in 1990, anticipating, in a way, that the Internet and World Wide Web would soon be the world's information superhighway, enabling American Memory's contents to reach vast numbers of people. According to its mission statement, American Memory is "a digital record of American history and creativity... [a] chronicle [of] historical events, people, places, and ideas that continue to shape America, serving the public as a resource for education and lifelong learning" ("Mission and History," n.d.). In 2000, with support and cooperation from many public and private partners, the Library reported American Memory had amassed more than 5 million items online—images, texts, recordings, films, speeches, paintings, and so on—and it has not stopped expanding. All materials in American Memory are accessible without charge ("Mission and History," n.d.).

An undated overview of the program states: "American Memory employs national-standard and well established industry-standard formats for many digital reproductions, e.g., texts encoded with Standard Generalized Markup Language (SGML) and images stored in Tagged Image File Format (TIFF) files or compressed with the Joint Photographic Experts Group (JPEG) algorithm. In other cases, the lack of well established standards has led to the use of emerging formats, e.g., RealAudio (for audio), Quicktime (for moving images), and MrSid (for maps)" ("Overview," n.d.). Although one can assume the specifics have evolved, they represent state-of-the-art standards at a point in time not very long ago. In 2003, the Library reported adopting the OAI (Open Archives Initiative) Protocol for Metadata Harvesting (Arms, 2003). The project promoted inclusiveness by employing the Dublin Core metadata schema as well as MARCXML (a shift from MARCSGML). That year, it also reported exploring the use of Metadata Object Description Schema (MODS) as a potential enrichment (Arms, 2003).

In 2005, American Memory is the umbrella for numerous initiatives, including training for teachers in educational uses of American Memory data, partnering with people and organizations that are sources for additional data, scanning programs, and research into technical and metadata development. One of the most exciting new programs in progress at this writing is StoryCorps, an effort to record and preserve the stories of ordinary Americans at do-it-yourself oral history stations. (These seem to be patterned after the do-it-yourself photo booths that were a staple in 20th-century dime-store emporiums.) At this writing, two stations have opened in New York City, one in Grand Central Terminal and one in the World Trade Center area, and the Library is funding two mobile stations to travel around the United States. Participants can use the station individually or in groups (such as families, friends, teams, colleagues) and record what they wish for up to 40 minutes, employing free online assistance in formulating appropriate questions and a productive format for their session. Afterward, they receive a CD-ROM containing the recording and are asked for permission to add their story to the American Memory archives. One can only imagine how many thousands of American stories StoryCorps will preserve.

VARIATIONS

VARIATIONS is not an acronym. It is the name given to the digital music library at Indiana University (IU), which originated in 1995. In its original version, VARIATIONS contained more than 7,000 digital audio titles, available at computer workstations in IU's Cook Music Library and other selected locations on the university campus network.

Sponsored jointly by the university's music library and digital library program, links on the original homepage, headed "Access to VARIATIONS," included the current semester's course reserves (VARIATIONS is still used for course reserves), an explanation of how to access nonreserve recordings via IU's public catalog, and an experimental prototype of online musical score access ("Indiana University VARIATIONS Homepage," n.d.). Other internal links were available to information about VARIATIONS, including two published papers and an announcement made when the project was initiated in 1995, as well as two presentations about it, daily usage statistics, and the project's staff. External links to the music library's homepage and the IU digital library homepage were also available.

In 2002, the project was redeveloped, and a new version was established, named VARIATIONS2, with the goal of creating a true multimedia digital music library. Grants of approximately $3 million from the National Science Foundation and the National Endowment for the Humanities helped to fund the project. Among its aims was researching metadata standards as well as system architecture and network services ("Variations2 Overview," n.d.).[3] One can imagine a variety of mark-up issues and technical problems surround digitizing musical media, which can involve just about all the printed, aural, and visual formats, both singly and in combination. Matters nonmusicians think of as simple and uniform, such as music notation, are actually extremely complex, with many notational systems in use in different countries and at different periods of time. When one thinks about it, one might remember that medieval notation looks different than modern notation, and a good many people also know that some modern composers take liberties with notation to allow "ad lib" in their pieces, going far beyond embellishments in cadenzas. However, these few examples barely begin to address the list of notational systems posted on the VARIATIONS Web site, all of which must be accommodated by metadata for digitized music materials. As previous mentioned, notation is only one such element.

VARIATION2's homepage offers many more links than the original project, twenty-two in all. Fourteen links go to an internal user guide and other units within IU, but nine more take the viewer to related projects elsewhere—five "related" links to the Distributed Digital Music Archives and Libraries project and projects at Johns Hopkins University, the University of Michigan, Michigan State University, and the Online Music Recognition and Searching project—OMRAS—a joint effort of the University of Massachusetts Amherst and Kings College London; four "other" links go to the Digital Libraries Initiative Phase 2, data from two ISMIR (Music Information Retrieval) conferences, and to a music-related project at the University of Washington.

Among the musical materials listed as available within the VARIATIONS2 digital library at this writing are both classical and popular pieces. Classical works include symphonic works, string quartets, concertos, and sonatas by well-known (Bach, Beethoven, Haydn, Mozart) and less well-known (Bristow, Chávez, Seeger, Bergsma) composers, and vocal selections including Gregorian chant, art songs, and operas. Digitized in connection with the pilot project's course support, a selection of twentieth-century classical works can also be accessed. Popular works include selections written by George Gershwin, Harry Warren, Benny Goodman, Miles Davis, Thelonius Monk, and Charlie Parker, along with selections by jazz ensembles. Many Beatles albums are included as are other rock music selections by Pink Floyd, Captain Beefheart, and Van Morrison and one rap selection ("Variations2 User Guide," n.d.).

Although VARIATIONS appears to be maturing more slowly than other projects described here, it is growing without neglecting its primary audience—IU music faculty and students. Whether the larger music world will embrace it fully and whether the University wishes to see VARIATIONS become a different kind of entity with a mission that places the needs of the larger music world first and foremost is yet to be seen.

Issues and Problems Encountered In Digital Projects

Three types of issues emerge from this small exploration of digital library projects: practical, political, and financial issues. In all three arenas, issues occur on at least two levels—the leadership level, where such things as policies, goals, and budget allocations are decided, and the operational level, where interfaces, services, and support systems are involved. Throughout a project, the focus of project leaders on real service outcomes is critical—namely, what useful products end users can get out of the digital library and at what cost to each individual in time, money, and effort.

In the planning phase of a digital library project, decisions on questions such as who should participate in the project and what roles participants can play may determine whether the project has the potential to flourish. Although any amount of digitized material, however small the total, might be helpful to a few, having enough material in all its appropriate varieties to be desirable to very large audiences is another story. Projects promulgated by institutions with long track records in cooperation accustomed to dealing with huge numbers of materials (such as OCLC and the University of California) seem well prepared for such ventures.

Dedicating enough money to see a project through to full-service operability is an obvious problem. It is not surprising that projects led by institutions or entities with large, readily available user populations (like the University of California and the State of Colorado, respectively) are able to obtain needed resources more easily than smaller ones attempting to "go it alone." Small institutions with visions that outweigh their pocketbooks seem to have found it advisable to join with peers to achieve a monetary critical mass. Envisioning a project large enough to be valuable to more than a small segment of local users should be considered, because thinking too small sometimes precludes sufficient potential growth for success.

Decisions in the implementation phase of a project, although seemingly less broad, visionary, and politically charged, can have equal impacts on the project's future success. These descussions involve the following:

1. *Standards*: Adoption of a uniform standard or a set of standards that can coexist without difficulty—a political issue.

2. *Costs*: High startup costs that may not show a dramatic payoff for some time—both a financial and a political issue.

3. *Staffing and Training*: Training staff to use the selected standards(s)—a practical issue involving funding, opportunities and time for the training, ongoing updating of skills, and the sustained commitment of the institution(s) involved over time.

4. *Commitment*: Sustained commitment to continuous improvement, development, and growth of a project—it is not terribly difficult to get people excited about the initial development of a digital library project, but it is hard to sustain the same level of commitment over time. When commitment to a project is linked to a single person within an institution and the person leaves, a project may languish from neglect, especially if the vacated position is not filled immediately. Further, the person or persons hired to replace the committed staff member may lack the same level of interest and commitment and be unwilling to "walk the walk and talk the talk" to keep it funded and staffed. In particular, when the committed staff member is a high-level administrator (e.g., the director of a library or chief curator of a museum), the whole project may fail should the person's replacement have priorities that do not include digital library project development.

The projects described in this chapter demonstrate features that seem to be important for the success of a digital library project:

1. *Long-term commitment.* At this writing, CDP is seven years old; CDL is eight. Their longevity attests to the nature of the commitment of their developers, which was not to experiment with a digital library and, then, after a year or two, letting the idea drop; but, instead, to start it, keep it operating, and ensure its continued growth as a high-priority program. The administrative positioning of CDL in the University of California President's Office attests to its priority and growing value to the University and the larger community beyond it.

2. *Continuous development and expansion.* The fact that the CDL Web site has been redesigned several times is evidence of continuous development. The huge number of institutions and publishers participating in JSTOR has grown from a tiny core of pioneers. In a digital library project, additions and improvements may be expected to go on indefinitely, unlike other services where, once an optimal level of activity is reached, a service may require only routine growth and maintenance (for example, an automated circulation system).

3. *Development of partnerships.* Although both the CDP and CDL began as statewide endeavors, both have developed into nationwide assets—perhaps, one could even say, global assets. The development of partnerships outside the project's immediate community—in the case of CDL, with nonuniversity partners; in the case of CDP, with non-library and

out-of-state partners—adds both to the growth of potential contributors to project resources and of potential audiences for project products. JSTOR demonstrated the value of partnering with commercial organizations as well as nonprofit institutions and organizations, having journal producers as well as consumers within its network of members. VARIATIONS and VARIATIONS2, while moving more slowly than the other projects in this area, indicated that it, too, seeks partners with whom it shares common interests in digitizing musical material. Being limited to a highly specialized discipline makes expansion somewhat more difficult.

4. *Careful planning and consensus building.* Thorough, collaborative, long-term planning was an integral part of the CDP program, evidenced by the formal establishment and public communication of multiyear plans. The first plan was initiated as soon as CDP's funding was secure and involved the dedication of many partners to its goals and objectives, evidence of successful consensus building. To some degree, consensus building was less of an issue for CDL because UC was a huge entity sizable enough by itself to require that outsiders who wanted to participate had to conform to its rules and regulations. But the very size of the UC nucleus prompted the need for careful planning so as to preclude wasting the university's inputs of money and staff time allocated to the project. Fortunately, UC had a strong tradition of cooperative planning for automated library services on which to build, going back many decades to the start of the Melvyl catalog.

5. *Securing the funding.* There is no doubt that digital libraries require large inputs of funds to pay for staff, the required technological infrastructure (equipment, software, telecommunications, etc.), and the myriad other costs involved in setting up a digital library. The examples listed here took millions of dollars to get started, provided in the main by government grants. Skimping on startup expenditures by minimizing the amount of material to be digitized, trying to run the project with insufficient staff, or adopting nonstandard methods because they cost less than conforming to standards is likely to have negative impacts down the line.

6. *Securing the personnel.* In addition to money, a digital library project must have knowledgeable, competent, reliable people to make needed decisions and run its operations. Finding such people is never an easy task, especially if planners want them to have professional library expertise as well as knowledge of computers and the digital world. Advertisements for metadata librarians sometimes offer larger salaries than are typical for comparable personnel but ask for the kinds of qualifications more frequently found in the business world, such as entrepreneurial skills and the ability to develop products and identify audiences.

7. *Adoption of standards.* In the case of CDP, a single metadata standard—the Dublin Core—was adopted. Perhaps Dublin Core was chosen as its standard because the project emerged from long-established statewide networking originating decades earlier through OCLC, originator of Dublin Core,[4] and also because a major impetus behind the digitization

project came from the library community. In recent years, however, the library community has embraced more metadata schemas, opening the door to new contributors and new communities of users for library-organized digital projects. In addition, research into developing "translations" from one metadata schema to another, called "crosswalks," has helped librarians and nonlibrarians bridge the gap that separates them. The Library of Congress, which also uses Dublin Core, has found it flexible and easily used by nonlibrarians as well.

8. *Inclusiveness.* All the projects described here have, at some point, begun to welcome newcomers to their circles. For example, the CDP invites all Colorado educational, cultural, and historical institutions into the project. Each of these institutions, no matter how small or seemingly insignificant, possesses unique resources that could potentially be added to the CDP, making it even more comprehensive and useful than it is at present. Even VARIATIONS, which seems to have the fewest collaborating partners, is expanding its reach beyond the borders of Indiana University.

9. *Participant education.* The Library of Congress, as might be expected, is investing heavily in training at all levels, from Library staff to participants in the StoryCorps program, but each of the projects described here involve some kinds of participant education. In the Colorado project, for example, educating and training as many members of the staffs of participating institutions and all other similar institutions as possible was a primary goal. Getting these participants to join the project and/or empowering them to be able to run their own mini-projects independently likely contributed to its rate of growth and economic viability. Unlike the CDL, which began with a "captive" audience of UC faculty and students, including many who could contribute scholarly material to the databases, CDP needed to consider how it might prompt the growth of both users and resources. Participant education seems to be a powerful tool. It ensures that users become proficient searchers and also empowers them to contribute to the ongoing development of the digital library.

More needs to be done to investigate the benefits of educating Web site users in becoming partners, themselves, in digital projects. Education in the processes of resource creation and delivery as well as in how to take advantage of resource provision may be a feature common to cooperative projects lacking profit making motives, simply because no member of such a partnership has enough money or staff to carry out such a project alone. JSTOR's history offers evidence of this model. Nevertheless, it is a feature worth emulating, even for projects having the usual commercial goal of making a profit.

Profits can be generated in more than one way. The ideal profit scheme is to charge high prices for something that costs very little along with selling a lot of it. Some companies increase their profits by reducing costs; others by raising prices; some by expanding their markets; others by diversifying their product line; and still others by doing combinations of some or all of these strategies. Consider the matter of costs. Resource provision alone, which is typically the path taken by commercial organizations (their attitude seems to be, "we'll give you access to the data, but how we get it, process it, and deliver it to you is totally and completely our company secret"), involves also supplying large amounts of user support costing enormous amounts of money. When users are ignorant about how data is created, processed, arranged, or delivered, they can hardly be faulted for failing to understand how to manipulate it effectively. Without knowledge of the backstory, they are always dependent on a disembodied kind of user support. If a company lowers costs by cutting its user support to the point where it fails to meet user needs, enthusiasm for the resources themselves, no matter how terrific they are, wanes. It seems obvious that when obtaining information is troublesome, searchers will do without it.[5] On the other hand, the notion that teaching a customer how to do what the company does in providing resources would destroy the monetary value of its products is a powerful barrier both to keeping costs low and maximizing development opportunities.

Successes and Failures of Metadata In Practice

Metadata does not succeed or fail by itself. One judges if it facilitates or obstructs access to the digital collections to which it has been applied. If the digital collection fails to include the kinds of materials its users want or does not have the range and depth of materials its users require, the best metadata available cannot improve it. Therefore, in evaluating metadata, it should be established that the digital collection itself includes the materials needed by its intended users in total numbers of documents as well as in document coverage, formats, variety, breadth, and depth. Once a good collection is gathered, however, metadata has real impacts on user success in locating wanted items from the mass of available materials. "Good" metadata is understandable and complete and facilitates user success as well as mitigates search failure; "bad" metadata (defined as failing to provide adequate routes of access for users) causes confusion and thwarts user success, despite wanted materials being present in the collection.

Consider library cataloging, which many think of as a kind of proto-metadata. Traditional library cataloging has had a checkered track record fulfilling its role as the primary finding tool for collections of books and other offline library materials. Library cataloging tends to be precise, but shortcuts dictated by technology (e.g., the limitations of card size), staffing (such as the need, in precomputer days, for armies of catalogers and filers), and cost (such as the high price of doing authority control) often resulted in less-than-optimal cataloging and made it difficult for users to locate and interpret the cards in the catalog. Even optimal cataloging has its problems. But torn between spending limited funds on materials or better cataloging for materials, many library directors opted for the former, believing that if they had the materials someone wanted, those users would ask librarians for help in finding them. Statistics were rarely gathered and almost never reported on how many people did not find what they wanted and left the library without seeking help.

It was not until the advent of computers, shared cataloging networks, and high volumes of resource sharing that the value of "good" cataloging—defined as full records conforming to authority control and formatted uniformly according to standard rules and protocols—became crystal clear. In the days of card catalogs, users who failed to decipher the library catalog were expected to consult a reference librarian. If they left without doing so, it was too bad, but no disaster. Going away empty-handed was considered a poor choice on the part of the user, because the library provided a catalog and reference assistance, and, if need be, users could browse the shelves until they found something that would "do," even if it was not the title originally sought. Since online cataloging became the rule in libraries, this has changed. Librarians now realize that good cataloging saves money by reducing the total amount of original cataloging work that must be done (whether in-house or outsourced) and increasing the amount of interlibrary borrowing that can be done. If libraries want to share in network riches, they must conform to standards.

Digital libraries differ significantly from traditional library collections, and not only because they are online, although that is the most important and obvious difference. Digital libraries are likely to be very large, quickly growing, frequently changing databases; they are likely to be collaborative efforts; they are likely to include more diverse types of materials; and their users do very little searching while they are at the digital library's home institution, if it has only one. As a result, asking a librarian how to find something one believes should be in the database but does not show up in answer to a search query may not be an option. (Some Web sites offer online chat with a librarian, but it is far from the rule, and for familiar reasons: high cost and lack of available staff with the requisite knowledge.) Without standard methods for describing database documents and their contents, maintaining authority control, and so on, access to the documents suffers.

Reports in the literature on experiments that evaluate the performance of several metadata schemas applied to the same digital library are rare. Numerous articles and book chapters as well as online advice discuss selecting an appropriate metadata schema if one is starting a digital library, and reports of already-established digital libraries often describe how the schema being used was selected (and, sometimes, why it was selected over other schemas that were not chosen). Once chosen, however, few people go back to ask about what the library's performance might be if a different schema was applied. That kind of critical evaluation remains a mystery.

An evolution has taken place since the 1990s, when digital library projects began flourishing, but it is not clear that one metadata schema was changed for another that could have been chosen in its place at the same point in time. Rather, metadata schemas seem to change because new schemas develop that possess features missing in the original schema. In fact, new schemas are developed *because* the added or changed features are desirable. One thing is clear, however—standard schemas are nearly always preferred over customized or proprietary schemas that cannot be incorporated easily into a multi-institutional, multi-database, multi-community environment.

Given a choice between a perfect but unique metadata schema utterly lacking in interoperability and a moderately good schema that gets high marks for interoperability, most experts recommend the latter. In part, this is because digital libraries are, by their very nature, better when they are bigger and more diverse, and to get as big and diverse as possible, it takes more than one institution, library, or other data generating entity. The likelihood that the originators of a digital library project intend to be the sole contributors to it for all time is minuscule compared with the likelihood they will seek partners. In a collaborative environment, interoperability trumps perfection every time.

Other features of "good" metadata are scalability, relevance, and adequate description of the kinds of data elements for which the library's users search. Some problems of library-oriented metadata are attributable to the fact that data elements considered essential in business and industry were not particularly important to libraries, such as copyright ownership, contract terms, user eligibility, and provenance. In the collaborative environment of digital libraries, relevance to multiple user communities may require the application of more than one metadata schema to the same digital data.

A Suggested Model

The foregoing discussions of six current digital library projects help to suggest a flexible model for establishing digital collections, including selecting appropriate metadata schemas. The individual projects arose within different types of parent bodies, having different missions, user populations, and materials, and each project differs from the others in its primary goals as well as in its size, contents, partnerships, growth patterns, usage, and so on. Nevertheless, they share some commonalities that can be useful in modeling new digital library projects.

Despite their differences, each of the six projects described in this chapter seems to exhibit the following ten characteristics:

1. Strong leadership able to achieve consensus about goals

2. Adequate funding

3. Substantial infrastructure

4. A pool of materials to be digitized

5. Commitment to a long-term future

6. Adoption of standards

7. Knowledgeable staff

8. Ongoing education and training

9. Continuing growth

10. Linking with partners

When one or more of these characteristics is lacking, a project is unlikely to make enough progress to meet its goals, offer cost-effective services, and appear desirable in the eyes of its user population. Although the ten factors listed here were not given in rank order, the first three appear to be especially important. It is no surprise that the institutions or organizations that initiated the digital library projects described here also were in the forefront of earlier networking ventures and/or already had succeeded in developing large cooperative programs in other areas. The old adage "nothing breeds success like success" seems to operate in the digital library world as well as in most commercial fields.

Conclusions

This chapter briefly described six digital library projects of different types and sizes, ranging from one based at a single institution that reached out very slowly to partners (VARIATIONS, at Indiana University) to one initiated through an international network that had numerous contributor-partners from the start (CORC, at

OCLC, Inc.). One project began and continues as a national effort but welcomes contributions from a variety of sources (LC's NDLP). Two projects began as statewide collaborations that grew beyond their borders (CDP in Colorado and CDL in California). One project began as a collaboration among U.S. research libraries (JSTOR) and grew to include partners located all over the world functioning in all the roles that participate in the information chain, including authors, publishers, distributors, and readers.

Although the six projects differ widely in many respects, all exhibit certain similarities, from which a suggested model was derived. Features of the projects that seem to point toward success include leaders who are able to create a strong consensus about goals; adequate funding; having a reliable, well-developed infrastructure; having access to a large pool of materials to be digitized; committing to a long-term future; adopting standard systems and methods; developing a knowledgeable staff; supporting ongoing education and training for both staff and users; ensuring the project continues to grow; and building links with partners.

The choice of a particular metadata schema seems less important than choosing to apply a standard metadata schema or configuring the digital library in such a way that it can accommodate more than one schema, as appropriate to the audiences for the materials in its collections. Digital libraries seem to morph rapidly from (relatively) small projects involving local entities to worldwide collaborations with partners that number in the thousands. Keeping barriers to participation low and encouraging new partners, new data sources, new services, and new users appear to be integral elements in the formula for success.

Notes

1. OCLC, Inc., owns the *Dewey Decimal Classification* (DDC). The Web-based version of DDC includes many *Library of Congress Subject Headings* associated with DDC numbers, gleaned from cataloging records contributed to WorldCat, OCLC's shared online catalog. Thus, the elements were in place for initiating the system of automatic compilation of subject-related Web sites.

2. Cooperative projects have a long history among the University of California (UC) campuses, located at Berkeley, Davis, Irvine, La Jolla, Livermore, Los Angeles, Richmond, Riverside, Sacramento, San Francisco, Santa Barbara, and Santa Cruz. Among them are the MELVYL online union catalog and a shared long-term storage facility for little-used materials.

3. No pointer, instruction, or information about the revised project is given to viewers of the initial VARIATIONS project homepage. One could easily be led to assume the project "died" as of May 13, 2002.

4. The "Dublin" in Dublin Core stands for Dublin, Ohio, the location of OCLC headquarters.

5. Known colloquially as "Mooer's Law," this principle is often cited to criticize hard-to-use library systems. The speaker actually said something different. Calvin N. Mooer's words, delivered in 1959, were as follows: "It is now my suggestion that many people may not want information, and that they will avoid using a system precisely because it gives them information.... Having information is painful and troublesome. We have all experienced this. If you have information, you must first read it, which is not always easy. You must then try to understand it.... Understanding the information may show that your work was wrong, or may show that your work was needless.... Thus not having and not using information can often lead to less trouble and pain than having and using it." Reprinted in the *Bulletin of the American Society for Information Science* (October/November 1996).

Bibliography

Agnew, Grace. (2003). "Metadata Assessment: A Critical Niche within the NSDL Evaluation Strategy." Available: http://eduimpact.comm.nsdl.org/evalworkshop/_agnew.php (accessed February 14, 2005).

Arms, Carolyn R. (2003). "Available and Useful: OAI at the Library of Congress." Available: http://memory.loc.gov/ammem/techdocs/libht2003.html (accessed February 9, 2005).

Blandford, Ann, and George Buchanan. (2003). "Usability of Digital Libraries: A Source of Creative Tensions with Technical Developments." *TCDL Bulletin* (Summer), Available: www.ieee-tcdl.org/Bulletin/current/blandford/blandford.html (accessed 11 February 2005).

Bluh, Pamela M., ed. (2001). *Managing Electronic Serials*. Chicago: American Library Association.

Building and Sustaining Digital Collections: Models for Libraries and Museums. (2001). Washington, DC: Council on Library and Information Resources.

"California Digital Library. Mission." (n.d.). Available: http://www.dclib.org/glance/overview.html (accessed January 31, 2005).

"Colorado Digitization Plan Program, Strategic Plan: Background." (n.d.). Available: http://www.cdpheritage.org/about/background.html (accessed January 20, 2005).

Conger, Joan E. (2004). *Collaborative Electronic Resource Management: From Acquisitions to Assessment.* Westport, CT: Libraries Unlimited.

Electronic Information for Libraries (eIFL). *eIFL.net: Electronic Information for Libraries.* eIFL Foundation and Open Society Institute (OSI), Available: www.eifl.net (accessed February 11, 2005).

"Facts and Figures." (n.d.). Available: http://www.jstor.org/about/facts.html (accessed February 8, 2005).

Fialkoff, Francine. (2005). "Access by Google" [editorial]. *Library Journal* (January): 8.

A Framework of Guidance for Building Good Digital Collections. (2001). Washington, DC: Institute of Museum and Library Services, 2001, Available: www.imls.gov/scripts/text.cgi?/pubs/forumframework.htm (accessed February 16, 2005).

Guidance on the Structure, Content, and Application of Metadata Records for Digital Resources and Collections. (2003). [Draft for worldwide review of the "Report of the IFLA Cataloguing Section Working Group on the Use of Metadata Schemas"] IFLA, October 27, 2003.

Guthrie, Kevin M. (2000, July 9). "Challenges and Opportunities Presented by Archiving in the Electronic Era" [working paper]. http://www.jstor.org/about/archiving.html (accessed February 8, 2005).

"The History of JSTOR." (n.d.). http://www.jstor.org/about/background.html (accessed February 8, 2005).

"Indiana University VARIATIONS Homepage." (n.d.). Available: http://www.dlib.indiana.edu/variations (accessed January 20, 2005).

Intner, Sheila S., et al., eds. (2003). *Electronic Cataloging: AACR2 and Metadata for Serials and Monographs.* New York: Haworth Information Press.

Jones, Wayne, et al., eds. (2002). *Cataloging the Web: Metadata, AACR, and MARC 21.* Lanham, MD: Scarecrow Press for the Association for Library Collections & Technical Services. (ALCTS Papers on Library Technical Services and Collections, no. 10).

Liu, Ying. (2003). "Geo-referenced Digital Libraries: Experienced Problems of Purpose and Infrastructure." *Library Philosophy and Practice* 6, no. 1 (Fall). Available: http://www.webpages.uidaho.edu/~mbolin/liu.html (accessed on February 11, 2005).

"Mission and History" [Library of Congress, American Memory]. (n.d.). Available: http://memory.loc.gov/ammem/about/index.html (accessed February 9, 2005).

Moen, William E., and E. Stewart. (1998). "Assessing Metadata Quality: Findings and Methodological Considerations from an Evaluation of the U.S. Government Information Locator Service (GILS)." Available: http://doi.ieeecomputersociety.org/10.1109/ADL.1998.670425 (accessed February 11, 2005).

OCLC. (n.d.). "Archived Projects." Available: http://www.oclc.org/research/projects/archive/default.htm, p. 1.(accessed February 11, 2005).

"OCLC Cooperative Online Resource Catalog (CORC) Project Invites Participants." (n.d.). *AMIGOS Library, OCLC Collections & Technical Services News.* Available: http://www.amigos.org/aaoc/1999/apr99/corc.html (accessed January 20, 2005).

"Overview" [Library of Congress, American Memory]. (n.d.). Available: http://memory.loc.gov/ammem/dli2/html/lcndlp.html (accessed February 9, 2005).

Quam, E. (2001). "Informing and Evaluating a Metadata Initiative: Usability and Metadata Studies in Minnesota's Foundations Project." *Government Information Quarterly* 18: 181–94.

Saracevic, Tefko, and Lisa Covi. (n.d.). *Digital Libraries: Challenges for Evaluation.* (PowerPoint screens). Available: http://www.ffzg.hr/infoz/lida/lida2000/dlib_evaluation.ppt (accessed on 14 February 2005).

"Technical Requirements for Database vendors 10/28/04." (n.d.). Available: http://www.dlib.org (accessed January 31, 2005).

"Variations2 Overview." (n.d.). Available: http://variations2.indiana.edu/overview.html (accessed February 8, 2005).

"Variations2 User Guide." (n.d.). Available: http://variations2.indiana.edu/use/content.html (accessed February 8, 2005).

Zhang, Ying, and Yuelin Li. (n.d.) "The MIC Metadata Assessment." Available: http://www.scils.rutgers.edu/~miceval/progress/NSDL_handout.doc (accessed February 15, 2005).

Chapter 8

Archiving and Preserving Digital Materials: Why? What? Who? How? How Much?

Why?

In his excellent article, "Cataloguing in an Electronic Age" Michael Gorman discusses many of the most thought-provoking issues, both historical and current, on this subject with wit and wisdom. He covers an impressively broad spectrum of topics, from origins of MARC to the future of metadata standardization and concludes, rather wistfully, with the following sentence: "Last, and most important, what is the point of all of this if the resources identified and catalogued are not preserved?" (Gorman, 2003, 16).

Electronic texts, unlike the fixed texts of print data, are subject to inadvertent destruction of both the physical medium on which they exist and the intellectual content of their information. Electronic texts, so easy to edit, manipulate, revise, and improve, have lost their assurance of permanence. There are many ways to destroy electronic data inadvertently. First, the *medium* is at risk. The medium itself is threatened in several ways: first by destruction due to natural or artificial causes: for example, a floppy disk that warps or becomes obsolete technologically. In the December 15, 2004, issue of *RLG DigiNews,* what is essentially a requiem for the floppy disk eloquently points up the second risk. Tracing the history of the floppy from its birth in 1971 as an 8-inch data loading peripheral IBM introduced for its System/370 mainframe computers, to its 5.25-inch version brought out five years later by Shugard Associates and dubbed the minifloppy, and through its third incarnation in 1981 when Sony debuted the 3.5-inch floppy that gradually became the predominant and ubiquitous form of floppy, the elegy to the floppy concludes:

There is no denying the facts. Whether it takes two years or five or ten, all floppy disk formats will be obsolete within the foreseeable future.... The history of the floppy disk provides an excellent object lesson in the management of content on digital media. All media is subject to obsolescence. Media types that are less mainstream, less standardized, and less widely adopted are hit harder and faster by obsolescence. (Entlich, 2004)

Neal Beagrie, in an interview a few months earlier, states the same problem in slightly different words: "Although, from a technical perspective, everyone can read a book from the 16th century, only few are able to access 15-year-old data stored on diskette" (Beagrie, 2004b).

Next, there is the bigger problem of *intellectual* preservation. Data may be destroyed inadvertently. Many types of accidental changes may occur: a document can be damaged accidentally or as a result of the nature of the electronic resource (e.g., a dynamic database by its nature is frequently updated, erasing previous data in the updating). Unauthorized tampering with one's own work—for example, to cover one's tracks or destroy evidence—or with the work of another person (or authorized tampering under dubious circumstances, as illustrated later) can also destroy electronic data. The most recent scandal of this type, as of this writing, was carried on numerous Web sites and newspaper front pages on December 18, 2004. An excerpt from one noted that "MILLIONS of e-mails to British government staff will be automatically wiped out on Monday, 11 days before freedom of information laws come into force" (*British Govt Orders Email Purge,* 2004). It seems that all government employees had been ordered to destroy all e-mail over three months old and that although the deleted e-mails will be stored on backup systems, these have been declared off limits to freedom of information requests because of the cost of accessing them. Reaction by the opposition was swift and unambiguous: "The Conservative opposition party said Blair's Labour government was deliberately trying to destroy embarrassing information" (*British Govt Orders Email Purge,* 2004).

Lack of metadata and systems documentation, electronic data in forms that cannot be preserved because the software or hardware becomes obsolete or the digital resources have been *designed* to prevent any copying, and finally a lack of empowering mechanisms to institutions willing and able to be caretakers of our electronic resources (although this last situation is gradually improving), all threaten our digital heritage. The desperate danger in which our digital heritage finds itself today has extended beyond the boundaries of the information and library community and reached the consciousness of the general public, as a recent article in the online version of Britain's *The Independent,* ominously titled "The End of History," demonstrates. The article begins by asking its readers to spot "the odd one out" in a list that includes the Magna Carta, the Dead Sea Scrolls, and the contents of Downing Street's e-mail inbox today (foreshadowing the earlier-mentioned e-mail deletion crisis a year and a half later!). "It will take the most valiant effort to read those emails in whatever form they have been preserved," the article points out, and then continues, "by contrast, you can be pretty confident that there will still be scholars AD2300 who will be interested by, and able to read, the parchment and paper documents that have already survived for centuries" (Arthur, 2003).

What?

The first act of digital preservation is identifying or selecting which material merits the effort of preservation. The fluidity and dynamic nature that digital data add to preservation raise questions such as which version of a resource is the "genuine" one. Furthermore the time frame within which selection choices must be made is shortened because of the problems of media instability and technological obsolescence. Dynamic databases, which change from moment to moment, add a further complication to the process of digital archiving because they can only be preserved through samples or snapshots. Digital resources also require decisions not only about what items to keep, but also which elements of the resource should be preserved. Features such as links to other documents and interactivity will be lost unless decisions are made to keep them. In the final analysis, the question is not only *what* should be preserved, but *how much* of each digital item should be preserved. Digital preservation thus may involve saving not only the resource, but also contextual information such as information on the medium (which may need to be changed frequently) and metadata about the contents. Finally, the issues involved in digital archiving are different for "born-digital" materials than they are for materials that have been digitized, because the original print source of digitized materials are usually both documented and preserved. Born-digital material, on the other hand, is in danger of disappearing without a trace unless it is properly identified, documented for future access, and preserved technologically.

Defining the digital resource, given this complex environment, is not simple. The Task Force on Archiving of Digital Information emphasizes that the central goal of digital preservation must be to preserve information integrity. It defines five components that constitute the integrity of digital documents: content (intellectual substance contained in information objects), fixity (content fixed in a discrete object as opposed to continuously updated documents), reference (reliable systems for locating and citing), provenance (a record of the document's origin and chain of custody), and context (a document's interaction with elements in the wider digital environment).

In addition, digital objects can be classified according to various typologies. The first major division of digital objects is into two main groups: *digitized* material, converted from documents or other media into electronic format, and *natively digital* (also referred to as "born digital") material, which was created in digital form. Within both groups they can be further divided according to their characteristics and forms. Typologies of electronic publications in the literature on electronic data archiving are numerous and varied.

The NSF-DELOS Working Group on Digital Archiving and Preservation, in its 2003 report and recommendations, for example, divides digital content into categories according to "institutional, legal, social, and technological contexts" (*Invest to Save,* 2003):

- E-government

- E-commerce

- Education and Research

- Digital Libraries

- E-heritage
- Personal Archives

Answers to the question of what to preserve, like the definitions and typologies of digital resources, are also numerous and varied. Collection policies and selection criteria of individual research institutions and digital archives give us perhaps the best examples of which electronic data should be preserved.

The National Library of Australia, for example, archives only internal links of digital objects it chooses for archiving, whereas the Libraries and Archives of Canada has chosen to archive the text of the linked object only if it is on the same server as the object that is being archived. In other words, the previous issue of the same periodical accessed through a hypertext link would be considered a part of the original publication, but another publication accessed through a hypertext link would not. Brewster Kahle's Internet Archive retains all links because the project aims to archive a snapshot of the entire Internet (Lazinger, 2004, p. 101).

The National Library of Wales opens the section on collection policy in its 2003 report on digital preservation policy and strategy by declaring that "as with traditional material, not all digital resources can or should be kept" (National Library of Wales, 2003). The report states that the library has to deal increasingly with born-digital resources and that these pose more of a problem for preservation than do digitized objects because "the library usually has little or no input or control at the creation stage, e.g., what standards are used." Noting that both its policies on retention of electronic records and its collection development policy are in the process of being reviewed, the report nonetheless puts forth a typology of digital objects already held by the library. The list of formats for the born-digital objects that it currently preserves includes:

- Digital publications received through voluntary deposit agreements, for example,
  - CD ROMs, disks
  - E-journals, e-books
  - Databases
  - Disks that accompany printed material
  - Online publications received via e-mail, etc.
  - Disks that form part of archival collections
  - Electronic records deposited by institutions as part of their archives
  - Web sites
  - Time-based materials, for example, sound and video (National Library of Wales, 2003)

Finally, in a 2004 article on Web archiving in Denmark, five aspects or characteristics of digital resources—that is, precisely *what* needs to be preserved when we preserve a digital object—are identified as relevant for the discussion of what the State and University Library Denmark needs to archive:

- **Readability:** A minimum requirement must be that the core elements can be read.

- **Comprehensibility:** Most text documents have more to them than just the raw text. Data may be lined up in columns, arrows may point at important features, text attributes may indicate particularly important words, and so on.

- **Appearance:** Some attributes of a file format are not necessary to understand the meaning of a file but are part of the overall impression.

- **Functionality:** Unlike analog objects, digital objects often have functionality beyond that of visual and audio characteristics.

- **"Look and Feel":** A perfect copy of a digital object would preserve not only the appearance and functionality of the original, but the entire "look and feel," for example, the design and operational quirks of GUI elements, the resolution of the monitor, and even the speed of the machine (Christensen-Dalsgaard, 2004).

Most of the major digital preserving institutions would agree with the approaches of the National University of Wales and the State and University Library Denmark. The National Library of Wales maintains that in the final analysis it is clear that despite the problem of the sheer diversity and numbers of formats that require digital preservation and despite the huge quantities of legacy, as well as current, digital material that all libraries and archives have, all of which needs to be accessed and preserved, the most cost-effective and efficient approach to digital preservation is to address the intellectual content, rather than the physical medium of each item (National Library of Wales, 2003). The State and University Library Denmark takes this approach a step further and declares that, in addition, we ideally need to preserve the appearance and functionality of the digital resource as well. Both agree, however, that at the same time this policy needs to be carried out while still aiming to slow the rate of deterioration of the physical media by ensuring proper environmental control and preventing physical damage to the media.

Who?

The stakeholders in the process of digital preservation include first the creators of the digital objects, who may be individuals, institutions, or organizations. Other stakeholders may be publishers, distributors, systems administrators, libraries, archives, and users. What unites all these stakeholders is their interest in adding to or making use of the value of digital information objects. Still, these stakeholders are a diverse collection of communities, some of whose interests may conflict with those of other communities within the list of stakeholders. For example, data creators are a different set of people from potential data users, and it is not always certain that the data creators have an incentive to collaborate with the users.

Stewart Granger, in a 2002 opinion piece, represents the "digital domain"—the stakeholders in digital preservation, access, rights management, interoperability, and so on—in the following Venn diagram:

Figure 8.1. Venn diagram of the "Digital Domain."

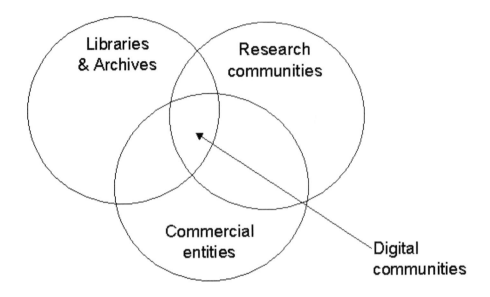

Source: Stewart Granger (2002). "Digital Preservation and Deep Infrastructure" [Online]. *D-Lib Magazine* 8, no. 2 (February). Available: http://www.dlib.org/dlib/february02/granger/02granger.html. Reprinted by permission of *D-Lib Magazine.*

The diagram shows the differing motives and cultures that exist in this domain: public and private, commercial and nonprofit, national cultures, and so on. Given their varied interests and cultures, these digital communities are likely to have differing priorities with regard to digital preservation, some of them in conflict, and it is against this background, he points out, that collaborative structures to ensure the preservation of our digital heritage and facilitate cost savings in doing it, must be put into place.

Libraries—both singly and in consortia—have so far been in the forefront of research into and implementation of the beginnings of far-reaching preservation policies for digital resources. Though using national libraries as our primary archiving institutions for electronic data is an attractive option, there are barriers to overcome. First, depository legislation for electronic information varies widely among countries that have depository arrangements. Second, copyright is a problem even for publications originating in the library's country. Finally, there is the possibility that no national library can truly commit to acquiring by deposit all electronic publications that should be acquired or that such programs will be subject to the vagaries of budget appropriations (Lazinger, 2004, p. 101).

All areas of digital preservation have expanded wildly in the slightly more than a decade since the problem of preserving the vast quantities of material being digitized, as well as the even more vast quantities of material being born digitally and existing only on the Internet, began to be recognized. None, however, has expanded more than the area of stakeholders—the "Who?" of digital preservation. The number of stakeholders who have entered the playing field—planning conferences, giving courses, funding projects, researching and writing publications, maintaining informative Web sites—has grown exponentially as awareness of the need to preserve our digital heritage has grown.

Sorting out the plethora of digital preservation initiatives, both collaborative and individual (single-country or single-institution) that have blossomed in the past few years can probably best be done by focusing on the most important groups and projects by geographic location. Therefore, we have divided these initiatives into U.S. initiatives, UK initiatives, European initiatives (both single country and pan-European), Australian initiatives, and global initiatives (primarily UNESCO-sponsored).

U.S. Initiatives

In January 2003, the U.S. Congress approved the Library of Congress's Plan for the National Digital Information Infrastructure (NDIIPP) to enable the Library to launch the first phase of building a national infrastructure for the collection and long-term preservation of digital resources. Along with this approval Congress released $35 million for the next phase of NDIIPP, of which $15 million dollars was to be matched by nonfederal sources. The majority of the funds were to be earmarked for testing various models to support the capture and preservation of digital content, focusing on a variety of digital media: e-books, e-journals, digital film, audio, and television. The Library was to work with other repositories and rights holders to test approaches that support a distributed digital preservation infrastructure (Campbell, 2003).

Nearly two years later, in September 2004, the Library of Congress announced awards of $15 million to eight institutions and their partners for identifying, collecting and preserving digital material within a nationwide digital preservation infrastructure. These include university libraries (University of Illinois at Urbana-Champaign, North Carolina State Libraries), a school of library and information science (University of Illinois at Urbana-Champaign Graduate School of Library and Information Science), university business schools and research consortia (University of Maryland Robert H. Smith School of Business), University of Michigan Inter-university Consortium for Political and Social Research), a broadcasting corporation (Educational Broadcasting Corporation), and the California Digital Library at the University of California, among others, each partnered with public and private institutions from all aspects of the information community, from OCLC to the Public Broadcasting Service (PBS). Laura Campbell, who is leading the NDIPP for the Library of Congress, speaking on the collaborative structures being funded, noted that these awards marked a milestone for the Library and the NDIPP and that "these formal partnerships mark the beginning of a new phase of this program to raise awareness of the need for digital preservation and to take steps to capture and preserve at-risk digital content that is vital to our nation's history" (*Library of Congress Announces Awards of $15 Million to Begin Building a Network of Partners for Digital Preservation*, 2004).

A privately funded U.S.-based initiative (with global content, however) is the Internet Archive, probably the best-known and the oldest of the Internet-archiving projects still in existence. It was founded as a nonprofit organization in 1996 by Brewster Kahle, founder and CEO of Alexa Internet (now a wholly owned subsidiary of Amazon.com) of which the Internet Archive is the noncommercial and sister organization. The two companies share technology, with Alexa's Web crawlers searching the Internet and accumulating Web pages and related information to those pages to add such functionalities as listing of related sites based on users' patterns and site's user ratings. After six months, the pages themselves go to the Internet Archive for preservation. As of January 2004, the Internet Archive stored more than 300 terrabytes of data, including more than 1,200 short films in MPEG-2 and MPEG-4 formats and more than 30 billion Web pages. In October 2001, the Internet Archive introduced the Wayback Machine, a custom-search engine that allowed users to enter a URL and receive from that URL links to pages that have been archived, whether the Web site is currently active or dead. Despite its technological efforts, however, the Internet Archive is missing material from the first four years of the Web and is unable to retrieve or archive restricted-access Internet or Web sites on secure servers.

In an announcement on December 15, 2004, on the Internet Archive Web site, its commitment to a new project, a Text Archive composed of e-books from libraries in five countries committed to putting their digitized books in open-access archives, was made public. The announcement went on to state that "over one million books have been committed to the Text Archive. Currently over twenty-seven thousand are available and an additional fifty thousand are expected in the first quarter of 2005" (*International Libraries and the Internet Archive collaborate to build Open-Access Text Archives,* 2004). Libraries from the United States, Canada, India, Egypt, China, and the Netherlands are listed as current participants.

The Internet Archive was conceived both as a repository of Internet material and as an Internet library formed to preserve, store, and provide access to artifacts in digital format. Over the years, it has run into trouble with regard to its perception of itself as a fair-use exception to the laws of access to copyrighted material, as exemplified by the letter to the *Chronicle of Higher Education* of Professor Stephen R. Brown of American University, who complained that "the Internet Archive is nothing more than an enormous copyright violation disguised as a library" (Edwards, 2004). In addition, there is a very limited notion of collection development within the Internet Archive, the goal of which is to archive as much of the Internet as its technology will allow without regard to the veracity or quality of the material. Still, according to Kahle, the Internet Archive is perhaps the only place in which artifacts that are considered to be ephemeral, both bibliographic and nonbibliographic, are stored for current and future scholars and the public. Among other things, it provides snapshots in time of historical events and extends the functionality of the Internet by providing archival copies of dead sites to allow for continued access to their content (Edwards, 2004).

The last large-scale U.S. digital preservation initiative we mention here is LOCKSS, the acronym for the whimsically named Lots Of Copies Keep Stuff Safe. LOCKSS was initiated at Stanford University as an open source software that provides librarians with an easy and inexpensive way to collect, store, preserve, and provide access to their own, local copy of authorized content they purchase. Running on standard desktop hardware and requiring almost no technical administration, LOCKSS converts a personal computer into a digital preservation appliance, creating low-cost, persistent, accessible copies of e-journal content as it is published. Because pages in these appliances are never flushed, the local community's access to that content is safeguarded. A library uses the LOCKSS software to turn a low-cost PC into a digital preservation appliance that performs four functions:

- It collects newly published content from the target e-journals using a Web crawler similar to those used by search engines.

- It continually compares the content it has collected with the same content collected by other appliances and repairs any differences.

- It acts as a Web proxy or cache, providing browsers in the library's community with access to the publisher's content or the preserved content as appropriate.

- It provides a Web-based administrative interface that allows the library staff to target new journals for preservation, monitor the state of the journals being preserved, and control access to the preserved journals.

Before LOCKSS appliances can preserve a journal, the publisher has to give permission for the LOCKSS system to collect and preserve the journal. They do this by adding a page to the journal's Web site containing a permission statement, and links to the issues of the journal as they are published. To add new publishing platforms, the LOCKSS system provides a fill-in-the-blanks tool that a librarian or administrator can use to collect this information and test that it is correct. The information is then saved in a file (the LOCKSS plug-in) and added to the publisher's Web site or to some other plug-in repository, so that it is available to all LOCKSS systems. As of this writing, more than 80 libraries and 50 publishers from around the world are using the software (*About LOCKSS*, 2004).

U.K. Initiatives

In 1995, the Joint Information Systems Committee (JISC) and the British Library hosted a Workshop at the University of Warwick to determine what needed to be done with regard to digital preservation, a matter that had been regarded as increasingly urgent for several years. In the nearly a decade since, there has been a great deal of activity in the United Kingdom aimed at building the infrastructure to support the long-term preservation if digital information, much of it led by the hosts of the Warwick Workshop JISC and the British Library.

In addition to running the high-speed academic network for the United Kingdom, JISC provides electronic content and therefore has a vested interest in digital preservation. It has been one of the leading organizations in the world in research and development on long-term preservation of digital materials through projects and services such as the Arts and Humanities Data Service (http://www.ahds.ac.uk), CEDARS (CURL Examplars in Digital Archiving; http://www.leeds.ac.uk/cedars/), CAMiLEON (Creative Archiving at Michigan and Leeds: Emulating the Old on the New; http://www.si.umich.edu/CAMILEON/), and the seven JISC/NPO Preservation Studies (http://www.ukoln.ac.uk/services/elib/papers/supporting). As part of its long-term digital preservation strategy, JISC has continued its tradition of funding a long list of projects for implementation of digital preservation strategies in its program for 2004–2006. These projects are as follows:

- Assessment of UK Data Archive and the National Archives compliance with OAIS/METS, to map the systems and metadata currently in use by UK Data Archive (UKDA) and the National Archives (TNA) against those in the OAIS Reference Model and the METS standards, and to explore the potential for interaction between existing metadata standards utilized within the two institutions and METS

- DAAT: Digital Asset Assessment Tool, to develop a digital preservation assessment tool for use within the United Kingdom higher education and research, learning, and teaching communities

- Digital Archival Exemplars for Private Papers, to develop best-practice guidelines rooted in practical experience in the archival and preservation aspects of digital private papers

- Digital Preservation Training Programme, to develop a modular training programme in digital preservation, with class-taught, online, and offline components

- eSPIDA: effective Strategic model for the Preservation and disposal of Institutional Digital Assets, to develop and implement a sustainable business focused model for digital preservation, as part of a knowledge management agenda in higher education institutions

- LIFE: Lifecycle Information for E-literature, to explore and develop a life-cycle approach to costing digital archiving for e-journals

- Managing Digital Assets in Tertiary Education (MANDATE), to produce a toolkit including templates, a database structure and a training programme that will enable colleges to bring a coherent approach to the management and preservation of digital assets

- Managing Risk: a Model Business Preservation Strategy for Corporate Digital Assets, to address the basic issues of who should do what, when, and how, and also review the use of external consultants and evaluate the benefits and cost of using external contractors to manage corporate digital assets

- METS Awareness Training: develop the existing introductory training materials on METS created by the Oxford Digital Library by making them less institutionally specific

- PRESERV: PReservation Eprint SERVices, to implement an ingest service based on the OAIS reference model for institutional archives built using Eprints software

- SHERPA Digital Preservation: Creating a Persistent Preservation Environment for Institutional Repositories, to bring together the SHERPA (Securing a Hybrid Environment for Research Preservation and Access) institutional repository systems with the preservation repository established by the Arts and Humanities Data Service to create an environment that fully addresses all the requirements of the different phases within the life cycle of digital information (Joint Information Systems Committee [JISC], 2004)

The British Library is focusing on four major of categories of digital content in building repositories for digital preservation:

- Deposited materials (a voluntary deposit scheme has been implemented and is pending legal deposit legislation)

- Web sites

+ Digitization (it has undertaken a number of digitization initiatives over the years, the largest of which is "Collect Britain," a collection of images and sounds selected from the BL's collection)

+ Digital materials purchased for the provision of services (Jones, 2003b)

The National Archives has been actively engaged in providing guidance to government departments in implementing good electronic records management practice and working with government departments to support the introduction of electronic management systems. In addition, it has built a digital archive capable of providing long-term storage of all electronic records that government departments produce and select for archiving. In addition, like the British Library, the National Archives is also engaged in preserving Web sites—in its case, government Web sites—and is working collaboratively with others in web archiving (JISC, 2004).

The Digital Preservation Coalition (DPC) was formed in January 2001 and formally launched at the House of Commons in 2002. From six founding members, it had grown to 25 members from a variety of sectors by June 2003. Despite its modest resources, it has succeeded in raising awareness of the importance of digital preservation in its short existence, launching a public relations campaign, packaging and disseminating relevant information, such as an electronic edition of the *Preservation Management of Digital Materials Handbook* (http://www.dpconline.org/graphics/handbook/) and publishing quarterly updates of *What's New in Digital Preservation* (http://www.dpconline.org/graphics/whatsnew/), Michael Day (UKOLN) and Gerard Clifton's (National Library of Australia) invaluable source of reference and current awareness in digital preservation.

Finally, the U.K. Digital Curation Centre (DCC) was formally launched in October, 2004 to support U.K. institutions in storage, management, and preservation of digital data across the life cycle of scholarly interest, while at the same time supporting reproducibility and reuse. The Centre will be run by a consortium made up of the Universities of Edinburgh and Glasgow, UKOLN at the University of Bath, and the Council for the Central Laboratory of the Research Councils (CCLRC) and will also establish a research program on wider digital preservation issues, promote links across community of practice, and develop services to evaluate tools and technical information for digital curation (*DPC/PADI What's New in Digital Preservation, 2004*).

European Initiatives

In Europe, harvester technology to preserve Web content has been the dominant approach to Web archiving by its national libraries, which have led the European stakeholders in this area of endeavor. The first harvesters—applications that retrieve and store Web content according to a set of user-defined parameters—were built in the mid-1990s to enable the creation of Web indexes such as Alta Vista. Around this time, the staff at the Internet Archive and the Royal Library of Sweden also started building tools for collecting and archiving the Web. Unlike the search engine harvesters, these harvesters were built specifically for the purpose of Web archiving. The NEDLIB harvester, developed in the European Union (EU) funded project Networked European Deposit Library (NEDLIB) (http://www.kb.nl/coop/nedlib) led by the Koninklijke Bibliotheek in the Netherlands in 1997–2000, is one of these. Other partners in NEDLIB included the following:

- Bibliothèque nationale de France

- National Library of Norway

- Die Deutsche Bibliothek (Germany)

- Biblioteca Nacional de Portugal

- National Library of Switzerland

- Biblioteca Nazionale di Firenze

- Helsinki University Library in Finland (Hakala, 2004)

The NEDLIB project ended as of January 31, 2001. The NEDLIB harvester, however, is freeware (available from http://www.csc.fi/sovellus/nedlib), the second version of which was tested in the national libraries of Norway, Estonia, and Iceland until September 2002, when version 1.2.2 of the harvester was finally deemed satisfactory. It has been used successfully in many countries and has retrieved hundreds of millions of Web pages.

The Nordic Web Archive (NWA; http://nwa.nb.no/) was a collaborative project of the Nordic national libraries that began in September 2000 and ended in June 2002. Because it did not have the financial resources to develop a text-indexing engine of its own, it acquired the search engine developed by a Norwegian company FAST Search and Transfer ASA (http://www.fastsearch.com/), with which it created and made available for free a global Web index that, as of March 2004, contained 3.15 billion files, "definitely sufficient for indexing even the union of all Nordic Web archives for the foreseeable future" (Hakala, 2004).

In 2002, several European national libraries and the Internet Archive began discussions about possible cooperation in developing new tools for Web archiving which resulted in the formation in the summer of 2003 of the International Internet Preservation Consortium (IIPC; http://netpreserve.org). This consortium consists of the Internet Archive and 11 national libraries and aims at developing standards, best practices, and tools for fostering Web archiving. It is led by the Bibliothèque Nationale de France, but it includes more than just European libraries. Its members are the Library of Congress, the British Library, Library and Archives Canada, the Biblioteca Nazionale Centrale di Firenze, the National Library of Australia, and all the Nordic national libraries. The IIPC Web site, citing the July 2003 formal chartering of the Consortium, states: "The initial agreement is in effect for three years. During that period, the membership is limited to charter institutions. The IIPC seeks to involve national libraries everywhere and will welcome inquiries in the summer of 2005 about future membership" (netpreserve.org, 2004).

In 2001, the European Commission and the Swiss Government, realizing that action was needed in the area of digital curation and preservation, set up ERPANET (European Resource Preservation and Access Network), led by the Humanities Advanced Technology and Information Institute (HATII) at the University of Glasgow (UK), and its partners Schweizerisches Bundesarchiv (Switzerland), ISTBAL at the Università di Urbina (Italy), and National Archief van Nederland (Netherlands). ERPANET's mission was to enhance the preservation of cultural and scientific digital objects, for which it received funding of some 1.2 million euros for its first 36 months until November 2004. During those 3 years, ERPANET has enjoyed, in addition, the commitment of professionals from across Europe, Australia and New Zealand, and Canada and the U.S., who have donated time, thought, effort, and knowledge. Specific objectives ERPANET set for itself in preparing its funding application in 2000 were as follows:

- To identify and raise awareness of sources of information about the preservation of digital objects across the broad spectrum of national and regional cultural and scientific heritage activity in Europe

- To appraise and evaluate information sources, to document developments in digital preservation, and to make available results of research, projects and best practice.

- To provide an online advisory service on digital preservation issues, practice, technology, and developments

- To implement thematic workshops to bring together experts from a range of disciplines to examine key preservation issues and to initiate associated thematic discussion

- To run training seminars based on best practice and to identify where and what further practitioner training and staff development initiatives might be undertaken

- To conduct research through case studies that would improve our understanding of practices, needs, and future developments

- To stimulate further research on digital preservation in key areas and encourage the development of standards where gaps and opportunities have been identified

- To stimulate ICT companies and software developers to incorporate some of the curation and preservation thinking into newer generations of software (Ross, 2004)

All these goals have been carried out to varying degrees in ERPANET projects in the past three years. In addition, ERPANET has worked to ensure that it provides its expertise and that of its community to the work of other projects, recognizing that preservation is a problem that demands collaborative action. For example, the European Commission's FP5 funded digital library activity DELOS and the National Science Foundation (NSF) established working groups to study the digital library landscape, and among the eight working groups, one examined Digital Archiving and Preservation. Colleagues from ERPANET contributed to the development of its 2003 report, *Invest to Save: Report and Recommendations of the NSF-DELOS Working Group on Digital Archiving and Preservation*. With their first phase of funding at an end, ERPANET is examining business scenarios to find one that will give them long-term viability "to develop effective preservation capabilities across public, commercial, and consumer sectors" (Ross, 2004).

Australian Initiatives

From the inception of the digital era, Australia has had a strong digital online culture. Internationally, Australia has one of the highest levels of Internet connections among its population (surpassed only by the US and Singapore) and, for a country with a relatively small population, it has had a large number of leading-edge online projects, including projects designed to archive these online materials. Both the National Library of Australia (NLA) and its national archive have been instrumental in carrying out activities and publishing guidelines that are frequently cited internationally as exemplars in the field of digital preservation (Beagrie, 2003a).

The NLA has led national collaborative initiatives for published digital materials, the best known of which is the PANDORA archive (Preserving and Accessing Networked Documentary Resources of Australia; http://Pandora.nla.gov.au/). PANDORA was initiated in 1996 by the NLA and is now built in collaboration with nine other Australian libraries and cultural collecting organizations. Australian online publications are selectively harvested by the NLA for inclusion in PANDORA, with all of the eight other partners having responsibilities for collecting and preserving Australian documentary heritage. Each partner identifies, selects, catalogs and archives the publications for which it accepts responsibility. The six main categories of resources collected are as follows:

1. Commonwealth and Australian Capital Territory government publications

2. Conference proceedings

3. E-journals

4. Publications of higher education institutions

5. Titles referred by indexing and abstracting agencies

6. Topical sites—in nominated subject areas (defined in PANDORA'S selection guidelines) documenting key issues of current social or political interest (Phillips, 2003)

PANDORA'S selective approach to archiving enables the partners to realize some important objectives (Phillips, 2003):

- Each item can be fully cataloged and included in the national bibliography.

- Each item can be made accessible because permissions to make publications available via the Web are negotiated with the publishers before the item is archived.

- The "significant properties" of resources being archived can be analyzed to enhance knowledge of preservation requirements and enable strategies for preservation to be put into place.

Another well-known Australian initiative is Preserving Access to Digital Information (PADI), a digital preservation gateway maintained by the NLA and other individual and institutional partners in Australia and abroad. It started as a voluntary initiative of several Australian organizations and later was transferred to the NLA to provide the program with the resources it needs. In 2001, PADI's functionality was extended to allow registered individuals outside the NLA to enter information directly into the PADI database. PADI has an international advisory board and is encouraging international participation in maintaining its database. For example, it now has a memorandum of understanding with the UK-based Digital Preservation Coalition (DPC), which will allow the DPC to input to PADI, an arrangement that could be mirrored in the future with other organizations worldwide (Beagrie, 2003a).

Global Initiatives

The Draft Charter on the Preservation of the Digital Heritage was published by UNESCO (2003a) for submission to UNESCO's General Conference. It is seen as "one very visible element in an international campaign to address the barriers to digital continuity and to head off the emergence of a 'digital divide', in which the tools of digital preservation are restricted to the heritage of a well-resourced few" (Webb, 2003). In addition to the charter, UNESCO'S campaign for promoting digital preservation includes widespread consultations, the development of practical technical guidelines and a number of pilot projects. Because UNESCO charters and declarations are meant to be "normative" rather than binding, that is, accepted by member states through a vote of acceptance rather than by individual ratification, the purpose of the Draft Charter is primarily to raise consciousness. It undertakes, therefore, to "focus worldwide attention on the issues at stake and to encourage responsible preservation action wherever it can be taken" (Webb, 2003). The charter asserts the responsibility of each member state to work with relevant institutions and organizations to encourage an environment that will maximize accessibility of the digital heritage; seeks a fair balance between the legitimate rights of creators and other rights holders; recognizes that some digital information is sensitive or personal and may require some restrictions on access; and calls for urgent action, ranging from awareness raising to practical programs addressing digital preservation threats, to preserve digital heritage materials.

Whereas the UNESCO Charter focuses on advocacy and public policy issues, the UNESCO (2003b) *Guidelines for the Preservation of Digital Heritage* concentrate on presenting practical principles on which technical decisions throughout the life cycle of a wide range of digital objects can be based. The nearly 200 pages of material in the Guidelines, currently available in English, Spanish, and French through the UNESCO portal, are organized around two approaches: basic concepts behind digital preservation and detailed discussions of processes and decisions involved in various stages of digital preservation, for example, what to keep, managing rights, protecting data, and maintaining accessibility. Colin Webb of the National Library of Australia culled 39 of the principles asserted in the Guidelines into a single list ("to give readers a sense of the approaches taken") appended to his article in RLG DigiNews describing the UNESCO campaign to save the world's digital heritage, from which we have further culled 14 of the principles we view as the most useful to keep in mind:

- ◆ Not all digital materials need to be kept, only those that are judged to have ongoing value: these form the digital heritage.

- ◆ Digital materials cannot be said to be preserved if access is lost. The purpose of preservation is to maintain the ability to present the essential elements of authentic digital materials.

- ◆ Digital preservation will happen only if organisations and individuals accept responsibility for it. The starting point for action is a decision about responsibility.

- Comprehensive and reliable preservation programs are highly desirable, but they may not be achievable in all circumstances of need. Where necessary, it is usually better for noncomprehensive and nonreliable action to be taken than no action at all. Small steps are usually better than no steps.

- Preservation programs must clarify their legal right to collect, copy, name, modify, preserve, and provide access to the digital materials for which they take responsibility.

- Authenticity is best protected by measures that ensure the integrity of data is not compromised and by documentation that maintains the clear identity of the material.

- The goal of maintaining accessibility is to find cost-effective ways of guaranteeing access whenever it is needed, in both the short- and long-term.

- Standards are an important foundation for digital preservation, but many programs must find ways to preserve access to poorly standardised materials, in an environment of changing standards.

- Preservation action should not be delayed until a single "digital preservation standard" appears.

- It is reasonable for programs to choose multiple strategies for preserving access, especially to diverse collections. They should consider the potential benefits of maintaining the original data streams of materials as well as any modified versions, as insurance against the failure of still-uncertain strategies.

- Preservation programs are often required to judge acceptable and unacceptable levels of loss in terms of items, elements, and user needs.

- Waiting for comprehensive, reliable solutions to appear before taking responsible action will probably mean material is lost.

- Digital preservation incorporates the assessment and management of risks.

- While suitable service providers may be found to carry out some functions, ultimately responsibility for achieving preservation objectives rests with preservation programs and with those who oversee and resource them. (Webb, 2003)

One other recent global initiative that deserves attention in any discussion of the "Who?" of digital preservation is the IFLA-CDNL Alliance for Bibliographic Standards (ICABS). The new alliance between IFLA and national libraries was established in August 2003 to continue and expand the coordination work formerly done by the IFLA Universal Bibliographic control and International MARC (UBCIM) Core Activity established 30 years ago.

In the mission statement of the ICABS strategic plan, it says that the ICABS alliance aims "to advance understanding of issues related to long-term archiving of electronic resources, including the promotion of new and recommended conventions for such archiving" (van Wijngaarden, 2003). The focus of the alliance is on offering practical ways to improve international coordination. These objectives will be realized through the following "Goals and Actions" agreed to during the IFLA Berlin Conference in 2003. Each of the partners in this alliance has agreed to be the lead support agency for one or more of the actions, shown here as the "responsible partner."

Goal

1. Maintain, promote, and harmonize existing standards and concepts related to bibliographic and resource control

Actions

1.1 ISBD maintenance and development

Support the work of the IFLA Cataloguing Section's ISBD Review Group in developing and maintaining the International Standards for Bibliographic Description. Encourage the harmonization of national practices to follow these standards. Promote the results of the ISBD revisions.

Responsible partner: Die Deutsche Bibliothek

1.2 FRBR maintenance and development

Support the work of the IFLA Cataloguing Section's FRBR Review Group in developing and maintaining the conceptual model and related guidelines for the Functional Requirements for Bibliographic Records (FRBR). Promote the use of this model.

Responsible partner: British Library

1.3 FRANAR project

Support the IFLA Division IV Working Group on Functional Requirements of Authority Numbering and Records (FRANAR). Promote the use of this model for authority control.

Responsible partner: British Library

1.4 UNIMARC

Promote the development and use of UNIMARC.

Responsible partner: Biblioteca Nacional de Portugal

1.5 MARC 21

Promote the development and use of MARC 21 and its XML derivatives.

Responsible partner: Library of Congress

1.6 Z39.50 and Z39.50-International: Next Generation (ZING)

Promote the application and use of Z39.50. Cooperate with Z39.50 implementers to continue development of ZING, and notably its XML-based Search/Retrieve Web Services (SRW) in order to evolve next generation implementations of Z39.50.

Responsible partner: Library of Congress

Goal

2. Develop strategies for bibliographic and resource control and ensure the promotion of new and recommended conventions

Actions

2.1 VIAF cooperative

Support and promote the idea of the Virtual International Authority File (VIAF) in cooperation with the Sections of IFLA's Division IV: Bibliographic Control and the partners in the current VIAF Proof of Concept project. Explore other VIAF models and promote the testing of prototypes.

VIAF Proof of Concept project partners: Library of Congress, Die Deutsche Bibliothek, and OCLC

2.2 Metadata and XML based metadata schemes

Explore Metadata requirements in close cooperation with the Information Technology Section and the Cataloguing Section of IFLA and their Working Groups. Collect and communicate information on existing Metadata schemes and application profiles.

Responsible partner: Library of Congress

2.3 Monitor work on persistent identifiers

Responsible partner: Library of Congress

Goal

3. Advance understanding of issues related to long-term archiving of electronic resources

Actions

3.1 Explore the requirements/conditions for long-term archiving of electronic resources.

Responsible partner: Koninklijke Bibliotheek

3.2 Migration and Emulation

Explore and promote strategies, methods and standards for migration and emulation.

Responsible partner: Koninklijke Bibliotheek

3.3 Web harvesting

Explore and promote methods to archive web-based publications collected by Web harvesting.

Responsible partner: National Library of Australia

3.4 Work out a survey of existing standards, guidelines, and codes for preservation of digital materials in co-operation with IFLA's Preservation and Conservation Section.

Responsible partner: National Library of Australia (IFLA Core Activity: IFLA-CDNL Alliance for Bibliographic Standards (ICABS), 2004)

Hilde van Wijngaarden, Digital Preservation Officer of the Koninklijke Bibliotheek, the Responsible partner for Actions 3.1 and 3.2, thinks that ICABS and its projects are not only important but also timely, a global initiative whose time has come:

> After years of discussing the problem and possible solutions, the last few years have seen an increase in actions that are taken to set up digital archives, organize the management of digital resources and define strategies for permanent access. This means now is a good time to take inventory and define best practices, evaluate emerging standards and describe issues that need extra attention. (van Wijngaarden, 2004)

How?

Technological obsolescence comes about as the result of the evolution of technology. A separate issue is that of media deterioration. As of this writing, there is no one unambiguous answer to the problem of technological obsolescence, but there are several clear options being explored to deal with this cycle of obsolescence. The options fall into three main categories: refreshing, migration, and emulation.

Refreshing is copying digital files from one storage medium to another storage medium of the same type in order to prevent media obsolescence. Refreshing does not solve the problem of backward compatibility if the software changes, and so it cannot be viewed as a solution to digital preservation, at least not in itself.

Migration—the periodic transfer of digital materials from one hardware/software configuration to another or from one generation of computer technology to the next—is the current favorite strategy for preserving electronic data. Media refreshing is a part of migration, but migration involves the transfer of the entire digital environment, not just the physical storage medium. Migration is necessary every time the operating environment, including the hardware and the software, changes. Migration strategies vary with the type of digital data being migrated and are still in the process of development.

The third digital preservation option being explored is emulation, or the development of software that performs the functions of obsolete hardware and other software. This strategy proposes that digital documents be stored in their original forms, along with the original software in which they were created and that additional software be created to permit a more advanced computer at some future time to mimic the obsolete hardware.

In preserving digital objects, it is access to the intellectual content (or visual content, if the digital object is an image or collection of images) that we are preserving rather than the physical object or medium. To preserve access to the intellectual content, we must preserve the integrity of the intellectual content, even as we discard the original storage medium, software and hardware on which the digital object was created and accessed originally. Preserving the integrity of digital objects also involves developing techniques for verifying the authenticity of a digital object, that is, whether the digital object has undergone alteration of any kind for any reason since its creation.

There are a number of different strategies for converting the form of digital information as technology changes. They include transferring digital information from less stable to more stable media, from highly software-dependent formats to less software-intensive formats, and from a multiplicity of formats to a smaller number of common formats; developing and imposing standards; developing backward compatibility paths; and developing process centers for migration and reformatting.

Proponents of emulation as the preferred digital preservation strategy contend that digital preservation needs a solution that is extensible because no one can predict what changes will occur, and that does not require labor-intensive examination or translation of individual documents. Migration does not supply these two essential conditions. Emulation, they state, does. Furthermore, running the original software under emulation on future computers is the only reliable way to recreate a digital document's original functionality, look, and feel.

In discussing the "how" of electronic archiving, there are additional issues, besides the method used to preserve the digital object, which must be taken into account both in choosing the preferred method and in implementing it effectively. They are *authenticity* of the digital object (i.e., that it is unaltered from the original; that it is what it purports to be), and *copyright,* or levels of permitted access to the digital object.

The concept of emulation, using physical or logical structures called "containers" or "wrappers" to provide a relationship between all information components such as the digital object and its metadata and software specifications, underlies the OAIS Reference Model (see Chapter 2), which utilizes the concepts of "information packages" (IPs) composed of "content information" and "preservation description information" contained by "packaging information." The content information includes the digital object itself and the representation information needed to interpret it. The preservation description information includes information about provenance and context, reference information such as unique identifiers, and a wrapper that protects the digital object against undocumented alteration.

In her article on digital preservation in the 2004 *Annual Review of Information Science and Technology,* Patricia Galloway calls emulation "the presumed 'gold standard' for carrying digital objects forward" (Galloway, 2004, p. 574), because no changes are made to the original object, and because software support is provided to make the original object accessible precisely as it was when it was created. On the other hand, this means that software emulators may have to be written to carry out the functions of the original hardware, the original operating system, and the retrieval and display capabilities of the original hardware and software. In addition—and Galloway notes that this must be taken into account—the systems on which emulators depend will themselves be subject to the need for conversion and migration from time to time (Galloway, 2004, p. 574). The most intensive investigation of emulation as the preferred digital preservation strategy was carried out by the CAMiLEON project (http://www.si.umich.edu/CAMiLEON/) under the auspices of the Universities of Michigan (USA) and Leeds (UK) and funded by JISC and NSF. CAMiLEON stands for Creative Archiving at Michigan and Leeds: Emulating the Old on the New. According to the CAMiLEON Web site, the project had three main objectives:

- To explore the options for long-term retention of the original functionality and "look and feel" of digital objects

- To investigate technology emulation as a long-term strategy for long-term preservation and access to digital objects

- To consider where and how emulation fits into a suite of digital preservation strategies (*Camileon,* 2003?)

One of the best-publicized results of the CAMiLEON project, which ended in 2003, was its part in the attempt to rescue the BBC Domesday Project. The BBC Domesday Project was a landmark multimedia resource that was produced to celebrate the 900th anniversary of the original Domesday book. School children and researchers from across the country collected a massive amount of material, which was recorded on two special videodiscs. Over a million people took part in the project, which was produced through a collaboration of the BBC, Acorn, Philips, and Logica. Information content was contributed to the community discs by thousands of school children from across the country, and the National Disc was filled with data from many different researchers, photographers, and scholars.

The Domesday project was built on hardware and software designed and manufactured in 1986, and many elements of this original setup are not compatible with today's computers. "Put simply, the BBC Domesday system is rapidly approaching complete obsolescence" (*Camileon,* 2003?).

The CAMiLEON team have implemented an emulator that runs BBC Domesday on a modern computer. In addition, the UK CAMiLEON team (now working on the JISC funded Representation and Rendering Project) is seeking funding to turn the demonstrator into a fully preserved system ready for archiving.

How Much?

The costs involved in digital archiving can be divided into two main categories: the costs for converting information into digital form (or for acquiring data already in a digital format) and the costs for maintaining digital information. Estimating the costs of these processes is complex, and the cost of each element in the processes varies according a variety of factors. For example, if materials need to be digitized, cost is affected by whether the digitization is implemented on-site or through a vendor. In addition, the type of material, the degree of digitization, and the resolution of the digitization all affect the cost, as well as the general condition of the material being digitized. High-quality, "preservation" projects cost more than access-oriented projects in which image quality is less important. Projects including both digital images of texts and machine-editable files converted from their paper originals through optical character recognition (OCR) technology or human keying are even more expensive. A number of projects have shown that digital imaging itself only accounts for about one-third of the overall costs for imaging projects with metadata creation often being as or more expensive than the physical conversion of materials into digital objects. Other studies have predicted that it will not be the conversion that will be the main cost of digital preservation, but rather the management of the project over the long term.

Digitization costs can be broken into "basic costs" and "technical costs." Basic costs include project planning, quality control, and document preparation activities. Technical costs include cost of moving the original materials through the scanning process and the cost of writing an output file to the required resolution, bit depth, and quality. It is much cheaper to scan individual sheets if they can be run through a sheet feeder than a bound volume or photographs, both of which must be scanned manually.

Several models for calculating costs have been developed. However, because cost studies are in themselves expensive and complex to carry out, there have really been only a few large-scale analyses of the costs of digital conversion and preservation. The most significant of these were Yale University Library's Project Open Book, Cornell University's Digital to Microfilm Conversion Project, and the Early Canadiana Online Project. There were also some comparative analyses carried out in the United Kingdom. Steven Puglia, from the National Archives and Records Administration (NARA), provided an extensive analysis of digitization project costs at NARA and other institutions in *RLG DigiNews,* and Kenney and Rieger reported on cost figures from the University of Michigan, University of Virginia, and Cornell University digitization projects. Yale's Project Open Book explored and produced figures primarily on the costs of conversion. Anne Kenney, in her final report on the Cornell Project, included estimates from various sources for archiving a digital book for 10 years as well. The costing study on the Early Canadiana Online Project included all costs associated with the production, cataloging, and sales of texts in microfiche or digital format.

One of the conclusions reached as a result of the Yale and Cornell studies was that despite predictions that microfilm could be replaced by digital imaging, many people have come to feel that digitization may increase access to materials but does not guarantee their continued preservation (Chapman et al., 1999). This attitude is reflected, for example, in a report on a Mellon Foundation–funded study on the future of Oxford's digital collections: "With reference to preservation, there was considerable unease within the library sector at the prospect of relying on a digital copy as a substitution for other formats; and most felt that film still provided the best preservation medium" (*Scoping the Future of Oxford's Digital Collections,* 1999).

The choice of a digital conversion path (film-first or scan-first) depends on which approach meets an institution's objectives for preservation (film) and access (digital images) at the lowest cost. Therefore, it is appropriate to compare the quality and costs of preservation microfilm to digital COM to determine whether the film-first or scan-first approach is more advantageous. The Cornell project established that digital COM can be of equal or superior quality to traditional 35 mm preservation microfilm and costs slightly less than $0.12 per page image. Both the Cornell and Yale reports point out, however, that the $0.12 per image for COM refers only to one generation of film and that these costs also presume that bibliographic targets have already been created and are stored with the digital images. Based on these findings, two preliminary conclusions were reached about the preservation component of the hybrid approach:

1. Film-first and scan-first offer comparable microfilm quality, but

2. COM production appears to be less expensive than microfilm production.

Other preliminary conclusions with respect to the digital images from the Yale and Cornell projects were that scanning from paper and scanning from film are comparable in cost, but the quality of scan-first digital image is better. The Hybrid Approach Decision Tree provided guidance for a number of situations:

1. When the goal is to produce digital preservation masters and preservation quality film when only brittle volumes are available, when both brittle volumes and microfilm are available, and when only microfilm is available.

2. When the goal is to produce digital access masters and preservation quality film when only brittle volumes are available, when both brittle volumes and microfilm are available and when only microfilm is available. (Chapman et al., 1999)

A 2004 article on library periodicals expenses compared nonsubscription costs of print and electronic journal formats over the long term. Nonsubscription costs include the following:

♦ All staff costs for current issues

♦ Staff costs for those backfile activities that are effectively one-time in nature

   Collection Development

   Licensing and Negotiations

   Subscription Processing, Routine Renewal, and Termination

   Receipt and Check-in

   Routing of Issues and Tables of Contents

   Cataloging

   Linking Services

   Physical Processing

♦ The depreciation of staff workstations, allocated on the same basis as the staff costs

♦ The total cost of binding, plus

♦ The total cost of subscription agents, plus

♦ The cost of space occupied by the current issues reading room during the year. (Schonfeld, 2004)

The authors state that "since we wanted to understand the long-term implications of the format choice, we adopted the life-cycle approach. In the life-cycle analysis that follows, we track the total non-subscription costs over the course of 25 years of accessioning one year of a typical periodical title (Schonfeld, 2004). They conclude that the long-term financial commitment associated with accessioning one year of a periodical is lower for the electronic format than for print, at every library in their study, and that the transition to electronic format is likely to afford reductions in libraries' long-term financial commitments to nonsubscription costs. At the same time, the authors acknowledge in their conclusion that "there is presently a total absence in the electronic format of any costs associated with the long-term archiving of the periodical content" (Schonfeld, 2004).

The LOCKSS project, discussed earlier in this chapter, consists of a large number of independent, low-cost, persistent Web caches of Web-published academic journals. Simulations run on the system show that it is capable of resisting for decades an "adversary" (i.e., someone trying to hack into the system and destroy it) capable of unlimited sustained effort. Among the design principles of the LOCKSS system is at least one principle with clear implications for the "how much?" of digital preservation: "*Cheap storage is unreliable. We assume that in our time-scale no cheap and easy to maintain storage is reliable*" (*Preserving Peer Replicas by Rate-Limited Sampled Voting*, 2003). At the same time that the system's designers state that cheap storage is unreliable, however, they maintain that first and foremost digital preservation systems must be very cheap to build and maintain, which precludes high-performance software (presumably including emulators) or complicated administration. LOCKSS, first of all, preserves access to the material via common techniques such as links, bookmarks, and search engines, making it appear to a library's patrons that pages remain available at their original URLs even if they are no longer available there from the publisher. To do this, participating libraries run persistent Web caches that

- *collect* by crawling the journal Web sites and preloading newly published material;

- *distribute* by acting as a limited proxy cache for the library's local readers, supplying the *publisher's* copy if it is available and the local copy otherwise; and

- *preserve* by cooperating with other caches that hold the same material to detect and repair damage. (*Preserving Peer Replicas by Rate-Limited Sampled Voting*, 2003)

The LOCKSS project may provide a cost-effective solution for longtime preservation of one category of digital objects—academic e-journals—whereas other categories, such as the diverse materials of the BBC Domesday Project, may require more expensive methods of preservation into the distant future, namely, emulator technology. As there is no single method of long-term digital preservation that guarantees beyond a doubt to be effective in preserving all types of digital objects for generations to come, there is not yet enough data to state conclusively which methods will be the most cost-effective because there has not yet been a long-term study. With regard to this issue, as with other issues in the complex scenario of preserving our digital heritage, only time will tell.

We can take heart, however, from the enormous growth in recent years of digital preservation projects being carried out by international organizations, academic institutions, private foundations, and government agencies throughout the world. At the end of December 2004, Google announced with considerable fanfare that it was preparing to make digital copies of the contents of some of the world's great libraries, including the Bodleian, the New York Public Library, and the libraries of the University of Michigan, Stanford University, and Harvard. Referring to the fate of the Domesday Project, Google tempered its announcement with a sober reminder that

none of this will happen quickly: the dull, manual process of scanning each page means that it will be a decade before 15m books from the libraries in Google's partnership are online. Nor have all the technical issues been settled: "future-proofing" is tricky, as evidenced by the BBC's 1986 Domesday Project, a digitalised version of the great book set on laser discs: what was cutting edge in 1986 was unreadable by 2000. Digital preservation seems an unlikely heritage issue to raise at this stage, but otherwise the time and energy spent by Google and others may yet go to waste. (*The World in 0s and 1s*, 2004)

Still and in spite of Google's stern and justified warning that digitization without preservation is futile, the sheer numbers of interested stakeholders willing to fund research projects and continue working on solutions for as long as it takes to ensure the safety of this invaluable and growing body of resources is our best guarantee that it will not perish after all.

Bibliography

Note: All URLs checked October 26, 2004, unless otherwise noted.

About ERPANET [Online]. (2004). Available: http://www.ERPANET.org/about.php

About LOCKSS [Online]. (2004). Available: http://www.LOCKSS.org/about/about.htm

Arthur, Charles. (2003). "The End of History." *Independent.co.uk* (June 30) [Online]. Available: http://news.independent.co.uk/business/analysis_and_features/story.jsp?story=420334

Ashworth, Susan, Mackie Morag, and William J. Nixon. (2004). The DAEDALUS Project, Developing Institutional Repositories at Glasgow University: The Story So Far. *Library Review* 53(5): 259–64.

Beagrie, Neil. (2003a). *National Digital Preservation Initiatives: An Overview of Developments in Australia, France, the Netherlands, and the United Kingdom and of Related International Activity* [Online]. Available: http://www.clir.org/pubs/reports/pub116/contents.html

Beagrie, Neil. (2003b). *A Continuing Access and Digital Preservation Strategy for the Joint Information Systems Committee (JISC) 2002–2005. Executive Summary* [Online]. Available: http://www.jisc.ac.uk/index.cfm?name=pres_continuing

Beagrie, Neil. (2004a). "The Continuing Access and Digital Preservation Strategy for the UK Joint Information Systems Committee (JISC)." *D-Lib Magazine* 10 no. 28 (July) [Online]. Available: http://www.dlib.org/dlib/july04/beagrie/07beagrie.html

Beagrie, Neil. (2004b). "Digital Information Will Never Survive by Accident." *SAPINFO* (August 11) [Online]. Available: http://www.jisc.ac.uk/index.cfm?name=news_digital

Beagrie, Neil. (2004c). "Launch of Digital Curation Centre Web site." *Digital-Preservation Announcement and Information List* (April 7) [Online]. Available: http://www.jiscmail.ac.uk/cgi-bin/webadmin?A2=ind0404&L=digital-preservation&T=0&F=&S=&P=789

British Govt Orders Email Purge. (2004). *Northern Territory News* (December 18) [On-line]. Available: http://www.ntnews.news.com.au/common/story_page/0,7034,11725496%255E1702,00.html (accessed December 19, 2004)

Burnhill, Peter. (2004). "In Brief: Digital Curation Centre (DDC) Established." *D-Lib* (February) [Online]. Available: http://www.dlib.org/dlib/february04/02inbrief.html

CAMiLEON [Online]. (2003?). Available: http://www.si.umich.edu/CAMILEON/about/aboutcam.html

Campbell, Laura. (2003). "National Digital Information Infrastructure and Preservation Program. " *RLG DigiNews* 7, no. 3 (June 15) [Online]. Available: http://www.rlg.org/preserv/diginews/v7_n3_feature1.html

Canadian <Metadata> Forum. (2003). *About the Forum [Online]. Available:* http://www.collectionscanada.ca/metaforum/index-e.html

Chapman, Stephen, Paul Conway, and Anne R. Kenney. (1999). Digital Imaging and Preservation Microfilm: The Future of the Hybrid Approach for the Preservation of Brittle Books *RLG DigiNews* 3 no. 1 (February 15) [Online]. Available: http://www.rlg.org/preserv/diginews/diginews3-1.html

Childress, Eric. (2003). "Faith, Trust, and Cooperation: Sharing the Load of Creating Metadata for the Web." *Journal of Internet Cataloging* 6 no. 1: 5–8.

Christensen-Dalsgaard, Birte. (2004). "Web Archive Activities in Denmark." *RLG DigiNews* 8 no. 3 (June 15) [Online]. Available: http://www.rlg.org/en/page.php?Page_ID=17661#article0

Coutts, John. (2003). "Digital Citizens." *Guardian Unlimited* (July 10) [Online]. Available: http://www.guardian.co.uk/online/story/0,,994662,00.html

Digital Preservation Coalition. (2003). "DPC Advocacy Campaign. Media and PR" [Online]. Available: http://www.dpconline.org/graphics/advocacy/

Digital Preservation Coalition. (2004). "Digital Preservation: The Global Context" [Online]. Available: http://www.dpconline.org/graphics/events/for040623.html

DPC/PADI. What's New in Digital Preservation 8 (February–June 2004) [Online]. Available: http://www.nla.gov.au/padi/qdigest/june2004.html

Edwards, Eli. (2004). "Ephemeral to Enduring: The Internet Archive and Its Role in Preserving Digital Media." *Information Technology and Libraries* 23 no. 1: 3–8.

Emulation: Context and Current Status (2003) [Online]. Digital Preservation Testbed White Paper. Available: http://www.digitaleduurzaamheid.nl/bibliotheek/docs/white_paper_emulatie_EN.pdf

Entlich, Richard. (2004). "One Last Spin: Floppy Disks Head Toward Retirement." *RLG DigiNews* 8 no. 6 (December 15) [Online]. Available: http://www.rlg.org/en/page.php?Page_ID=20492

Fleischhauer, Carl. (2003). "Preservation, Security, and Digital Content." *Journal of Library Administration* 38 no. 3/4: 141–47.

Galloway, Patricia. (2004). "Preservation of Digital Objects." *Annual Review of Information Science and Technology* 38: 549–90.

Gatenby, Pam. (2004). "Collecting and Managing Web Resources for Long-Term Access: Web Harvesting and Guidelines to Support Preservation (ICABS Actions 3.3 and 3.4)." World Library and Information Congress: 70th IFLA General Conference and Council, 22–27 August 2004, Buenos Aires, Argentina [Online]. Available: http://www.ifla.org/IV/ifla70/papers/026e-Gatenby.pdf

Geser, Guntram, and John Pereira, eds. (2004). *The Future of Digital Heritage Space: An Expedition Report. DigiCULT* (Thematic Issue 7, December) [Online]. Available: http://www.digicult.info/downloads/dc_thematic_issue7.pdf

Gorman, Michael. (2003). "Cataloguing in an Electronic Age." *Cataloging & Classification Quarterly* 36 no. 3/4: 5–17.

Granger, Stewart. (2002). "Digital Preservation and Deep Infrastructure." *D-Lib Magazine* 8 no. 2 (February) [Online]. Available: http://www.dlib.org/dlib/february02/granger/02granger.html

Hakala, Juha. (2004). "Archiving the Web: European Experiences." *Program: Electronic Library and Information Systems* 38 no. 3: 176–83.

IFLA Core Activity: IFLA-CDNL Alliance for Bibliographic Standards (ICABS) [Online]. (2004). Available: http://www.ifla.org/VI/7/icabs.htm

International Libraries and the Internet Archive Collaborate to Build Open-Access Text Archives. (2004). Announcements: December 15 [Online]. Available: http://www.archive.org/iathreads/post-view.php?id=25361

Invest to Save. Report and Recommendations of the NSF-DELOS Working Group on Digital Archiving and Preservation [Online]. (2003). Available: http://delos-noe.iei.pi.cnr.it/activities/internationalforum/Joint-WGs/digitalarchiving/Digitalarchiving.pdf

The Joint Information Systems Committee (JISC). (2004). *Supporting Digital Preservation and Asset Management in Institutions: Projects Funded Under the JISC Circular 4/04 Programme Have Been Announced* [Online]. Available: http://www.jisc.ac.uk/index.cfm?name=programme_404

Jones, Maggie. (2003a). *Archiving E-Journals Consultancy—Final Report: Report Commissioned by the Joint Information Systems Committee (JISC)* [Online]. Available: http://www.jisc.ac.uk/uploaded_documents/ejournalsfinal.pdf

Jones, Maggie. (2003b). "Digital Preservation Activities in the U.K.—Building the Infrastructure." *World Library and Information Congress: 69th IFLA General Conference and Council, 1-9 August 2003, Berlin* [Online]. Available: http://www.ifla.org/IV/ifla69/papers/129e-Jones.pdf

Lavoie, Brian. (2004). "Thirteen Ways of Looking at … Digital Preservation." *D-Lib Magazine* 10 no. 7/8 (July/August) [Online]. Available: http://www.dlib.org/dlib/july04/lavoie/07lavoie.html

Lazinger, Susan. (2004). "Issues of Policy and Practice in Digital Preservation: Why? What? Who? How? How Much?" In: *Digital Libraries: Policy, Planning and Practice.* Edited by Judith Andrews and Derek Law. London: Ashgate, pp. 99–112.

Library of Congress Announces Awards of $15 Million to Begin Building a Network of Partners for Digital Preservation: Eight Institutions and Their Partners to Participate in National Program [Online]. (2004). Available: http://www.digitalpreservation.gov/about/pr_093004.html

Lynch, Clifford A. (2003). "The Coming Crisis in Preserving Our Digital Cultural Heritage." *Journal of Library Administration* 38 no. 3/4: 149–61.

Martin, Ruth. (2003). "ePrints UK: Developing a national e-prints archive." *Ariadne* 35 (April 30) [Online]. Available: http://www.ariadne.ac.uk/issue35/martin/

Masanes, Julien. (2002). "Towards Continuous Web Archiving: First Results and an Agenda for the Future ." *D-Lib Magazine* 8 no. 12 (December) [Online]. Available: http://www.dlib.org/dlib/december02/masanes/12masanes.html

National Digital Information Infrastructure and Preservation Program (Digital Preservation). (2004). *Update to the NDIIPP Architecture* [Online]. Available: http://www.digitalpreservation.gov/repor/NDIIPP_v02.pdf

National Library of Wales. (2003). *Digital Preservation Policy and Strategy* [Online]. Available: http://www.llgc.org.uk/adrodd/digital_preservation_policy_and_strategy.pdf

netpreserve.org: National Internet Preservation Consortium. Mission [Online]. (2004). Available: http://netpreserve.org/about/mission.php

The OceanStore Project: Project Overview [Online]. (2002). Available: http://oceanstore.cs.berkeley.edu/info/overview.html

Phillips, Margaret E. (2003). "PANDORA. Australia's Web Archive, and the Digital Archiving System that Supports it." *Digicult.Info* 6 [Online]. Available: http://www.digicult.info/downloads/digicult_thematic_issue6.pdf

Preserving Our Digital Heritage: Plan for the National Digital Information Infrastructure and Preservation Program: A Collaborative Initiative of the Library of Congress [Online]. (2002). Available: http://www.digitalpreservation.gov/index.php?nav=3&subnav=1

Preserving Peer Replicas by Rate-Limited Sampled Voting [Online]. (2003). 19th ACM Symposium on Operating Systems Principles (SOSP '03), October 19–22, 2003, Bolton Landing, New York, USA. Available: http://www.cs.rochester.edu/sosp2003/papers/p140-maniatis.pdf

Ross, Seamus. (2004). "The Role of ERPANET in Supporting Digital Curation and Preservation in Europe." *D-Lib Magazine* 10 no. 7/8 (July/August) [Online]. Available: http://www.dlib.org/dlib/july04/ross/07ross.html

Schlicke, Priscilla. (2003). "Digital Preservation Strategies." *Information Management Report* (July): 1–4.

Schonfeld, Roger C. (2004). "Library Periodicals Expenses: Comparison of Non-Subscription Costs of Print and Electronic Formats on a Life-Cycle Basis." *D-Lib Magazine* 10 no. 4 (January) [Online]. Available: http://www.dlib.org/dlib/january04/schonfeld/01schonfeld.html

Scoping the Future of Oxford's Digital Collections. A Study Funded by the Andrew W. Mellon Foundation [Online]. (1999). Available: http://www.bodley. ox.ac.uk/scoping/

Searle, Sam. (2003). "Preservation Metadata: Pragmatic First Steps at the National Library of New Zealand." *D-Lib Magazine* 9 no. 4 (April) [Online]. Available: http://www.dlib.org/dlib/april03/thompson/04thompson.html

Spedding, Vanessa. (2003). "Data Preservation: Great Data, But Will It Last?" *Research Information* (Spring) [Online]. Available: http://www.researchinformation. info/rispring03data.html

Stanescu, Andreas. (2004). "Assessing the Durability of Formats in a Digital Preservation Environment: The INFORM Methodology." *D-Lib Magazine* 10 no. 11 (November) [Online]. Available: http://www.dlib.org/dlib/november04/ stanescu/11stanescu.html

Steenbakkers, Johan F. (2004). "Treasuring the Digital Records of Science: Archiving E-Journals at the Koninklijke Bibliotheek. *RLG DigiNews* 8 no. 2 (April 15) [Online]. Available: http://www.rlg.org/en/page.php?Page_ID=17068

UNESCO. (2003a). *Draft Charter on the Preservation of the Digital Heritage* [Online]. Available: http://unesdoc.unesco.org/images/0013/001311/131178e.pdf

UNESCO. (2003b). *Guidelines for the Preservation of Digital Heritage* [Online]. Available: http://portal.unesco.org/ci/en/ev.php-URL_ID=8967&URL_DO=DO_ TOPIC&URL_SECTION=201.html

UNESCO Adopts a Convention on the Preservation of Intangible Heritage and a Declaration on Human Genetic Data [Online]. (2003). Available: http://portal. unesco.org/en/ev.php-URL_ID=16797&URL_DO=DO_TOPIC&URL_ SECTION=201.html

Van Wijngaarden, Hilde. (2004). "An Exploration of Strategies and Recent Developments in Digital Preservation: Outline of an International Inquiry by the *Koninklijke Bibliogheek*." World Library and Information Congress: 70th IFLA General Conference and Council, August 22–27, 2004, Buenos Aires, Argentina [Online]. Available: http://www.ifla.org/IV/ifla70/papers/025e-Wijngaarden.pdf

Webb, Colin. (2003). "Saving Digital Heritage—A UNESCO Campaign." *RLG DigiNews* 7 no. 3 (June 15). [Online]. Available: http://www.rlg.org/legacy/ preserv/diginews/diginews7-3.html#feature3

Williamson, Andrew. (2003). "Awareness of Quality Assurance Procedures in Digital Preservation." *Library Review* 53 no. 4: 204–6.

The World in 0s and 1s [Online]. (2004). *The Guardian* (December 20). Available: http://education.guardian.co.uk/print/0,3858,5089297-108229,00.html

Chapter 9

Impact of Digital Resources on Library Services

Some digital libraries are independent of traditional libraries and their onsite collections of books, paper periodicals, and undigitized audiovisual materials and function without library oversight, even though the projects that created them may have originated within traditional institutions. Others remain under the administrative umbrella of traditional libraries. Either way, the proliferation of digital library projects has affected all libraries and the services traditional libraries offer. This chapter explores the changes in library services that can be attributed to the maturation of digital library projects, such as online reserves, reference services, user instruction, and the like. The chapter also addresses the kinds of education and training needed for librarians and archivists to function effectively in the digital environment.

New and Changed Services

To some degree, the online services the library world is witnessing—whether entirely new services or traditional services now offered online—are the result of maturing networking as much as they are by-products of digital library projects. The ability to send materials electronically to any outlet deemed eligible to receive them is the key feature prompting online library services, whether the materials are stored in a repository called a digital library or any other kind of database or data center. Having access to one or more digital libraries, however, speeds the process and makes it possible to search repositories whose contents have been preselected to match the needs of a defined audience. An example of this kind of preselection is the VARIATIONS project, built to serve the needs of Indiana University's music scholars. A digital library is not a necessary prerequisite to initiating online services but goes hand-in-hand with it.

Online Reserves

Online reserves are, by definition, specified groups of materials in electronic form related to particular college or university courses. Accordingly, they qualify as a kind of digital library. One easily goes beyond this simple, materials-oriented defini-tion to one that is more user-oriented, because online reserves have clearly defined target audiences—namely, the groups of students enrolled in the courses for which the materials have been gathered. Indiana University's VARIATIONS is a good ex-ample. When VARIATIONS was launched, one of its principal services was provid-ing course reserves to students. Course reserves are such an important service that when VARIATIONS2 was launched, it did not supersede VARIATIONS. The orig-inal digital library project was retained and continues to support online reserves. (Had they chosen to do so, VARIATIONS2's designers could have incorporated the online course reserve system into one unified project. The authors are not implying that maintaining both projects simultaneously and having them supply different services was the only option, but some advantage must have prompted the decision to do so.)

Building digital libraries for course reserves enables librarians to streamline the management of the reserve collection process, which was extremely labor-intensive in precomputer days, even though new problems are encountered in doing so. At this writing, online reserves often require converting paper documents to electronic form, with all the attendant legal and contractual, technical scanning, and biblio-graphical/metadata problems. Sometimes, electronic documents contracted for an-other purpose cannot be used for online reserves without new contract specifications (and new fees). But once the problems are resolved and the materials are in electronic form, librarians circumvent the traditional process—picking materials off the shelves; processing them for the reserve collection, including preparing new biblio-graphic data pertaining to reserves; storing them in separate locations; retrieving them from the shelves on request throughout the hours the library is open; monitor-ing their prompt return; de-processing them at the end of the semester, including re-moving the bibliographic data pertaining to reserves; and, finally, physically returning them to their original locations.

A college offering several hundred courses, each having reserve collections involv-ing 20 or 30 documents (some have many more), results in the pick, process, store, re-trieve, monitor, de-process, and return operations for thousands of documents. Even when everything in the traditional system is working smoothly, users may be unable to obtain requested materials because other students borrowed them first and are entitled to a specified length of time before being asked to return them. At the end of the day, both librarians and users have much to gain from adopting online reserves.

Online Reference Services

Experimentation with online reference services, sometimes available 24 hours a day, seven days a week (24/7 reference), has been going on for years, improving rapidly as new communication options were made available to librarians and users. If the pro-totype for online reference was the 20th century's telephone reference service, the on-line prototype was e-mail. At this writing, e-mail is still employed for reference service communications, chosen mainly by users who have requests that are not time-sensitive or are likely to involve time-consuming searches through multiple databases.

Online reference—especially 24/7 reference—seems ideally suited to the world of serious research. Its users might be graduate students, faculty members, and pro-fessional researchers working in business, medicine, the sciences, or other subject ar-eas. Working during the night or on weekends and holidays is not unusual for university-based scholars and other serious researchers, who sometimes prefer it when most people are gone and they are not disturbed by telephone calls, visitors, or interactions with colleagues. Faculty members have obligations that consume many daytime hours—teaching classes, meeting with students and advisees, serving on departmental and university committees, attending seminars and conferences—but leave the evening, weekend, and holiday hours for their personal research. Sometimes faculty members prefer working at "off" hours to avoid using databases they know are heavily used by their students during regular study hours. Users may be located in different time zones than the service headquarters (not an unusual occurrence for participants in "virtual" classes and workshops), or they may wish to take advantage of lower rates for telecommunications charges during nonpeak hours.

E-mail has a distinct advantage over telephone service in that it does not demand instant attention from librarians receiving the messages and answering queries. Too often, telephone reference desks have short periods during which many calls are received at once and long periods during which only a few calls are received. E-mail queues allow librarians to answer messages in turn (e-mail automatically queues messages according to the time they are received) as quickly as possible, but without the haranguing of ringing telephones, which is stressful for librarians, or keeping users on hold for long periods, which tends to anger them, because the "desk" is busy.

Digital libraries have streamlined the process of answering online queries. They enable librarians to search for materials at the same computer on which they receive the query, "letting their fingers do the walking," as the saying goes, instead of having to leave the desk to find materials in nonelectronic format shelved at a distance. Once found, the electronic versions of materials can be electronically transferred to the user's online mailbox or, if that is not feasible, information about the materials can be sent to the user electronically.

Online chat is now a typical medium for online reference service. It has several advantages over e-mail, the main one being that the user and the librarian can exchange information in real time, without the time lags inherent in sending and receiving e-mail messages. Such exchanges of information are especially important when the user's inquiry is not sharply focused or the librarian interprets a query in a way that the user believes is going in the wrong direction. Online chat is also useful when a query is time-sensitive. Online chat can either provide the user with an immediate answer or the knowledge that an immediate answer is not possible. For some people, knowing right away that an answer will take time or be difficult to obtain is better than waiting for an e-mail that could take several hours to arrive, while each tick of the clock adds to the person's psychological stress. Knowing an immediate reply is not possible empowers the user to change direction, ask a different question, or try a new approach that might afford a quicker resolution to the person's information need.

When online chat is combined with digitized collections, a librarian can send a sample of retrieved material and ask the user if the material is appropriate, if he or she believes the material answers the question completely, or if the user wants more material with similar or different features.

Online User Instruction

Library Web sites provide an immediately obvious, easily and frequently accessed place to situate user instruction. Questions arise about where instructional links should appear, how they are navigated, and how to evaluate them. More questions ask how to design instructional links that are sufficiently clear, complete, and detailed to warrant dropping traditional forms of instruction involving face-to-face interactions between library instructors and users.

Although it is clear that offsite users can benefit from online instruction because they have few opportunities to receive onsite instruction, it is less clear that onsite users would be equally as well served by it. Several issues have an impact on the answer, at least in the academic environment, although they have little to do with how the instruction is delivered:

1. Is user instruction required or voluntary? If the answer is "voluntary," it is likely that some proportion of students will fail to take advantage of it. It can be argued that posting instruction on the library's Web site attracts more voluntary users than requiring their presence in a classroom, simply because Web-based delivery is both more convenient and not time-sensitive.

2. Is user instruction offered as a general aid to using the library or linked to particular courses or assignments within a course? Linking user instruction to specific coursework tends to make it both more attractive and more likely to be remembered and employed than when it is given solely as a general aid to library activities. On the other hand, Web-based instruction could be valuable because it is available at the point of use, whereas classroom-based instruction is not.

3. Do students of user instruction receive grades for their work or merely gain the satisfaction of the knowledge gained? Earning grades for user instruction creates an incentive for paying attention and doing the work. Grade-free classes seem less important, however valuable the knowledge they impart.

In academic venues, answers to these questions may make the difference between user participation or user indifference, whether instruction is offered via the Web, in the library, or in regular classrooms.

In the public library environment, user instruction issues are different. Public libraries never require instruction, even when it would be an advantage both to the users and the libraries; and, of course, no classes, assignments, credit, or grades are involved. Public library users who take advantage of user instruction generally are motivated by a need to find materials they have been unable to obtain on their own, but some might participate merely because they have time on their hands and they like the library.

Well-designed web-based user instruction is the subject of several professional publications,[1] although many more discuss library Web site design in general. Typically, instruction provided on the same screen as a database's search menu (or directly linked to it) tends to be so cryptic it is hard to believe it succeeds in reaching anyone who is not already familiar with the process. Instructions may include statements such as, "Enter as much of the author's name as you know: au = Wolfe, T." If a user knows an author search involves specifying an index using a mnemonic tag (au) and a search command represented by punctuation (=) the statement will suffice. If, however, users are real novices to online searching, they may not recognize the search command "au =," understand and copy the proper spacing, or even realize they must enter the author's name surname first. People who are unaware of exactly what an example demonstrates are prone to interpret it incorrectly.

Even trickier to interpret than the highly abbreviated instructions for searching author names are those for searching subject headings and keywords as well as clarifying the kinds of title sets each will retrieve, or using Boolean operators to combine terms. The terms "subject headings" and "keywords" may not have the same meaning to laypeople that they have to librarians and other database professionals. Combine users' lack of knowledge with poor typing skills and one has a recipe for failure instead of an opportunity to engage users' interest and empower them to maximize the return on their effort.

Other Services to Off-site Users

Library Web sites are useful locations for a variety of local services, including requesting interlibrary loans, renewing borrowed materials, checking library records, communicating with library offices, and so on. Such services take advantage of telecommunications to streamline local activities and enable users to engage in them without going to the library building. They depend on local internal files such as circulation files and should be given high priorities when library Web sites are designed. A useful service is enabling a user to access personal accounts and local library offices while searching in a digital library, that is, to request access to a limited-access item or to pay fines that block access.

Other valuable services that go beyond local internal files include alerting users to new materials in the digital library that meet criteria they used in previous searches—an electronic version of current awareness services—and prompts that offer suggestions for refining searches and using alternative strategies for finding material on a topic. In her book *Collaborative Electronic Resource Management*, Joan Conger (2004, 207) envisions a "smart" library account that would gather information for users and anticipate their needs:[2]

"The dynamic environment would create an opening screen with the following:

- General resources pertinent to the student's current classes

- Resources similar to resources used during [recent] months

- New items the library has cataloged in the past week that may help

- Suggested resources not yet used"

One area that would seem ripe for development is automatically combining subject headings, classification numbers, and keywords for a subject area in which a user is interested, no matter which type of search is initiated. For example, if a user enters the word "digits" as a search term in a digital library, a response might ask: "Are you searching for materials about numbers (digit = number) or fingers (digit = finger)?" If the user answers "Fingers," the response might combine the terms "digits" and "fingers" as keywords with the corresponding Dewey and LC classification numbers, and produce a retrieval set containing titles such as *Diseases Affecting Human Appendages, Anatomy of the Human Hand, Strategies for Successful Aging: Caring for the Extremities, Painting the Human Hand, Hands across the Ocean, Finger Plans and Other Means of Creating Your Cyberpersonality,* and so on. Synonyms might be pre-programmed into the system for "digits" and "fingers," such as "appendages," "hand(s)" and "extremities," or the classification number assigned to titles containing the search term(s) might prompt the retrieval of materials containing the same or synonymous terms. Either way, a more comprehensive retrieval set would appear than if the computer matched only the keywords, only the subject headings, or only the classification numbers.

Prompts that ask the user if he or she wants more material similar to any of the retrieved items might be augmented by asking if the user wants to "browse the shelves" for similar materials. Browsing the shelves might mean showing 10 titles available in the digital library having classification numbers preceding the title in question and 10 titles available in the digital library having classification numbers that succeed it. In addition, the user could be empowered to continue browsing forward and backward from any point. In this way, online searching could overcome the physical inability of offsite users to discover items serendipitously.

To sum up, services based on materials in digital libraries are branching out from merely enlarging the holdings as much as possible while continuing to use the kinds of search techniques common to online public access catalogs and commercial databases of the 20th century to developing genuinely new types of service. New services tend to be based on ideas that help users find more of what they need without spending more time doing it. Engaging the ability of computers to match multiple search elements rapidly and display the results as suggestions, even if not specifically requested to do so, might help users move beyond their immediate search terms to plumb digital libraries more effectively.

Education and Training for the Digital Environment

Formal Coursework

Most of the 56 library schools in the United States and Canada accredited by the American Library Association[3] preparing new professionals have responded to the need for formal coursework focusing on digital libraries by instituting courses on them or related subjects, generally parsing the subject area as a whole into its component parts. Groups of courses cover metadata creation, metadata schemas, and similar topics (some coursework in this group covers a single schema); database design and management, including collection development and indexing (some coursework in this group covers one type of database, such as numeric or visual image databases); Web site design and management; digital information services; managing electronic serials; copyright and legal matters; telecommunications; and other topics that are part of the larger subject area. However, "Building and Managing Digital Libraries" is not, typically, the title of a course embracing all the parts and approaching them as a whole. Both the broad approach to overall project design, implementation, and management, and the nonlibrary skills, such as entrepreneurship, if taught at all, must be sought in the less formal venues.

Continuing Education

Academic institutions offering degree programs in library and information science and professional associations catering to library and information science practitioners make great efforts to fill the gap for working professionals between what they learned while they were in school earning their professional degrees and what they need to know in order to keep up with changes in the field after graduation. Workshops offered by library networks also provide formal training for practitioners. Formal continuing education workshops generally are designed and taught by credentialed faculty and often offer credit toward postgraduate certificates. Relevant workshops cover the skills needed to build and maintain Web sites, create metadata, and function in the high-tech world of digital libraries. More and more continuing education workshops are offered online, enabling persons located far from the sponsors to participate fully in the training experience.

Sponsors of formal continuing education workshops generally are responsive to suggestions from the field, even if the individuals offering the suggestions are not affiliated with the sponsoring institution or organization. Sponsors seek feedback from participants and area employers as well as from individuals affiliated with them such as alumni, faculty, members, and friends.

Informal and On-the-Job Training

Among the skills needed for effectiveness in the digital environment are a good many not taught in library school courses, such as leadership, entrepreneurship, costing and pricing products, and marketing. These skills appear more likely to be taught in a business school than one preparing librarians and information specialists. Nevertheless, job advertisements for metadata librarians ask for these skills as well as the ability to design new services and imagine new audiences for digital libraries—one could call it "creativity"—which is difficult to imagine being part of any formal training program. When confronted with a dearth of candidates having all the requisite skills, administrators can choose to hire people with library skills and teach them the necessary business skills or hire people with business skills and teach them the library skills.

One of the problems of providing good on-the-job training is the absence, at this writing, of a cadre of experienced professionals to do the training. Libraries are at the beginning of digital library development and still seem to be feeling their way in the dark. The few truly experienced master professionals are too busy doing their jobs to take on major training obligations. The vague wordings of metadata librarian advertisements indicate a fundamental lack of knowledge of what the job should entail, along with hopes that the successful candidates who take these jobs will be able to define it for them.

The Downside of Online Services

Given the many benefits described here in changing traditional onsite services to online services and initiating entirely new services, both based on digital libraries, what possible downside can one imagine? Critics point to several negative results, including the possibility that traditional libraries could disappear and, simultaneously, that library users are being lulled (or lulling themselves) into accepting mediocre online sources because they are online, when they might find much better sources in traditional offline formats such as books or printed journals. Other negatives include losing the talents and skills of experienced professionals who do not wish to work in the electronic environment (they may take early retirement rather than be moved to electronic formats); investing large sums of money in digital library ventures that fail to function successfully; and neglecting or ignoring the needs of traditional, in-person, onsite users because librarians are focused on the online users. For the foreseeable future, libraries are going to be hybrid institutions with hybrid collections, services, and programs; but finding staff members who are comfortable in both venues and sufficient funds to maintain two "shows" is likely to be elusive.

The fact that the knowledge and services of well-educated professional librarians and information specialists might be needed more than ever to help people evaluate information in our current chaotic digital environment is beside the point. How can people be convinced of the importance of professional service if they avoid making contact with librarians and information specialists in the first place? Outstanding library Web sites are one answer to this conundrum, especially if a high-priority goal is to make visitors want to return to the site. If, however, the principal goal of library Web sites is to impart no-nonsense, no-frills information, this strategy seems doomed.

Libraries once were, very nearly, the only game in town, especially when it came to "free"[4] information service. For better or worse, they no longer are. In the twenty-first century world of digital information, libraries are one of a variety of choices; and, like their rivals, they must compete to succeed. What market share do libraries hold? No one reports on it or speaks in those terms, and, therein is the problem.

Conclusions

This chapter has examined the ways in which traditional library services have changed as a result of the initiation of digital library projects. Among the new and changed services are online full-text serials and reserve collections, online reference, and online user instruction. In addition are online services that offer assistance to searchers during the search process and better searching techniques. Online browsing (i.e., the ability to browse by call number) adds opportunities for patrons to find materials in the digital library serendipitously, because they are located near items that meet initial search parameters.

Perhaps the most important differences between today's digital libraries and yesterday's traditional libraries are not so much the services themselves but in the altered expectations of users, librarians, and library administrators for rapid service that includes provision of full-text sources, not merely bibliographic information that points to wanted sources but does not deliver them.

Notes

1. A search for the keywords "library web design" and publication dates of 2000 or later in the Simmons College Libraries catalog retrieved nine titles, a relatively small number. Three with relevant content were as follows: *Web Site Design with the Patron in Mind: A Step-by-Step Guide for Libraries*, by Susanna Davidsen and Everyl Yankee (Chicago: American Library Association, 2004); *Web-based Instruction: A Guide for Libraries*, by Susan Sharpless Smith (Chicago: American Library Association, 2001); and *Community College Instruction Web Pages*, compiled by Marcia Krautter Suter and Elizabeth Burns (Chicago: Community and Junior Colleges Library Section, Association of College and Research Libraries, 2004).

2. The author actually suggests ten different types of information for the welcome screen.

3. The schools are listed on the Association's Web site, www.ala.org, following links for library education.

4. "Free" is enclosed in quotation marks to highlight the fact that library service is never free—even the materials available to be used or borrowed without charge. All library service has a cost, even if the cost is borne by large groups of taxpayers or members and not by the individuals using the services.

Bibliography

Ariadne Magazine. Available: http://www.ariadne.ac.uk

Bennett, Scott. (2003). *Libraries Designed for Learning.* [Report of the Council on Library and Information Resources.] Available at http://www.clir.org/pubs/reports/pub122/pub122web.pdf

Building and Sustaining Digital Collections: Models for Libraries and Museums. (2001). Washington, DC: Council on Library and Information Resources.

Conger, Joan E. (2004). *Collaborative Electronic Resource Management: From Acquisitions to Assessment.* Westport, CT: Libraries Unlimited.

Cotler, Deborah. (2005). "Electronic Resources: A Foundation of Successful Online Courses." [Unpublished term paper submitted for Simmons College class LIS408-20]

ERIL-L: Electronic Resources in Libraries listserv. (n.d.). Available http://www.joanconger.net/ERIL

IFLA Publication 99: Education and Research for Marketing and Quality Management in Libraries. (2002). Munich: K. G. Sauer.

Intner, Sheila S. (2003). "Dollars and Sense: Metadata and Its Impact on Collections Work in Libraries." *Technicalities* 23, no. 2 (July/August), 1, 14–15.

Jurewicz, Lynn, and Todd Cutler. (2003). *High Tech, High Touch: Library Customer Service through Technology.* Chicago: American Library Association.

LIBREF-L: Reference listserv. Available: http://www.library.kent.edu/libref-l.

The Resource Shelf: Resources and News for Information Professionals. (n.d.). Available: http://www.resourceshelf.com

Tenopir, Carol. (2003). *Use and Users of Electronic Library Resources: An Overview and Analysis of Recent Research Studies* (Report of the Council on Library and Information Resources). Available: www.clir.org/pubs/reports/pub120/contents.html

Wilson, A. Paula. (2004). *Library Web Sites: Creating Online Collections and Services.* Chicago: American Library Association.

Chapter 10
Future Possibilities

What does the future hold for metadata in libraries? What trends can be followed closely to discern indications about the future? Are discussions of metadata in libraries simply the province of a small and insular nucleus of the most advanced "techies" among us? Given the passage of time, are these discussions unlikely to reach increasingly larger groups of ordinary librarians? These questions are explored in this chapter.

Trends to Follow

In a scan of the literature for the single most mentioned issue with regard to the future of metadata, interoperability emerges as the hands-down winner. Brian Schottlaender, in his article answering the questions "Why Metadata? Why Now? Why Me?" states unequivocally that "perhaps more than anything, interoperability issues will be challenging" (Schottlaender 2003, 27).

Jane Greenberg (2003a) concurs; discussing the major issues in metadata research, she cites three recent trends that she has observed in the most recent literature, which she lists in the following order:

- *Interoperability*

- *Crosswalks*

- *Metadata Functionality. Descriptive metadata*

Defining interoperability as the sharing of resource data, if not the resource itself, and establishing logical connections among two or more projects, Greenberg then identifies the three types of interoperability—semantic, structural, and syntactic—and notes that achieving a degree of interoperability is a research trend evident in many digital initiatives, such as, for example, the Open Archives Initiative (OAI). For that matter, the second research trend Greenberg identifies—crosswalks—is also about interoperability. Crosswalks are, in fact, semantic mappings of metadata element definitions across metadata scheme specifications, constructed to achieve semantic interoperability (a mapping of elements with the same meaning but different field names).

The third trend Greenberg identifies as leading current metadata research is a concern with how descriptive metadata, such as "author/contributor" and "title," support not only the obvious function of resource discovery but also other functions such as resource administration and authentication, acquisitions, circulation, provenance tracking, and acquisitions. Extensive efforts by metadata researchers to classify metadata by type (see Chapter 1) indicate that today's metadata researchers feel strongly that classifying and understanding metadata's functionality can aid information professionals in the future in developing excellent information systems and schemas (Greenberg, 2003a).

Another trend in metadata research seems to be a move toward application design research, that is, research aimed toward developing specific applications for specific tasks. Themes Greenberg observed in this area include the development and implementation of (1) metadata schemas, (2) metadata generation tools (templates, editors, and generators to facilitate metadata creation), (3) project architectures, and (4) engines to search and retrieve digital resources via metadata. The rationale for this trend toward specific application development is, most likely, the tremendous speed at which information technology is advancing and the consequent race to keep up with these new technologies, limiting the time researchers can devote to more leisurely research activities, such as reviewing the literature and formulating and testing hypotheses (Greenberg, 2003b).

In a slightly later article (Greenberg, 2003b), Greenberg examines one of these areas of current metadata research—metadata generation tools—by analyzing the capabilities and potential of two Dublin Core automatic metadata generation applications, Klarity and DC-dot. Here again, it is standardization of the Dublin core, making the metadata of many communities of interest interoperable, which gave rise to the development of a wide variety of automatic metadata generators. Greenberg's research on automatic generators showed that generators using both *metadata extraction* (an algorithm that automatically extracts metadata from a resource's content displayed via a Web browser, as many commercial search engines produce in response to a search) and *metadata harvesting* (automatically collecting metadata from META tags found in the "header" source code of an HTML resource or encoding from another resource format, such as Microsoft Word documents), have the best potential for creating useful metadata.

The advantages of automatic generation seem obvious—it saves metadata creation time, fosters metadata consistency, and costs much less than manual metadata creation. The disadvantages are perhaps no less obvious—the metadata created by these generators, at least at present, is likely to be less rich, less accurate, and less sophisticated than the metadata created by experienced information professionals. Therefore, at least for the present, "the best metadata generation option is to integrate both human and automatic processes" (Greenberg, 2003b, p. 77), perhaps having the human metadata creator, for example, start the process by assigning keywords or, alternatively, letting the automatic metadata generator create a basic record, and then letting the human metadata creator enrich and refine the rough automatically created record.

Although examining the subjects of current research is one of the most important ways one can identify trends worth following, analyzing the future roles librarians might be expected to play in the creation of new metadata schemes and the adaptation of existing ones is no less important. El-Sherbini and Klim, in a 2004 article on metadata and cataloging practices, list the seven roles Kuny defined for librarians with regard to metadata in 1997 (Kuny, 1997) as still valid today and for the foreseeable future:

- Selection, evaluation, and description of networked information
- Coding metadata records
- Standards setting
- Training
- Advocacy
- Document repositories
- Registries (PURLs; metadata naming) (El-Sherbini and Klim, 2004, p. 240)

Is Interest in Metadata Limited to a Few Librarians?

Since librarians have always worked with the cataloging and classification concepts that form the basis of metadata, their practical experience has made it easy for them to adapt to the new concept of metadata. The concept is not new to them but rather part of the main current of cataloging and classification tradition.

Michael Gorman (2003), who puts cataloging in the electronic age into such eloquent perspective, sums up his examination of the strategies needed to solve the problems of cataloging the Internet and his prediction of how metadata will evolve with a list of difficult questions:

> Metadata is a buzzword that is losing its buzziness, but real problems and real issues lurk behind all the pomposity and techno-babble. What are we going to do about identifying and making accessible the valuable records of humanity that are only available in electronic form? How are we going to deal with the mutability and evanescence of those records? How are we going to preserve those resources and transmit them to posterity? (p. 16)

Like Gorman, we believe that the community of information professionals who have organized and preserved the world's written treasures for thousands of years will not fail to continue to organize and preserve the world's digital treasures in the future, demonstrating their usual sensitivity and creativity, remembering the lessons history has taught them, and keeping in mind the interests of all their user communities, present and future, as they have always done.

As these words are being written, knowledge of metadata still is limited to a small circle of librarians and information specialists working in libraries determined to find ways to expand the intellectual opportunities they offer the scholars and researchers whose work they support. Just because desirable information is being generated in a new medium does not put it "off limits" as far as these librarians are concerned. On the contrary, when information is generated electronically, it has many advantages for today's world of scholarship, making it more, not less, important for research support. Digital information is easy, rapid, and inexpensive to disseminate and already exists in a form that can be searched effectively. Librarians accustomed to supporting research are the ones who have acquired the knowledge themselves, or joined with knowledgeable colleagues from many fields, including library and information science, to establish metadata beachheads in their institutions.

Informal observation of the professional scene, however, seems to indicate that substantial interest in metadata now goes beyond the cadre of research librarians to the profession at large. The metadata conferences sponsored by the Association for Library Collections & Technical Services have not only been well attended but over-subscribed, attracting large audiences not once or twice, but six times. Publications about metadata are increasingly being marketed to librarians in nonresearch settings and seem to have numerous readers among librarians of all types, as evident by new listings in the professional literature such as *Metadata in Practice* edited by Hillman and Westbrooks, Priscilla Caplan's *Metadata Fundamentals for Librarians*, as well as this book. Examination of library and information science courses at 12 universities indicates expanded offerings that cover, or at least mention, metadata in half of them. Thus, it may not be overly optimistic to believe that the interest in metadata will continue to spread to librarians working in all types of libraries supporting all sorts of information-related activities.

The Future of Metadata in Libraries

The question of whether metadata has a future in libraries is really part of the larger issue of whether information delivered through the Internet has a future in libraries. In a fully wired world, will the library continue to be a viable node for information seeking, gathering, organization, and dissemination? The authors see no reason to believe otherwise.

It also is important not to underestimate the timetable for the spread of metadata throughout the library world. It would not do for predictions of metadata to emulate those made for the paperless society, which was supposed to arrive decades before the spread of computers began making that a reality (although many continue to complain that computers help generate much more paper information than ever). Nothing would hamper the viability of metadata-based projects more than assuming they will pervade the profession years before the required infrastructure is in place. Metadata projects require more than strong interest. They require adequate levels of computing ability among staff, an existing technological infrastructure or willingness to commit enough of the library's resources to build one, and astute leadership in planning and implementing projects that succeed in bringing something new and valuable to members of the libraries' public. If the result of a metadata project is not valuable to those who use it, the project cannot be called a success.

The library world is starting down a new path to acquiring information, processing it, and disseminating it. In the same spirit with which Gorman challenges librarians to address the issues surrounding metadata, this book offers an introduction to the history, methods, tools, and models the authors believe will smooth the path and help readers traverse it with confidence.

Bibliography

Note: All URLs checked on January 3, 2005, unless otherwise noted.

Caplan, Priscilla. (2004). *Metadata Fundamentals for All Librarians.* Chicago: American Library Association.

El Sherbini, Magda, and George Klim. (2004). "Metadata and Cataloging Practices." *The Electronic Library* 22, no. 3: 238–48.

Gorman, Michael. (2003). "Cataloguing in an Electronic Age." *Cataloging & Classification Quarterly* 36, no. 3/4: 5–17.

Greenberg, Jane. (2003a). "Metaviews in the Millennium: Research and Education." *Journal of Internet Cataloging* 6, no. 1: 9–14.

Greenberg, Jane. (2003b). "Metadata Extraction and Harvesting: A Comparison of Two Automatic Metadata Generation Applications." *Journal of Internet Cataloging* 6, no.4: 59–82.

Hillman, Diane I., and Elaine L. Westbrooks, eds. (2004). *Metadata in Practice.* Chicago: American Library Association.

Kuny, Terry. (1997). "Metadata, Libraries and Librarianship: Speech Notes." 63rd IFLA Council and General Conference. UDT Core Program Workshop, 4 September [Online]. Available: http://www.aiim.org/fbia/documents/63kuny2.pdf

Schottlaender, Brian E. C. (2003). "Why Metadata? Why Me? Why Now?" *Classification Quarterly* 36, no. 3/4: 19–29.

Acronyms

Acronyms are ubiquitous in the metadata world. The following is a handy reference guide to both metadata and library-related acronyms mentioned in this book.

AACR2	Anglo-American Cataloguing Rules, 2nd edition
AAT	Art and Architecture Thesaurus
AIP	Archival Information Package
AITF	Art Information Task Force
ALCTS	Association of Library Collections & Technical Services
ARIADNE	Alliance of Remote Instructional Authoring and Distribution Networks for Europe
CAMiLEON	Creative Archiving at Michigan & Leeds: Emulating the Old on the New
CCLRC	Central Laboratory of the Research Councils
CDL	California Digital Library
CDNL	Conference of Directors of National Libraries
CDP	Colorado Digital Project
CDWA	Categories for the Description of Works of Art
CEDARS	CURL Exemplars in Digital Archiving
CHIO	Cultural Information Online
CIDOC	International Commission for Documentation
CIMI	Computer Interchange of Museum Information
CRM	Conceptual Reference Model
CNRI	Corporation for National Research Initiatives
CORC	Cooperative Online Resource Catalog
CSDGM	Content Standards for Digital Geospatial Metadata
CURL	Consortium of University Research Libraries
DAAT	Digital Assessment Tool
DC	Dublin Core
DCC	Digital Curation Centre
DCMI	Dublic Core Metadata Initiative
DDC	Dewey Decimal Classification
DELOS	Digital ERCIM Library Operational System (ERCIM = European Research Consortium for Informatics and Mathematics)
DIP	Dissemination Information Package
DOI	Digital Object Identifier
DPC	Digital Preservation Coalition
DTD	Document Type Definition

EAD	Encoded Archival Description
eLib	Electronics LIBrary Programme
ERPANET	European Resource Preservation NETwork
eSPIDA	effective Strategic model for the Preservation and Disposal of Institutional Digital Assets
FGDC	Federal Geographic Data Committee
FP5	Fifth Framework Programme
FRANAR	Functional Requirements of Authority Numbering and Records
FRBR	Functional Requirements for Bibliographic Records
GEM	The Gateway to Educational Materials
GIF	Graphics Interchange Format
GILS	Government Information Locator Service
HATII	Humanities Advanced Technology and Information Institute
HTML	HyperText Markup Language
HTTP	Hypertext Transfer Protocol
ICABS	IFLA-CDNL Alliance for Bibliographic Standards
IEEE	Institute of Electrical and Electronics Engineers
IFLA	International Federation of Library Associations and Institutions
IIPC	International Internet Preservation Consortium
<indecs>	Interoperability of Data for Electronic Commerce Systems
ISBD	International Standard Bibliographic Description
ISBN	International Standard Book Number
ISO	International Organization for Standardization
ISSN	International Standard Serial Number
ISTBAL	Istituto di Studi per la Tutela dei Beni Archivistici e Librari (Institute of Studies for the Protection of Archival and Library Heritage, University of Urbina, Italy)
JISC	Joint Information Systems Committee
LC	Library of Congress
LCC	Library of Congress Classification
LCCN	Library of Congress Control Number
LCNAF	Library of Congress Name Authority File
LCSH	Library of Congress Subject Headings
LIFE	Lifecycle Information for E-literature
LOCKSS	Lots Of Copies Keep Stuff Safe
LOM	Learning Objective Metadata
MANDATE	Managing Digital Assets in Tertiary Education
MARC	Machine Readable Cataloging
MCN	Museum Computer Network

MeSH	Medical Subject Headings
METS	Metadata Encoding and Transmission Standard
MIME	Multipurpose Internet Mail Extensions
MODS	Metadata Object Description Schema
NARA	National Archives and Records Administration
NDIIPP	National Digital Information Infrastructure and Preservation Program
NDLP	National Digital Library Program
NEDLIB	Networked European Deposit Library
NSF	National Science Foundation
NWA	Nordic Web Archive
OAI	Open Archives Initiative
OAI-PMH	Open Archives Initiative Protocol for Metadata Harvesting
OAIS	Open Archival Information System
OCLC	Online Computer Library Center
OCR	Optical Character Recognition
OSI	Open Source Initiative
PADI	Preserving Access to Digital Information
PANDORA	Preserving and accessing networked documentary resources of Australia
PCC	Program for Cooperative Cataloging
PDF	Portable Document Format
PRESERV	Preservation Eprint SERVices
RDA	Resource Description and Access
RDF	Resource Description Framework
RLG	Research Libraries Group
RLIN	Research Libraries Information Network
SGML	Standard Generalized Markup Language
SHERPA	Securing a Hybrid Environment for Research Preservation and Access
SICI	Serial Item and Contribution Identifier
SIP	Submission Information Package
TCM	Toolkit for Conceptual Modeling
TCP/IP	Transmission Control Protocol/Internet Protocol
TEI	Text Encoding Initiative
TGN	Thesaurus of Geographic Names
TIFF	Tagged Image File Format
TNA	The National Archives
UBCIM	Universal Bibliographic Control and International MARC

UDT	Universal Dataflow and Telecommunications
UKDA	United Kingdom Data Archive
UKOLN	United Kingdom Office for Library Networking
UPC	Universal Product Code
URI	Uniform Resource Identifier
URL	Uniform Resource Locator
URN	Uniform Resource Name
VIAF	Virtual International Authority File
VRA	Visual Resources Association
W3C	World Wide Web Consortium
XML	eXtensible Markup Language
ZING	Z39.50 International: Next Generation

Glossary

AACR2. *See Anglo-American Cataloguing Rules,* second edition.

Access. The process of choosing and formulating headings for bibliographic records. Also refers to the larger processes of providing bibliographic access (i.e., cataloguing), intellectual access (i.e., classification and indexing), and physical access to material.

Access point. Any name, word, or phrase by which a catalog record can be retrieved from the catalog, known also as an entry, heading, or retrieval point.

Added entry. A secondary access point; any heading by which a catalog record can be retrieved other than the first (or main entry).

Administrative metadata. Metadata used in managing and administering information resources.

***Anglo-American Cataloguing Rules,* second edition.** The dominant set of rules for the descriptive cataloging of library materials. Since its initial publication in 1978, it has been revised and updated several times.

Area of description. A major area of the bibliographic description.

Bibliographic description. The part of a catalog record that identifies the item it represents, exclusive of access points, call numbers, and control numbers other than the ISBN and the ISSN.

Bibliographic level. *See* Levels of description

Book mark. *See* Cutter number; Shelf mark

Book number. *See* Cutter number; Shelf mark

Call letter. *See* Shelf mark

Call number. The shelf address of an item, usually consisting of its classification number and shelf marks.

Chief source of information. In descriptive cataloging, the main location from which bibliographic data are taken, such as the title screen(s) of an electronic resource.

Classification. The process of determining where an item fits into the hierarchy of a classification schedule.

Collocation. The act of bringing related data together.

Continuing resource. A bibliographic resource that is issued with no predetermined conclusion. *See also* Integrating resource; Serial.

Corporate body. A named group of people that acts as an entity.

Crosswalk. A mapping of the relationships among elements, semantics, and syntax from one metadata format to another.

Cutter number. An alphanumeric code designed to arrange items in alphabetic order, first formulated by Charles Ammi Cutter.

Dataset. A collection of computer-readable data records.

Descriptive metadata. Metadata used to describe or identify information resources.

Digital object identifier. A unique identifier assigned to electronic intellectual property.

Document type definition. A formal description in SGML or XML syntax of the components to be used for describing a specific document.

Dublin Core. A set of 15 identifying elements used to create metadata used to create metadata for electronic resources.

Encoded Archival Description. A set of protocols for editing text for computer input and communication.

Extensibility. An element that has the potential to be expanded in scope, area or size.

Extensible Markup Language (XML). A subset of Standard Generalized Markup Language, that allows designers to create their own customized tags for Web documents.

Faceted. A classification or subject-heading list in which topical components (i.e., facets) are listed and the cataloger builds an appropriate class number or heading by combining the appropriate components.

Federal Geographic Data Committee metadata standard. A set of metadata terminology and definitions for geospatial data (e.g., maps).

General material designation. A term used in the first area of description to name the media group to which an item belongs. When applied to metadata, this term is "electronic resource."

Heading. *See* Access point

HyperText Markup Language (HTML). A set of protocols for editing text in documents for the World Wide Web.

Instantiation. The creation of an object from its class; an identifiable occurrence.

Integrating resource. A bibliographic resource that is added to or changed by updates and that is integrated into the whole (e.g., updating loose-leaf publications and updating Web sites).

Interoperability. The ability of multiple systems, using different hardware and software platforms, data structures, and interfaces, to exchange and share data.

Joint Steering Committee for Revision of AACR. An international body consisting of representatives of the library associations and national libraries of Australia, Canada, the United Kingdom, and the United States (i.e., the Library of Congress) charged with determining the contents of the *Anglo-American Cataloguing Rules*. Also known as JSC.

Level of description. One of three standard styles of description prescribed by AACR2, each containing varying amounts of bibliographic information from the least (level 1) to the most (level 3).

MARC (MAchine Readable Cataloging). A group of identifying codes used to communicate bibliographic and other types of data using computers.

MARC 21. The current version of MARC issued in 1998; revisions are issued when appropriate.

MARCXML. A metadata scheme for working with MARC data in a XML environment.

Markup language. A way of indicating the structure of a document by using embedded encoding tags and providing a computer with information about how to process and display the documents.

META tag. The HTML element used to demarcate metadata on a Web page, or example, <META>.

Metalanguage. A document creation language.

Modularity. The ability to create new metadata applications by combining elements from various previously established metadata schemas.

Monograph. An item published or produced in full within a limited time period.

Namespace. The method in the in Resource Description Framework to tie a specific use of a metadata element to the scheme where the intended definition is to be found. (FROM NISO). *OR* A unique name that identifies an organization that has developed an XML schema. A namespace is identified via a Uniform Resource Identifier (a URL or URN). (from DC). *OR* The set of unique names used to identify objects within a well-defined domain, particularly relevant for XML applications.

Paris Principles. A statement of descriptive cataloging principles adopted by participants in the International Conference on Cataloguing Principles held in Paris in 1961.

Preservation metadata. Metadata related to the preservation management of information resources.

Protocol. A set of rules that mandates the way computers communicate with each other across networks.

Resource Description Framework. A language for writing metadata about Internet resources that can be exchanged between applications without loss of meaning.

Schema. A metadata element set and rules for using it.

Serial. An item published or produced in parts intended to go on without end.

Shelf mark. Any code or system of marks designed to arrange items on shelves, excluding the classification number.

Standard Generalized Markup Language. A language used to mark up electronic documents with tags that define the relationship between the content and the structure.

Structural metadata. Metadata that describes how an item is structured.

Subject analysis. A method of determining the subject matter of a bibliographic resource.

Subject heading. (1) A word or phrase identifying the intellectual content of an item being cataloged and used as an access point. (2) A term from an authorized list of terms to be used as access points.

Syntax. Rules that define the way metadata elements and their content are encoded.

Technical metadata. Metadata related to how a system functions or metadata behaves.

Text Encoding Initiative. A set of protocols for editing text for computer input and communication.

Uniform Resource Identifier (URI). A method for identifying all names or addresses that refers to resources on the Internet (e.g., uniform resource locator, uniform resource name).

Uniform Resource Locator (URL). A unique address for locating a resource on the Internet.

Uniform Resource Name (URN). A name given to an Internet resource.

Uniform title. A title created to collocate editions and versions of a work that appear under different titles. This title may be one by which the item is commonly known, the original title of a work published in translation, or a title constructed by a cataloger.

Use metadata. Metadata related to the level and type of information resources.

World Wide Web Consortium. An international consortium that develops common protocols and specifications to ensure the interoperability of the World Wide Web.

Z39.50. A NISO and ISO standard protocol for cross-system search and retrieval.

Chapter 4

Figure 4.6

```
Type: a     ELvl: I      Srce: d     Audn:        Ctrl:         Lang: eng
BLvl: m     Form: s      Conf: 0     Biog:        MRec:         Ctry: dcu
            Cont:        GPub:       LitF: 0      Indx: 0
Desc: a     Ills:        Fest: 0     DtSt: e      Dates: 2004,08,
040         $c
020         1-932326-11-1
050
082 0 4     025.17/82 $b Sm51 $2 22
049
100 1       Smith, Abby.
245 1 0     Survey of audio collections in academic libraries $h
[electronic resource] / $c by Abby Smith, David Randall Allen, and
Karen Allen.
260         Washington, D.C. : $b Council on Library and Information
Resources, $c August 2004.
538         Mode of access: World Wide Web.
500         Title from title screen (viewed Mar. 10, 2005).
530         Also published in print: Washington, D.C. : Council on Library
and Information Resources, 2004. (Optimizing collections and services
for scholarly use).
650    0    Academic libraries $x Special collections $x Sound recordings
$x Preservation.
650    0    Sound recordings $x Conservation and restoration $z United
States.
650    0    Sound archives $x Conservation and restoration $z United
States.
650    0    Library surveys $z United States.
700 1       Allen, David Randall.
700 1       Allen, Karen.
710 2       Council on Library and Information Resources.
856 4 0     $u http://www.clir.org/pubs/reports/pub128/contents.html
```

Figure 4.7

```
Type: a      ELvl: I      Srce: d      GPub: f      Ctrl:        Lang: eng
BLvl: i      Form: s      Conf: 0      Freq:        MRec:        Ctry: onc
S/L: 2       Orig:        EntW: h      Regl: x      ISSN:        Alph: a
Desc: a      SrTp:        Cont:        DtSt: c      Dates: 2003,9999
040          $c
020
050
082 0 4      920/.071 $b Di561 $2 22
049
245 0 0      Dictionary of Canadian biography online $h [electronic
resource].
260          [Ottawa] : Library and Archives of Canada, 2003-.
538          Mode of access: World Wide Web.
500          Title from title screen (viewed Mar. 10, 2005).
500          "This first phase presents people who died between the years
1000 and 1930".
530          Also published in 14 print vols. And on CD-ROM by the
University of Toronto Press covering people who died between 1000 and
1920.
530          French language ed. also published in print, CD-ROM, and
online.
504          Includes bibliographical references.
651          Canada $x Biography $v Dictionaries.
856 4 0      $u http://www.biographi.ca/EN/index.html
```

Figure 4.8

```
Type: a      Elvl: I      Srce: d      Audn:        Ctrl:        Lang: eng
BLvl: m      Form: s      Conf:        Biog:        MRec:        Ctry: nyu
             Cont:        GPub: i      LitF:        Indx:
Desc: a      Ills:        Fest:        DtSt: s      Dates: 1998,
040          $c
020
050          JC571 $b Un3 1998
082
049
110 1        United Nations. $b General Assembly.
245 1 0      All human rights for all $h [electronic resource] $b the
fiftieth anniversary of the universal declaration of human rights,
1948-1998 : universal declaration of human rights adopted and
proclaimed by General Assembly resolution 217A (III) of 10 December
1948.
246 3 0      Universal declaration of human rights
246 3 0      Declaration of human rights
260          New York : $b United Nations, $c [1998].
538          Mode of access: World Wide Web.
500          Title from title screen (viewed Mar. 14, 2005).
500          Also available in many languages.
650     0    Human rights
856 4 0      $u http://www.un.org/Overview/rights.html
```

Figure 4.9

```
Type: a      ELvl: I      Srce: d      Audn:        Ctrl:        Lang: eng
BLv1: m      Form: s      Conf:        Biog:        MRec:        Ctry: xxc
             Cont:        GPub:        LitF:        Indx:
Desc: a      Ills:        Fest:        DtSt: s      Dates: 2004,
040          $c
020
050
082 0 4   020.7071 $b L616 $2 22
049
245 0 0   Library education chronologies $h [electronic resource]
Library Education Anniversary Committee, Ex Libris Association.
260          [Canada] : $b Ex Libris Association, $c 2004.
538          Mode of access: World Wide Web.
500          Title from title screen (viewed Mar. 10, 2005).
500          "Special anniversary issue of ELÄN, fall 2004, Library and
information studies in Canada".
505 0     Dalhousie University - McGill University - Université de
Montréal - University of Alberta - University of British Columbia
University of Toronto - University of Western Ontario - Library
technician programs in Canada.
650     0   Library schools $z Canada $v Chronology.
650     0   Library technicians $x Education $v Chronology.
710 2     Ex Libris Association. $b Library Education Anniversary
Committee.
770 0     $t ELAN special anniversary issue 2004.
856 4 0   $u http://exlibris.fis.utoronto.ca/history/Chron/
chron.html
```

Figure 4.10

```
Type: a      ELvl: I      Srce: d      GPub:        Ctrl:        Lang: eng
BLv1: i      Form: s      Conf: 0      Freq:        MRec:        Ctry: onc
S/L: 2       Orig:        EntW:        Regl: x      ISSN:        Alph: a
Desc: a      SrTp: w      Cont:        DtSt: c      Dates: 1993?, 9999
040          $c
020
050     4   TK5105.888 $b G78 2000
082
049
100 1     Graham, Ian.
245 1 0   Introduction to HTML $h [electronic resource] / $c Ian Graham.
260          Toronto : $b University of Toronto.
362 1     Began publication in 1993?
538          Mode of access: World Wide Web.
500          Title from title screen (viewed Mar. 15, 2005).
500          "Last update: 20 September 2000".
650     0   HTML (Document markup language) $v Handbooks, manuals, etc.
856 4 0   $u http://www.utoronto.ca/webdocs/HTMLdocs/NewHTML/
htmlindex.html
```

Authors' notes: Although this document was found on the University of
Toronto Web site, the university shares no responsibility for the
content of the document and, therefore, an added entry was not made for
the university.

Jay Weitz, "Cataloging Electronic Resources: OCLC-MARC Coding
Guidelines" (www.oclc.org) states "if the beginning date is not
explicitly stated in the resource, omit 260 subfield $c and give the
beginning date in 362/1 if ascertainable." This date was supplied by
Dr. Graham.

Chapter 5

Figure 5.8

```
Type: p       ELvl: I      Srce: d      GPub: f      Ctrl:         Lang: eng
BLvl: i       Form: s      Conf: 0      Freq:        MRec:         Ctry: mdu
S/L: 2        Orig:        EntW:        Regl: x      ISSN:         Alph: a
Desc: a       SrTp: w      Cont:        DtSt: c      Dates: 2003,9999
040       $c
020
050     4  QH587 $b St41 2005
082
049
245 0 0  Stem cell information $h [electronic resource] : $b the
official National Institutes of Health resource for stem cell research.
Betheseda, Md. : $b National Institutes for Health.
Mode of access: World Wide Web.
362 1     Began in 2003.
500       Title from home page (viewed Mar. 16, 2005).
650     0 Stem cells.
650     0 Stem cells $x Research.
650     0 Stem cells $x Government policy $z United States.
710 2     National Institutes of Health (U.S.).
856 4 0  $u http://stemcell.nih.gov/index.asp


Authors' note: See note at bottom of figure 5.2.  This date was
supplied by the National Institutes for Health.
```

Figure 5.9

```
Type: a       ELvl: I      Srce: d      GPub:        Ctrl:         Lang: eng
BLvl: s       Form: s      Conf: 0      Freq: f      MRec:         Ctry: onc
S/L:          Orig:        EntW:        Regl: r      ISSN: 4       Alph: a
Desc: a       SrTp: p      Cont:        DtSt: d      Dates: 2002, 9999,
040       $c
022       1709-1179
050
082 0 4  020.5 $b El12 $2 22
049
245 0 0  ELAN $h [electronic resource] : $b Ex Libris Association
newsletter.
246 3 0  Ex Libris Association newsletter
260       [Toronto] : $b Ex Libris Association, $c 2003-
310       Semi-annual
362 0     No. 33 (spring 2003)-
538       Mode of access: World Wide Web.
538       System requirements: Adobe Acrobat.
500       Title from title screen (viewed Mar. 16, 2005).
530       Also issued in print ed.
500       Print ed. issues no. 1 (1989)-32 (spring 2002) have title Ex
Libris news.
650     0 Libraries $z Canada $x History $v Periodicals.
650     0 Librarians $z Canada $x Biography $v Periodicals.
740 0     Ex Libris news.
710 2     Ex Libris Association.
856 4 0  $u http://exlibris.fis.utoronto.ca/ELAN/elan.html
```

Figure 5.10

```
Type: p      ELvl: I      Srce: d      GPub: f      Ctrl:        Lang: eng
BLvl: i      Form: s      Conf: 0      Freq: u      MRec:        Ctry: dcu
S/L: 2       Orig:        EntW:        Regl: u      ISSN:        Alph: a
Desc: a      SrTp: w      Cont:        DtSt: n      Dates: uuuu,uuuu

040          $c
020
050     4    RA776 $b Un3 2005
082
049
110 1        United States. $b Department of Health and Human Services.
245 1 0      United States Department of Health & Human Services [Web site]
             $h [electronic resource].
246 3        United States Department of Health and Human Services
260          Washington, D.C. : $b U.S. Dept. of Health & Human Services.
538          Mode of access: World Wide Web.
500          Title from home page (viewed Mar. 18, 2005).
650     0    Health $x Popular works.
650     0    Health $x Political aspects.
856 4 0      $u http://www.hhs.gov
```

Figure 5.11

```
Type: a      ELv1: I     Srce: d     GPub:        Ctrl:        Lang: eng
BLv1: s      Form: s     Conf: 0     Freq: z      MRec:        Ctry: ilu
S/L:         Orig:       EntW:       Regl: x      ISSN:        Alph: a
Desc: a      SrTp:       Cont:       DtSt: c      Dates: 2002, 9999,
040          $c
020
050    4     Z701.3.E38 $b P926 2002
082
049
245 0 0      Preservation education directory $h [electronic resource].
260          Chicago : $b Association for Library Collections & Technical
Services, $c2002-  .
310          Frequency varies
362 0        8th ed.-
538          Mode of access: World Wide Web.
500          Title from title screen (viewed Mar. 18, 2005).
530          Editions 1-7 issued in print format.
500          Includes indexes.
650    0     Library materials $x Conservation and restoration $x Study and
teaching $v Directories.
650    0     Library schools $z United States $x Curricula.
650    0     Library schools $z Canada $x Curricula.
710 2        Association for Library Collections & Technical Services.
856 4 0      $u http://www.ala.org/ala/alctscontent/alctspubsbucket/
webpublications/alctspreservation/preseddir/home.htm


Cataloged as a remote access monograph

Type: a      ELv1: I     Srce: d     Audn:        Ctrl:        Lang: eng
BLv1: m      Form: s     Conf:       Biog:        MRec:        Ctry: ilu
             Cont:       GPub:       LitF:        Indx: 1
Desc: a      Ills:       Fest:       DtSt: s      Dates: 2002,
040          $c
020
050
082 0 4      025.84/071 $b P926 $2 22
049
100 1        Wiseman, Christine.
245 1 0      Preservation education directory $h [electronic resource] / $c
compiled by Christine Wiseman and Julie Arnott.
260          Chicago : $b Association for Library Collections & Technical
Services, $c 2002.
538          Mode of access: World Wide Web.
500          Title from title screen (viewed Mar. 18, 2005).
530          Editions 1-7 issued in print format.
500          Includes indexes.
650 0        Library materials $x Conservation and restoration $x Study and
teaching $v Directories.
650    0     Library schools $z United States $x Curricula.
650    0     Library schools $z Canada $x Curricula.
700 1        Arnott, Julie.
710 2        Association for Library Collections & Technical Services.
856 4 0      $u http://www.ala.org/ala/alctscontent/alctspubsbucket/
webpublications/alctspreservation/preseddir/home.htm
```

Index

About the Authors

SHEILA S. INTNER is Professor Emerita and Founding Director of the Simmons Graduate School of Library and Information Science master's degree program at Mount Holyoke College. She has received several awards, including the Margaret Mann Citation Award from the American Library Association (ALA) for outstanding contributions to education for cataloging and classification. She has served as an ALA Councilor-at-Large, Chairperson of the Cataloging and Classification Section of Associations for Library Collections & Technical Services (ALCTS), and as President of ALCTS. She is the author or principal editor of 20 books, including *Standard Cataloging for School and Public Libraries* (Libraries Unlimited, 2002), *Electronic Cataloging* (Haworth, 2003), and *Cataloging Correctly for Kids* (ALA Editions, 2006).

SUSAN S. LAZINGER is Senior Lecturer (Emerita), School of Library, Archive and Information Studies, Hebrew University of Jerusalem, Israel, where she was Head of the Academic Program. She is the author of two other books and numerous articles on cataloging and metadata, as well as a number of invited chapters in books edited by others. Susan is currently Adjunct Lecturer in digital preservation and metadata at the Department of Information Studies and Librarianship, Haifa University.

JEAN WEIHS has worked in university, public, school, and special libraries as a reference librarian, a bibliographer, and a school librarian. Most of her career has involved teaching cataloguing to librarians, library technicians, and school librarians in Canada and the United States. She represented the Canadian Committee on Cataloguing for nine years on the Joint Steering Committee for Revision of AACR, five of these as JSC Chair. She has held 45 positions on national and international committees. Jean Weihs has written 17 books, 6 separately published pamphlets/documents, 10 chapters in books edited by others, and more than 125 articles and book reviews in professional journals. She is the recipient of 13 national and international awards.